Dionysia Metaphysica

DIONYSIA METAPHYSICA
A Reiteration of Nietzsche's *The Birth of Tragedy*

by

James Chester

James Chester Publishing

Copyright © 2020 James Chester

All rights reserved. No part of this publication may be reproduced, distributed, or transmitted in any form or by any means, including photocopying, recording, or other electronic or mechanical methods, without the prior written permission of the publisher, except in the case of brief quotations embodied in reviews and certain other non-commercial uses permitted by copyright law. For permission requests, contact the publisher at the address below.

Published in the United States by James Chester Publishing, Boston Massachusetts

All inquiries may be made at https://www.JamesChester.org

Library of Congress Control Number: 2020914080

ISBN: 978-1-7350167-0-2 (paperback)

First edition 2020.
Front cover image by Rembrandt van Rijn, Philosopher in Meditation - 1632.

Book design by James Chester.

Printed in the United States of America

Acknowledgements

Nietzsche, F. W. (1910). *The Birth of Tragedy; or Hellenism and pessimism* (W. A. Haussmann, Trans.). Edinburgh, UK: Foulis.

TABLE OF CONTENTS

INTRODUCTION XV
1: ART AS MYTHOPOEIA 1
    A Definition of Human Being 1
    The Value of Intuitive over Conceptual Thought 2
        An Apprehension vs. A Conception of Nietzsche's Thalesian Insight 5
    Art as Mythopoeia 5
    Mythopoeia as Life and Beauty 6
    Proto-Tragedy vs. Modern, Theatrical Tragedy 7
    A Definition of "Apollonian" and "Dionysian" 9
    The Illusoriness of Visionariness Imparts Redemption ... 11
    Mythical Self as the Principium Individuationis 17
    Proto-Tragedy as the Collapse of Principium Individuationis 17
    Proto-Tragedy Is Redemptive 19

2: THE DOMAIN OF SELF AND THE REALMS OF SENSATION AND IDEATION 25
    Life as Expansion of the Limits of Mythical Self Via Will 25
    A Fraternal Union Between Sensation and Ideation 27
    Proto-Tragedy Invokes Mythopoeia 28
        The Realms of Sensation and Ideation Can Be Cultivated and Amplified 28
        Absent a Union, The Sensation and Ideation Realms Behave Antagonistically 35
        The Dithyramb Is A Symbolic Representation Whose Decryption Requires Initiation 36

3: THE ROLE OF MYTHOPOEIA IN LIFE 39
    Whence Arises Mythopoeia? 39
    Mythopoeia Fulfills a Need for Delight that Sustains Life 41
    Mythopoeia Empowers Man 45
    Mythical Self Cloaks Suffering in Ameliorative Naivete 46

4: MYTH HEALS AND ENABLES LIFE 51
Mythical Being (Self) Arises Out of a Need Created by Suffering 51
Mythical Self Is the Principium Individuationis 56
Ancient Greek Culture Lived as an Embodiment of Nietzsche's Thalesian Insight 58
Proto-Tragedy Is Symbiosis of the Two Realms of Sensation and Ideation 60

5: THE ROLE OF ART IN LIFE 61
Art Speaks from the Belly of Being 63
Tragic "Music" as Will Prompts Mythopoeia as Reverberation .. 67
The Consummation of Life as an Aesthetic Phenomenon 76
Dithyrambic Drama as a Close Approximation of Art in Nature . 77

6: THEORY OF DITHYRAMBIC MUSIC 79
Dithyrambic Drama as an Admixture of Epic and Lyrical Poetry. 80
First Mention of Dithyrambic Music 81
Music as Will 84
"Music" as Mythopoeia 86
Reality vs. Actuality 88
The Representation of "Music" in Metaphor 90

7: ACTUALITY VS. REALITY 95
The Role of the Chorus in Tragedy 95
Dithyrambic Drama as an Embodiable Representation of Human Will 97
The Tragic Chorus a Wall Against Ho-Hum, Egotistical Reality . 100
The Tragic Chorus as an Ideal Domain 101
The Tragic Chorus as Aborning Reality 105
In Comparison, The Satyr Is to Tragedy as the Idyllic Shepherd Is to Opera 107
Art as Savior from Nausea 108

8: THEORY OF DITHYRAMBIC DRAMA 117
The Meaning of the Tragic Satyr 117

The Chorus Walls Off the Worlds of Ego and Self 120
The Dithyramb is an Embodiable Representation 120
The Dithyramb Is Communicative as Passion and Dischargeable as Vision 123
The Concept of Dithyrambic Transport 126
Myth as only One Aim of Dithyrambic Drama 129
The Tragic Wisdom that Drives Continual Mythopoeia 130
The Chorus as Reality 131
Tragic Mythopoeia as Supra-Self 134

9: GENIUS AS AN EXPANSION OF THE LIMITS OF INDIVIDUATION VIA TRAGEDY 139

Mythical Self as a Healing Mirror of the World 139
Evolution of Mythical Self Via Life 142
An Analysis of Sophoclean Tragedy 142
An Analysis of Aeschylean Tragedy 147
The Origin of Aeschylean Tragedy in the Natural Imposition of Justice 153
Greek Suffering as Folly and Semitic Suffering as Sin 153
Genius as Transcendence of the Limits of Individuation 154
Tragedy as a Reunion with the "One Universal Being," Beyond Individuation 156

10: IMPORTANT CONCEPTS 161

Genius as Attainment of "One Universal Being" 161
A Yearning for Oneness with Nature Beyond Individuation as Will to Power 165
The All-Important Takeaway from *The Birth of Tragedy* 167
A Practical Definition of "Dionysian" and "Apollonian" 170
A Practical Definition of Living Myth 171
Self as Assimilative Living Myth 171
A Definition of "Music" 173
Actuality vs. Reality and Mysticism 174
Actuality as "Music" 174
Mythical Assimilation as an Aesthetic Phenomenon 175
A Second Form of Myth: Gateway Myth 176

Dying Myth Entrenches Itself in an Historical Foundation 176
The Growth of Mythical Self via the Assimilation of Sensation 177
The Dithyramb as Actuality and "Music" 178
The Errors of Euripides 180

11: THE FAILURE OF MODERN TRAGEDY 183
Dithyrambic Poetry as Dithyrambic Music 184
Euripi-dean Tragedy and Everyday Reality 187
Euripides Chose an Audience of Mass 192
Euripides Applied Scientific Thought to Tragedy 195

12: TRAGEDY, MYTH. AND WILL 197
Proto-Tragedy as the Production of Myth 197
Euripides Uprooted of Myth from Proto-Tragedy 198
Proto-Tragedy Is Rooted in Passion, Not Epic Concept 202
The Production of Myth Requires Embodiment, Not Mere Contemplation 204
Tragedy and the Role of the Prologue 208
Tragedy and Mysticism 213

13: AN ANALYSIS OF THE FAILURE OF WESTERN THOUGHT IN SCIENCE 217
Socrates and the Value of Consciousness 219
Socrates and the Indiscriminate Lust for Knowledge 219
Nietzsche vs. Socrates on the Value of Instinct....................... 222

14: SCIENCE IN TRAGEDY 229
Tragedy Requires Mysticism 229
The Socratic Version of Tragedy....................... 234
Dialectic Uprooted the "Musical" Foundation of Tragedy 236
Culture Requires the Co-Existence of Science and Art 237

15: THEORETICAL MAN 241
Theoretical Man Cannot Understand Tragic "Music" 241

Science as Driven by the Pleasure of Discovery 245
Myth as a Gateway.. 247
Art Makes Life Liveable 249
The Failure of Art Fails Life 250
When Science Realizes its Limits, Only Art Can Save It 251
Science Is Antipodal to Life 254
The New Dithyramb Restores Tragedy.. 256

16: THEORY OF DITHYRAMBIC TRAGEDY...................... 257

Dithyrambic Music as a Representation of Human Will............ 262
Nietzsche Learns the Theory of Dithyrambic Music from
Schopenhauer 263
Myth as Progenitor of Image and Concept 268
Concept Is a Representation of Music... 269
Concept Is an Abstraction but Music Is an Essence 270
Unlike Concept, Music Is Gripping 270
Music Is Communicative Absent Any Manifestation................. 271
Music Is a Representation of the Thing-In-Itself, of Will 272
Myth as Imbued Will 274
Will as Music 274
Will as Progenitor of Concept 276
Dithyrambic Music as Will 278
The Reality of Dithyrambic Music in the Melos 279
Concept Lacks a Melos 280
Old and New Concept 281
Mythopoeia and "Music" 282
Find your Self in Dithyrambic Drama 283
Tragedy Is Celebrated in the Will, Not in the Self 286

17: THEORY OF SUPRA-SELF AND OVER-SELF.............. 291

Tragedy as the Greater Joy in Becoming, Not Being 291
The Over-Self as a State of Existence Granting the Highest
Freedom to Will... 295
The Dithyramb Communicates Will, Not Concept, which Must Be
"Heard," Not "Seen" 298
Tragedy and Mysticism Are Closely Related 299

The Danger of Science 301
Euripi-dean Tragedy Is Composed in Concept, Not Will 305
Concept as a Copy of a Copy of the Will 306
Dithyrambic Music Requires a Universality of Appeal 310

18: THEORETICAL MAN VS. TRAGIC MAN 317
Art as the Enabler of Will 317
An Assessment of Western Culture in the 21st Century 320
Theoretical vs. Tragic Man in Modern Western Culture 321
Science and Democracy are Doomed by their Requirement for a Slave Class 324
Only Religion can Spare Impending Doom, but Science Precludes Religion 325
Nietzsche Predicts the Demise of Science and the Advent of Tragedy 326
Science Mistakenly Enshrines Actuality Under Veil of Reality .. 328
Science as a Detriment to Healing Culture 330
Nietzsche's Use of the Phrase "Metaphysical Comfort" 331
Nietzsche Writes an Obituary for Science 337

19: THE FAILURE OF OPERA IN MODERN TRAGEDY 339
Opera Is an Invention of Science 340
Opera Focuses on Speech and Concept 341
In Opera, the Combination of Concept and Music Is Unnatural 342
In Opera, Theoretical Man Claims a Pretense of Culture 347
Nietzsche's Wall in Dithyrambic Drama Keeps Out Theoretical Man 349
In Opera, the Idyllic Shepherd Is a Lame Imitation of the Satyr 351
Opera Is a Failed Attempt to Recreate Ancient Tragedy 353
Modern Man as the Moral Hero in Operatic Tragedy 354
The Primary Function of Art in Life Is to Heal 358
Nietzsche Predicts the Rebirth of Tragedy 361

20: THE BIRTH OF DIONYSIA 365
Moving Forward with the Demise of Theoretical Man and the Advent of Tragic Man 365

A New Culture Is upon Us 370
The Failure of Science as Psychiatry 372
A New Way of Thinking About the World 372

21: PROTO-TRAGEDY AND THE NEW DITHYRAMB AS THE NEW HOPE 377

The Apollonian Realm as a State-Forming Force on Human Nature 378
A Clue for Rendering the Dithyramb "Of the New Idol" 379
Genius as a Balance of Apollonian and Dionysian Forces 380
Tragic Myth as Supra-Self and Tragic Hero as Liberator of the Subconscious 383
Proto-Tragedy as Suffering Man's Greatest Hope 385
The Dithyramb as the Great Communicator 386
Myth Induces a Yearning for Life 391
Reality as Mythical Self 392
Will Produces and Empowers Myth 397

22: THEORY OF GENIUS 401

Man Achieves a Depth and Height of Soul from the Dionysian and Apollonian Realms, Respectively 401
A Characterization of Tragic Man and Vision of Supra-Self 404
A Definition of Genius as the Incarnation of the Over-Self 407
Dithyrambic Music and the Art of "Hearing" 410

23: THEORETICAL MAN IS BANNED FROM THE NEW DITHYRAMB 415

Dithyrambic Music Cannot Be "Heard" by Theoretical Man 415
Myth as Imbued Will 417
Nihilism Derives from the Demise of Myth 419
The Dithyramb is for Him Who Seeks His Self 421

24: THE BIRTH OF TRAGEDY FROM DISSONANCE 427

Salvation as a Fraternal Union of the Apollonian and Dionysian Realms 427

Introduction

Salvation is Found in Self but Originates in Emotion 429
A Metaphysical Supplement as an Aesthetic Phenomenon that Justifies Life 432
Dissonance of Will as the Spirit of Tragedy out of which Tragedy Is Born 433
Tragedy as the Originator of the Supra-Self 435
Mankind's Greatest Gift 439

25: DIONYSIA AND REDEMPTION 441
Prepare for a Cataclysmic Confrontation via Dithyrambic Drama Followed by Redemption 441

Introduction

What follows is the original text of Nietzsche's *The Birth of Tragedy Out of the Spirit of Music* (BT), word for word, as translated by William August Hausmann and included in the 1910 Oscar Levy edition of *The Complete Works of Friedrich Nietzsche*. Following the text is my reiteration of it, paragraph by paragraph, with the exception of the two prefaces, which I have not included. In addition, there are some passages of original text in which I found nothing noteworthy, though they are very few. Nonetheless, I included those passages without comment in order to qualify the reiteration as being complete and full. Lastly, all but a very few of the footnotes (exceptions noted) were added by the translator.

The first sentence of Francis Golfing's translation of Nietzsche's *The Birth of Tragedy* states "Much will have been gained for aesthetics once we have succeeded in apprehending directly — rather than merely ascertaining — that art owes it continuous evolution to the Apollonian-Dionysian duality...." The key phrase upon which the reader's understanding of Nietzsche's insight succeeds is "direct apprehension." However, his essay itself offers nothing more than a concept of how art evolves out of an "Apollonian-Dionysian duality." In fact, it is only in his book *Thus Spoke Zarathustra* that the reader is offered an apprehension, which differs from concept in the same way that experience differs from fanciful imagination. But

INTRODUCTION

Thus Spoke Zarathustra is a dithyrambic drama, specifically a dithyrambic tragedy, which is a fact I established most demonstrably in my book *The Birth of Dionysia*. And dithyrambic drama is an entirely new art form whose reading and practice requires substantial education. I achieved that education in autodidactic manner over a period of time that lasted two decades. And then I spent another three decades acting out his drama. I claim that education not only as a distinctive qualification to write about Nietzsche's ideas of Übermensch and the will to power, but, more specifically, to write about his theory of art as an evolution arising out of an Apollonian-Dionysian duality because I have achieved the direct apprehension he speaks of in the first sentence of *The Birth of Tragedy* but which he offers his readers only in *Thus Spoke Zarathustra*. On the basis of that education and that achievement, I now present a reiteration of Nietzsche's essay, *The Birth of Tragedy*.

The "art" that Nietzsche references in this very fundamental insight, as stated in the first sentence, is the process of creation that takes place *as life* within "human being," by which I mean the inner world of man comprising the mind, the will, the idea of Self, and the sense of being amidst the swirl of emotion. And that single substitution for the word "art" in that sentence, in contrast with the commonly accepted reference to the art in literature and music, along with numerous other substitutive and more practical references, drastically and fundamentally changes the entire purview of Nietzsche's disquisition in *The Birth of Tragedy*, which amounts to a *theory of art as life*, not a theory of art as literature or music.

What follows from that single — and what I call Thalesian — insight about art as life is a very complicated articulation of the process by which "human being," or Self, grows via an evolution that plays out between the two Apollonian and Dionysian realms of ideation and sensation, respectively. And proto-tragedy, which is a re-definition of tragedy that is different from modern tragedy, plays a religious role in that process by enabling it, all of which is explained in his essay via the reiteration I provide in this book.

Central to Nietzsche's theory of art as life is the concept of myth and its artistic creation, mythopoeia. But Nietzsche never makes that point explicitly. In fact, he only mentions the word "myth" mostly tangentially. And he never mentions the word mythopoeia, though he mentions the word mythopoeic (four times). But mythopoeia is precisely the art that Nietzsche references in his fundamental Thalesian insight about the evolutionary process that plays out between the Apollonian realm of ideation and the Dionysian realm of sensation. And that fact is only confirmed via an undertaking of his dithyrambic tragedy, *Thus Spoke Zarathustra*, which is his vehicle for providing the "apprehension" that he urged in his Thalesian insight.

When Nietzsche goes on to elucidate the tragic chorus as a wall and as a representation of a higher reality, it is not about Greek tragedy that he writes; it is about his own dithyrambic tragedy. When he writes about epic and lyrical poetry, it is about dithyrambic poetry that he writes in comparison. And when he writes about music, it is not about traditional auditory music that he writes; it is about dithyrambic music, which is a literary representation of the will to power. He also writes about a type of person whom he calls "theoretical man," who thinks conceptually and delights in the appearance of things, and it is precisely this type of scientifically minded person whom he has "walled off" from reading his dithyrambs, let alone undertaking their dramatization via a plausible embodiment, which explains

INTRODUCTION

the one-hundred and thirty plus years that passed before someone broke down his wall.

Thus, while *The Birth of Tragedy* is a metaphysica that reveals Nietzsche's view of the entire inner world of man, it is also a disquisition on his theories of dithyrambic music, dithyrambic drama, and dithyrambic tragedy, all of which are made practical in his *Thus Spoke Zarathustra*. All in all, however, it is not an essay about ancient Greek tragedy, though it certainly sheds light on some aspects of it, particularly its demise through science. But most books written about *The Birth of Tragedy* focus almost entirely on BT's *supposed* analysis of ancient Greek tragedy.

Dionysia Metaphysica is intended as a reiteration, not a commentary or an analysis, that claims to tell the reader "Here is what Nietzsche was trying to say," paragraph by paragraph, for all twenty-five chapters. Thus far, again, it is the only reiteration. Everything else is a commentary or an analysis.

1: Art as Mythopoeia

> We shall have gained much for the science of æsthetics, when once we have perceived not only by logical inference, but by the immediate certainty of intuition, that the continuous development of art is bound up with the duplexity of the *Apollonian* and the *Dionysian:* in like manner as procreation is dependent on the duality of the sexes, involving perpetual conflicts with only periodically intervening reconciliations.

A Definition of Human Being

We will have gained much for an understanding of how beauty becomes manifest within human being, by which, hereinafter, I mean the inner spiritual body comprised of mind, emotion, spirit and will and not the outer, physical body of flesh and bones, once we come to an understanding via instinctive intuition rather than deductive conception that human being is purely mythical and that mythopoeia, or the creation of mythical being, is driven by an evolution arising out of a periodically reconciliatory agon existing between the two realms of sensation and ideation, with that evolution being similar in nature to the procreation of the human species being driven by the never-ending conflicts and periodic reconciliations of the two sexes.

I equate the above statement, that art owes its continuous evolution to events arising out of the dual existence of that which is Dionysian and that which is Apollonian, on a level of significance to that with Thales statement that "All is water." Thus, I identify it as Nietzsche's Thalesian insight. And what Nietzsche said about Thales' insight will tell us something about his own Thalesian insight.

The Value of Intuitive over Conceptual Thought

In *Philosophy in the Tragic Age of the Greeks* (PTAG), he said "What drove him [Thales] to it [the insight that all is water] was a metaphysical conviction which had its origin in a mystic intuition."[1] Thales' insight is an insight into the workings of all things that come into being here on Earth and everywhere else. The other point to note in Nietzsche's characterization is that it comes to light out of nowhere, or, as Nietzsche calls it, out of mysticism, which, in my opinion, makes it more significant and more valuable than if it came into being via logic or reasoning.

As I explained in *The Birth of Dionysia* and which Nietzsche emphasizes in PTAG, the most fruitful philosophical thinking does not proceed upon logic or dialectic but rather upon intuition and mysticism.

---

[1] Nietzsche, Friedrich. *Philosophy in the Tragic Age of the Greeks*. Translated by Marianne Cowan. Washington, DC: Regnery Publishing, Inc, 1962, p. 39.

Philosophy leaps ahead on tiny toeholds; hope and intuition lend wings to its feet. Calculating reason lumbers heavily behind, looking for better footholds, for reason too wants to reach that alluring goal which its divine comrade has long since reached. It is like seeing two mountain climbers standing before a wild mountain stream that is tossing boulders along its course: one of them light-footedly leaps over it, using the rocks to cross, even though behind and beneath him they hurtle into the depths. The other stands helpless; he must first build himself a fundament which will carry his heavy cautious steps. Occasionally this is not possible, and then there exists no god who can help him across. What then is it that brings philosophical thinking so quickly to its goal? Is it different from the thinking that calculates and measures, only by virtue of the greater rapidity with which it transcends all space? No, its feet are propelled by an alien, illogical power — the power of creative imagination. Lifted by it, it leaps from possibility to possibility, using each one as a temporary resting place. Occasionally it will grasp such a resting place even as it flies. Creative premonition will show the place; imagination guesses from afar that here it will find a demonstrable resting place. But the special strength of imagination is its lightning quick

> seizure and illumination of analogies. Subsequent reflection comes with measuring devices and routinizing patterns and tries to replace analogy with equation and synchronicity with causality. But even if this should not work, even in a case such as that of Thales, non-provable philosophic thinking has its value. Even if all the footholds have crumbled by the time logic and empiric rigidity want to cross over to such a proposition as "all is water," even after the total demolition of any scientific edifice, something remains.[2]

In fact, the efficacy of intuitive thought, in comparison to the stumbling and impotent inefficiency of logical thought, is much more demonstrable during an undertaking of Nietzsche's dithyrambic tragedy, *Thus Spoke Zarathustra*. Proto-tragedy specifically, which is what Nietzsche's *Birth of Tragedy* essay is all about (it is not about modern, theatrical tragedy) seems totally unmoved by reasoning but moves forward most assuredly under the sway of mystical thought, despite the monumental obstacles that stand in its way. And that is an observation that can come only from experience, and specifically experience with dithyrambic tragedy.

---

[2] Ibid., pp. 40-41.

An Apprehension vs. A Conception of Nietzsche's Thalesian Insight

Returning to Nietzsche's Thalesian insight, he says that he requires us to use intuition and insight rather than reasoning and concept to understand it, and that is not possible without undertaking his dithyrambic tragedy. Indeed, I have seen it written many times that the most important insight that *Thus Spoke Zarathustra* teaches is Nietzsche's idea that the world recurs eternally. Actually, the most important insight that the drama teaches is Nietzsche's Thalesian insight as stated above. And the one quality that makes it the supreme insight is its ability to impart life to its beholder. But if this insight cannot be achieved except through mystical intuition, and if that mystical intuition derives solely from an experience with *Thus Spoke* Zarathustra, what good, then, would a constructed conception of it be to anyone? I see only one: to illuminate its extraordinary goodness, thereby encouraging, if not assisting, the reader to an achievement of that apprehension via an undertaking of *Thus Spoke Zarathustra*. And it is toward that aim that I present this reiteration.

Art as Mythopoeia

In the first place, the art he speaks of in the above statement is not the making of physical art we see in the physical world, such as a painting or a symphony or an epic poem. The art he speaks of is the creation of myth (or mythopoeia) within the inner spiritual world, the human soul. And specifically, the myth he references later in his essay is mythical being. Since both the outer world and the inner world are totally devoid of being, its creation out of nothing constitutes the act of art. However, the creation of other myths as well, specifically the gateway myths of Übermensch and the eternal recurrence, also fall under the purview of this artistic creation out of the realms of that which is Dionysian and that which is Apollonian.

Mythopoeia as Life and Beauty

Thus, it is not just for the science of aesthetics that so much will be gained with an achievement of this mystical apprehension; it is more for our understanding of how *life* manifests itself within human being as an artistic process of creation that we should gain the most. But, regarding aesthetics, indeed, Nietzsche's Thalesian insight also reveals how beauty becomes manifest within human being as well, insofar as the creation of being, which is entirely illusory, also creates sophrosyne and sophrosyne exudes beauty.

> These names we borrow from the Greeks, who disclose to the intelligent observer the profound mysteries of their view of art, not indeed in concepts, but in the impressively clear figures of their world of deities.

Here, Nietzsche references art as the creation of the gods in the instance of the ancient Greeks. In other words, the Greek gods were fictive beings that existed only in the minds of the ancient Greeks. But those gods were as real to an ancient Greek to an extent equal to how much an ancient Greek believed in his Self, which is another fictive being that exists only in the mind of its beholder. Thus, the reader should focus his attention on art as mythopoeia, the creation of fictive being, not art as the creation of physical works in poetry, literature, and music.

> It is in connection with Apollo and Dionysus, the two art-deities of the Greeks, that we learn that there existed in the Grecian world a wide antithesis, in origin and aims, between the art of the shaper, the Apollonian, and the non-plastic art of music, that of Dionysus: ...

Apollo is referenced as the god that gives form to things, just as mythical being gives form to the inner world, most obviously with the creation of the highly defined Self. Thus, in such a way is the word "plastic" referenced. Dionysus, on the other hand, does not give form but rather intoxicates those who behold him with emotion.

Proto-Tragedy vs. Modern, Theatrical Tragedy

> ... both these so heterogeneous tendencies run parallel to each other, for the most part openly at variance, and continually inciting each other to new and more powerful births, to perpetuate in them the strife of this antithesis, which is but seemingly bridged over by their mutual term "Art"; till at last, by a metaphysical miracle of the Hellenic will, they appear paired with each other, and through this pairing eventually generate the equally Dionysian and Apollonian art-work of Attic tragedy.

1: ART AS MYTHOPOEIA

Without stating explicitly what he means by the two tendencies, Apollonian and Dionysian, which he has not yet done, it is impossible to understand how they "run parallel to each other," openly in variance," and "continually incite each other." Notwithstanding that shortcoming, it is important to note his claim that it is when the normally opposed tendencies unite that tragedy arises as a particular phenomenon.

By tragedy, Nietzsche means an inner phenomenon that enables a process of growth, which is life itself as it becomes manifest within human being. Without tragedy, life or growth is not possible. Thus, it is a critical phenomenon.

It was the ancient Greeks who discovered this phenomenon. But then something happened that resulted in this knowledge being lost. Specifically, as we are about to discover, two things happened. One, myth, as something that occurred naturally and was then developed into an art form, was lost. And two, logical thought, under the tutelage of Socrates, rose to prominence. Tragedy requires mystical thought, which was deemed unworthy under Socrates' teaching of scientific thought.

Subsequently, tragedy evolved into the purely theatrical spectacle we know today. Thereafter, it was no longer an inner spiritual event, which is what it truly is. In addition, it then became moralized, which only deepened the loss by making the discovery of its original form that much more difficult.

For the purpose of our discussion, let us distinguish between these two forms of tragedy, the modern and the ancient, the theatrical and moralized event and the inner spiritual event, by calling the ancient, original form proto-tragedy. And it is the ancient form, proto-tragedy, about which we want to form a concept. But remember that a concept of proto-tragedy will not help us nearly as well as its apprehension will help us. And the apprehension cannot come except via an undertaking of *Thus Spoke Zarathustra*, which is a dithyrambic tragedy.

A Definition of "Apollonian" and "Dionysian"

> In order to bring these two tendencies within closer range, let us conceive them first of all as the separate art-worlds of *dreamland* and *drunkenness;* between which physiological phenomena a contrast may be observed analogous to that existing between the Apollonian and the Dionysian. In dreams, according to the conception of Lucretius, the glorious divine figures first appeared to the souls of men, in dreams the great shaper beheld the charming corporeal structure of superhuman beings, and the Hellenic poet, if consulted on the mysteries of poetic inspiration, would likewise have suggested dreams and would have offered an explanation resembling that of Hans Sachs in the Meistersingers:—

It is very important to understand what Nietzsche references when he speaks of that which is Dionysian and that which is Apollonian. To call Apollonian a reference to a physiological condition akin to dream is close but still far off. But to call Dionysian a reference to drunkenness is a miss. Kaufmann translated the German word as intoxication, which is a bit closer but still a long way off.

That which Nietzsche calls Dionysian is anything that is revealed in a speaker's facial gestures and tone of voice while speaking, which would be passion, volition, will, a problem between conscience and passion, or, in short, a state of mind that arises from emotional circumstances. That which he calls Apollonian is revealed in the speaker's beliefs and ideas, or, in short, a state of mind arising from belief or idea. That which is Dionysian is physical, inasmuch as it is based in emotion. And that which is Apollonian is fictive, inasmuch as it exists only within the mind. The most important thing to understand here is that the Dionysian aspect of the human soul does indeed reveal itself, while the Apollonian side, which is entirely fictive, reveals nothing. Another important point to understand is that the Dionysian side is perceptible to an observer's intuition, but the Apollonian side is not perceptible and is revealed only in the communication of concept comprising the Apollonian state of mind and articulated only by the subject. In other words, you can read a person's feelings, but you obviously cannot read their mind.

Nietzsche's Thalesian insight reveals a relationship between these two realms of the human soul. And it is an account of that relationship within the creation of myth, and most importantly the creation of mythical Self but other ideational myths as well, that will become the focus of his essay in *The Birth of Tragedy*. Remember that the goal of Nietzsche's essay is to give the reader a concept of proto-tragedy for no other reason than to encourage him or her to an undertaking of its *apprehension* via *Thus Spoke Zarathustra*. And, since the destruction of myth as an art form was one of the two factors that led to the demise of proto-tragedy, an understanding of myth is necessary for the re-birth of tragedy.

Continuing with the original text, Nietzsche begins to compare the Apollonian realm with dream. I think the most that can be taken from this comparison is that the Apollonian realm gives rise to visionariness. And the comparison between visionariness and emotion is quite significant in their dissimilarity.

> Mein Freund, das grad' ist Dichters Werk,
> dass er sein Träumen deut' und merk'.
> Glaubt mir, des Menschen wahrster Wahn
> wird ihm im Traume aufgethan:
> all' Dichtkunst und Poeterei
> ist nichts als Wahrtraum-Deuterei.
>
> My friend, just this is poet's task:
> His dreams to read and to unmask.
> Trust me, illusion's truths thrice sealed
> In dream to man will be revealed.
> All verse-craft and poetisation
> Is but soothdream interpretation.

The poet's task is to unmask and read dreams so that the truth in illusion is revealed. All poeticizing originates in the interpretation of dreams, which includes day dreams.

The Illusoriness of Visionariness Imparts Redemption

> The beauteous appearance of the dream-worlds, in the production of which every man is a perfect artist, is the presupposition of all plastic art, and in fact, as we shall see, of an important half of poetry also. We take delight in the immediate apprehension of form; all forms speak to us; there is nothing

indifferent, nothing superfluous. But, together with the highest life of this dream-reality we also have, glimmering through it, the sensation of its appearance: such at least is my experience, as to the frequency, ay, normality of which I could adduce many proofs, as also the sayings of the poets. Indeed, the man of philosophic turn has a foreboding that underneath this reality in which we live and have our being, another and altogether different reality lies concealed, and that therefore it is also an appearance; and Schopenhauer actually designates the gift of occasionally regarding men and things as mere phantoms and dream-pictures as the criterion of philosophical ability. Accordingly, the man susceptible to art stands in the same relation to the reality of dreams as the philosopher to the reality of existence; he is a close and willing observer, for from these pictures he reads the meaning of life, and by these processes he trains himself for life. And it is perhaps not only the agreeable and friendly pictures that he realises in himself with such perfect understanding: the earnest, the troubled, the dreary, the gloomy, the sudden checks, the tricks of fortune, the uneasy presentiments, in short, the whole "Divine Comedy" of life, and the Inferno, also pass before him, not merely like pictures on the wall—for he too lives and suffers in these

> scenes,—and yet not without that fleeting sensation of appearance. And perhaps many a one will, like myself, recollect having sometimes called out cheeringly and not without success amid the dangers and terrors of dream-life: "It is a dream! I will dream on!" I have likewise been told of persons capable of continuing the causality of one and the same dream for three and even more successive nights: all of which facts clearly testify that our innermost being, the common substratum of all of us, experiences our dreams with deep joy and cheerful acquiescence.

There are several points to note in this paragraph.

- He equates the production of dream with man being an artist. In other words, dream is to the dreamer what the painting is to the painter. And this should not go unnoticed because he is moving to the point that the art he speaks of in the creation of myth is an artistic endeavor. Mythopoeia is an act of art, and it occurs within the human soul, with the individual as his own artist.

- The visionariness that becomes manifest in dreams should be noted for the fact that it imparts form, unlike sensation that is emotional and imparts, shall we say, intoxication, such as intoxication with emotion, like pleasure or even displeasure.

1: ART AS MYTHOPOEIA

- The "forms" that become manifest in dreams exude beauty. And they speak to us intuitively, without the need for interpretation or conceptualization. Moreover, dreams, or the visions of form we see within our minds, are distinguishable from emotion for their quality of appearance. We recognize them as visions, not emotions.

- He then begins to move to the point that our visions are illusions. And it is the very illusoriness of these Apollonian visions that arouse delight in us and makes them redemptive.

- Then he makes a grand leap of insight to say that the same form-giving visions we have in our waking life (like our vision of Self but which also imparts a sense of Self that is not a vision) are also illusions and that they reflect the meaning we find in life. And these visions of being, specifically, though he does not say it, the vision of Self, make life interpretable for us. But it is not just our joys that find meaning in these illusory visions of being but also are suffering.

> This cheerful acquiescence in the dream-experience has likewise been embodied by the Greeks in their Apollo: for Apollo, as the god of all shaping energies, is also the soothsaying god. He, who (as the etymology of the name indicates) is the "shining one," the deity of light, also rules over the fair appearance of the inner world of fantasies. The higher truth, the perfection of these states in contrast to the only partially

intelligible everyday world, ay, the deep consciousness of nature, healing and helping in sleep and dream, is at the same time the symbolical analogue of the faculty of soothsaying and, in general, of the arts, through which life is made possible and worth living. But also that delicate line, which the dream-picture must not overstep—lest it act pathologically (in which case appearance, being reality pure and simple, would impose upon us)—must not be wanting in the picture of Apollo: that measured limitation, that freedom from the wilder emotions, that philosophical calmness of the sculptor-god. His eye must be "sunlike," according to his origin; even when it is angry and looks displeased, the sacredness of his beauteous appearance is still there. And so we might apply to Apollo, in an eccentric sense, what Schopenhauer says of the man wrapt in the veil of Mâyâ[3]: *Welt als Wille und Vorstellung,* I. p. 416: "Just as in a stormy sea, unbounded in every direction, rising and falling with howling mountainous waves, a sailor sits in a boat and trusts in his frail barque: so in the midst of a world of sorrows the individual sits quietly supported by and trusting in his *principium individuationis.*" Indeed, we might say of Apollo, that in him the

---

[3] Cf. *World and Will as Idea,* 1. 455 ff., trans, by Haldane and Kemp.

1: ART AS MYTHOPOEIA

> unshaken faith in this *principium* and the quiet sitting of the man wrapt therein have received their sublimest expression; and we might even designate Apollo as the glorious divine image of the *principium individuationis,* from out of the gestures and looks of which all the joy and wisdom of "appearance," together with its beauty, speak to us.

Notice in the above that he mentions the quality of "healing" in our Apollonian visions, that we attain a "deep consciousness of nature" through them, in contrast to only a partially intelligible "everyday" world in their absence, and that life is "made possible and worth living" through them. These are significant points because, as we move forward, we will come upon the revelations via Nietzsche's Thalesian insight that subliminal suffering (i.e., that which we call our demons) is both unbearable and incomprehensible outside of our vision of Self, but as soon as we attribute them to our Self as a dimension of our being, as our emotions, then they become interpretable and, most importantly, bearable. In such a way, the illusion and beauty of mythical Self makes life worth living and meaningful. Illusion heals. But that attribution of sensation to Self becomes possible only through proto-tragedy and, more than anything else, makes proto-tragedy so desirable and thaumaturgic and an integral part of life as it plays out within human being.

Mythical Self as the Principium Individuationis

Continuing with the above cited text, the illusion of mythical Self also adds a boundary and a restrictive governance between emotion and a ruling idea of being such that a man who is moved by extreme anger nevertheless retains his composure. On the other hand, a man who lacks the integrity of Self would become enraged and wild when moved by anger. In other words, Self, as myth, imparts sophrosyne. But the benefit of mythical Self goes much deeper than mere sophrosyne. Mythical Self provides an edification amidst the torrent of overpowering and titanic emotions moving this way and that within the human soul. And that edification is what we commonly call "mind," which, in the above quote, is referenced as the principium individuationis (hereinafter, the PI) because mythical Self individuates man by adding an idea and a sense of being to the inner world of man. Mythical Self adds form to a world that is otherwise universally formless.

Proto-Tragedy as the Collapse of Principium Individuationis

> In the same work Schopenhauer has described to us the stupendous *awe* which seizes upon man, when of a sudden he is at a loss to account for the cognitive forms of a phenomenon, in that the principle of reason, in some one of its manifestations, seems to admit of an exception. Add to this awe the blissful ecstasy which rises from

the innermost depths of man, ay, of nature, at this same collapse of the *principium individuationis,* and we shall gain an insight into the being of the *Dionysian,* which is brought within closest ken perhaps by the analogy of *drunkenness.* It is either under the influence of the narcotic draught, of which the hymns of all primitive men and peoples tell us, or by the powerful approach of spring penetrating all nature with joy, that those Dionysian emotions awake, in the augmentation of which the subjective vanishes to complete self-forgetfulness. So also in the German Middle Ages singing and dancing crowds, ever increasing in number, were borne from place to place under this same Dionysian power. In these St. John's and St. Vitus's dancers we again perceive the Bacchic choruses of the Greeks, with their previous history in Asia Minor, as far back as Babylon and the orgiastic Sacæa. There are some, who, from lack of experience or obtuseness, will turn away from such phenomena as "folk-diseases" with a smile of contempt or pity prompted by the consciousness of their own health: of course, the poor wretches do not divine what a cadaverous-looking and ghastly aspect this very "health" of theirs presents when the glowing life of the Dionysian revellers rushes past them.

Take notice of Nietzsche's statement that a blissful ecstasy arises from the innermost depths of man when the PI collapses. He is moving to the point that the Apollonian realm of the mind establishes an idea of being amidst the swirl of emotion that serves to individuate man, but it also imposes restrictions upon him that mitigate the power of the Dionysian realm, his emotions. And when the PI collapses with the surge of overwhelming emotions, as with the arrival of spring after a hard winter or when two people fall in love, man is reminded of the full power of his emotions and he rejoices in the intoxication, the sway, and the transport that his emotions provide him. Thus, while the power of the Apollonian forces, the mind, are essential to man's existence, so too are the forces from within the Dionysian realm, his passions. But intermittently, one realm becomes dominant over the other — to the point of enfeebling the other, and this enfeeblement is only overcome when the PI collapses and the emotions are given freedom again to well up.

It is important to note also that, in some people, there is less of a prominence of the Apollonian forces (the mind) so that emotion runs wild more often than not. Thus, a balance between the two realms, wholesomeness, is the most desirable state of existence. But occasionally, where a strong mind and a strong sense of individuation are present, a collapse of PI can be invigorating.

Proto-Tragedy Is Redemptive

What Nietzsche does not state at the outset of his essay, but which we can now, is that the shattering of the PI can be a very good thing just as much as it can be a very bad thing. The single difference that makes one shattering good and the other bad is the condition of the individual in which the shattering occurs.

Losing one's mind is a very bad experience, as when the horrific emotions of pain, humiliation, and fear overwhelm an individual to the point wherein he cannot bear it. But, as we will shortly see, what follows from a bad "shattering" of the PI is a phenomenon that we will call dismemberment, wherein the individual reins in the limits of his consciousness to avoid the emotions that have overwhelmed him and shattered his PI. And dismemberment is necessary because overwhelming emotions that shatter the PI *do not go away;* they recur — eternally. Under those circumstances, re-drawing the limits of consciousness is the *only* solution. But in that re-drawing, yet another sense of Self arises upon the ruins of the old dead Self, which we call Ego, which is more impoverished and less interpretive than the original, whole Self. It is also more cerebral, prone to excessive thought, and less rooted in feelings. And this should be easy enough to understand. When an individual suffers and loses his sense of Self, he becomes more egotistical, which means emotional, insecure, unbalanced, and unwholesome. The best healing that such an individual could possibly undergo is a reunion with his old suffering Self, along with an effort to free himself from the grip of his demons. And that is what proto-tragedy provides. Proto-tragedy heals by reuniting suffering man with his old Self, so that he may then begin to heal himself once and for all. But, in order for that reunion to take place, the Ego that arose in the wake of the collapse of suffering Self must itself expire and let loose its grip; it must undergo its own shattering of the PI. And this, too, is easy enough to understand *conceptually — but very difficult to achieve instinctually.* And it should also be easy enough to understand also that a suffering individual who finally lets go of the grip his Ego holds on him and is reunited with his deeper true Self would rejoice in the collapse of his old tyrannical Ego. That joy in the curative release from Ego and subsequent reunion with true Self is the joy that the ancients found in the catastrophic shattering of the PI, which they called tragedy and which we will call proto-tragedy. Notice that in both instances, one being the shattering of mind and the subsequent devolution into Ego if not madness, and the other being the curative shattering *are both catastrophic*. But, clearly, one is very bad and one is very good.

But, as I said, Nietzsche does not come out with that articulation right away. Instead, he begins building up to it very slowly by showing how the shattering of the PI, as it occurs naturally (as opposed to being willed) with the arrival of spring, for instance, and in dance festivals, is a good thing. In the next passage, he points to *how* the shattering is a good thing by showing the benefits it provides.

> Under the charm of the Dionysian not only is the covenant between man and man again established, but also estranged, hostile or subjugated nature again celebrates her reconciliation with her lost son, man. Of her own accord earth proffers her gifts, and peacefully the beasts of prey approach from the desert and the rocks. The chariot of Dionysus is bedecked with flowers and garlands: panthers and tigers pass beneath his yoke. Change Beethoven's "jubilee-song" into a painting, and, if your imagination be equal to the occasion when the awestruck millions sink into the dust,

1: ART AS MYTHOPOEIA

you will then be able to approach the Dionysian. Now is the slave a free man, now all the stubborn, hostile barriers, which necessity, caprice, or "shameless fashion" has set up between man and man, are broken down. Now, at the evangel of cosmic harmony, each one feels himself not only united, reconciled, blended with his neighbour, but as one with him, as if the veil of Mâyâ has been torn and were now merely fluttering in tatters before the mysterious Primordial Unity. In song and in dance man exhibits himself as a member of a higher community, he has forgotten how to walk and speak, and is on the point of taking a dancing flight into the air. His gestures bespeak enchantment. Even as the animals now talk, and as the earth yields milk and honey, so also something super-natural sounds forth from him: he feels himself a god, he himself now walks about enchanted and elated even as the gods whom he saw walking about in his dreams. Man is no longer an artist, he has become a work of art: the artistic power of all nature here reveals itself in the tremors of drunkenness to the highest gratification of the Primordial Unity. The noblest clay, the costliest marble, namely man, is here kneaded and cut, and the chisel strokes of the Dionysian world-artist are accompanied with the cry of the Eleusinian mysteries: "Ihr stürzt nieder,

> Millionen? Ahnest du den Schöpfer, Welt?"[4]

According to this, the shattering of the PI leads to a reunion with one's innermost human nature. And it also leads to a restoral of a measure of fraternity between individuals. Both the reunion and the restoral make sense when you consider that the shattering leads to a temporary suspension of egocentric individuality. But the shattering also leads to a certain enchantment within the affected individual. And then Nietzsche says something very significant: that the individual in whom the PI has been shattered becomes himself a work of art, kneaded by nature's hand. This harkens back to the original Thalesian insight about art, and it is important to understand, as I said earlier, that the art he speaks of is art as it plays out within the human soul, not art as a work of literature or music. He means man as a work of art.

---

[4] Te bow in the dust, oh millions?
Thy maker, mortal, dost divine?
Cf. Schiller's "Hymn to Joy"; and Beethoven, Ninth Symphony.—TR.

2: The Domain of Self and the Realms of Sensation and Ideation

Life as Expansion of the Limits of Mythical Self Via Will

> Thus far we have considered the Apollonian and his antithesis, the Dionysian, as artistic powers, which burst forth from nature herself, *without the mediation of the human artist,* and in which her art-impulses are satisfied in the most immediate and direct way: first, as the pictorial world of dreams, the perfection of which has no connection whatever with the intellectual height or artistic culture of the unit man, and again, as drunken reality, which likewise does not heed the unit man, but even seeks to destroy the individual and redeem him by a mystic feeling of Oneness. Anent these immediate art-states of nature every artist is either an "imitator," to wit, either an Apollonian, an artist in dreams, or a Dionysian, an artist in

> ecstasies, or finally—as for instance in Greek tragedy—an artist in both dreams and ecstasies: so we may perhaps picture him, as in his Dionysian drunkenness and mystical self-abnegation, lonesome and apart from the revelling choruses, he sinks down, and how now, through Apollonian dream-inspiration, his own state, *i.e.*, his oneness with the primal source of the universe, reveals itself to him *in a symbolical dream-picture.*

It is important to remember that what we want to understand from Nietzsche's essay is the phenomenon of proto-tragedy. And the most we can hope for from this essay is a concept because an apprehension will come only from an experience which is provided only by his dithyrambic tragedy. To that end, we must also understand the Apollonian-Dionysian duality as the antagonistic relationship that exists between sensation and idea. Simply put, idea arouses sensation, and sensation prompts the formulation of idea, such as we see in a conflict between conscience and passion where idea is generated as a solution to the conflict, thus allowing the will to move forward. With that, we see that the dynamics unfolding within the human soul are not just between idea and sensation but that the will is also involved. Moreover, there is a fourth factor and that is mythical being or Self. And the creation of mythical Self is the art in progress — such that the interplay between sensation and idea, or between the Apollonian realm and the Dionysian realm, is precisely what leads to the expansion of the dominion of Self, of being: expansion of the limits of its ability to bear sensation and, consequently, expansion of the limits of its percipience, but also expansion of the realm of ideation as the conflicts in which the will becomes mired are overcome with idea, therewith unharnessing the will and giving it free rein.

A Fraternal Union Between Sensation and Ideation

In the above paragraph, he states that forces from within the Apollonian and Dionysian realms arise naturally, without any intervention, including any intervention by the will, which means that their activity is instinctual. And he says that the forces immediately find satisfaction, both in the creation of a vision and in the creation of an intoxicating enchantment with that vision. And in that juxtaposition, between a vision within the mind and the beholder's intoxicating enchantment with that vision, we clearly see how the two disparate realms complement each other. The vision itself provides a certain satisfaction, but the enchantment with the vision provides that much more satisfaction, while that which is being satisfied, one, the need for a vision, and, two, the need for an arousal of sensation, arise from within two very different realms of the human soul. And all this happens, all this artistic creativity, without any willfulness on the part of the subject, man. It happens naturally — and instinctively.

Then he goes on to say that the Dionysian forces can destroy man insofar as titanic or severely disharmonious emotion can shatter the PI. If the shattering is good, as in the case when egotistical or egocentric being is shattered, then the shattering leads to a reunion with human nature, which, as we have already seen, makes sense, given the detrimental nature of egocentricity.

Proto-Tragedy Invokes Mythopoeia

But then, lastly, he says something that is very telling and should not go unnoticed. He says that the restoral of human nature within the subject whose egocentric being has been shattered *reveals itself* in an Apollonian manifestation, which is to say that the subject beholds a deeper and truer Self that is much stronger and much more comprehensive than the impoverished Ego. This is moving closer to an elucidation of the proto-tragic phenomenon and specifically its power to invoke mythopoeia, with mythopoeia being the quintessential act of artistic creation.

The Realms of Sensation and Ideation Can Be Cultivated and Amplified

> After these general premisings and contrastings, let us now approach the *Greeks* in order to learn in what degree and to what height these *art-impulses of nature* were developed in them: whereby we shall be enabled to understand and appreciate more deeply the relation of the Greek artist to his archetypes, or, according to the Aristotelian expression, "the imitation of nature." In spite of all the dream-literature and the numerous dream-anecdotes of the Greeks, we can speak only conjecturally, though with a fair degree of certainty, of their *dreams*. Considering the incredibly precise and unerring plastic

> power of their eyes, as also their manifest and sincere delight in colours, we can hardly refrain (to the shame of every one born later) from assuming for their very dreams a logical causality of lines and contours, colours and groups, a sequence of scenes resembling their best reliefs, the perfection of which would certainly justify us, if a comparison were possible, in designating the dreaming Greeks as Homers and Homer as a dreaming Greek: in a deeper sense than when modern man, in respect to his dreams, ventures to compare himself with Shakespeare.

In the above first sentence, do not overlook his assertion that the Apollonian and Dionysian forces within man can be developed. In other words, they are subjectable to a graduated cultivation that plays out in stages. And we see this in nature, as in the case of great leaders who possess extraordinary passions, and not just modest or common ambitions, as well as the ability to think in leaps and bounds that not all human beings possess. In other words, in genius we see an extraordinary development or amplification or the Apollonian and Dionysian forces, sensations and ideas. And that point will also go directly to Nietzsche's philosophy, whose aim is a culture that heals man and, in that healing, cultivates the production of genius.

> On the other hand, we should not have to speak conjecturally, if asked to disclose the immense gap which separated the *Dionysian Greek* from the Dionysian

barbarian. From all quarters of the Ancient World—to say nothing of the modern—from Rome as far as Babylon, we can prove the existence of Dionysian festivals, the type of which bears, at best, the same relation to the Greek festivals as the bearded satyr, who borrowed his name and attributes from the goat, does to Dionysus himself. In nearly every instance the centre of these festivals lay in extravagant sexual licentiousness, the waves of which overwhelmed all family life and its venerable traditions; the very wildest beasts of nature were let loose here, including that detestable mixture of lust and cruelty which has always seemed to me the genuine "witches' draught." For some time, however, it would seem that the Greeks were perfectly secure and guarded against the feverish agitations of these festivals (—the knowledge of which entered Greece by all the channels of land and sea) by the figure of Apollo himself rising here in full pride, who could not have held out the Gorgon's head to a more dangerous power than this grotesquely uncouth Dionysian. It is in Doric art that this majestically-rejecting attitude of Apollo perpetuated itself. This opposition became more precarious and even impossible, when, from out of the deepest root of the Hellenic nature, similar impulses finally broke forth and made way for themselves: the Delphic god, by a seasonably effected reconciliation, was now contented with taking the destructive arms from the hands of his powerful antagonist. This reconciliation marks the most important moment in the history of the Greek cult: wherever we turn our eyes we may observe the revolutions resulting from this event. It was the reconciliation of two antagonists, with the sharp demarcation of the boundary-lines to be thenceforth observed by each, and with periodical transmission of testimonials;—in reality, the chasm was not bridged over. But if we observe how, under the pressure of this conclusion of peace, the Dionysian power manifested itself, we shall now recognise in the Dionysian orgies of the Greeks, as compared with the Babylonian Sacæa and their retrogression of man to the tiger and the ape, the significance of festivals of world-redemption and days of transfiguration. Not till then does nature attain her artistic jubilee; not till then does the rupture of the *principium individuationis* become an artistic phenomenon. That horrible "witches' draught" of sensuality and cruelty was here powerless: only the curious blending and duality in the emotions of the Dionysian revellers reminds one of it—just as medicines remind one of deadly poisons,— that phenomenon, to wit, that pains beget joy, that jubilation wrings painful sounds out of the breast. From the highest joy sounds the cry of horror or the yearning wail over an irretrievable loss. In these Greek festivals a sentimental trait, as it were, breaks forth from nature, as if she must sigh over her dismemberment into individuals. The song and pantomime of such dually-minded revellers was something new and unheard-of in the Homeric-Grecian world; and the Dionysian *music* in particular excited awe and horror. If music, as it would seem, was previously known as an Apollonian art, it was, strictly speaking, only as the wave-beat of rhythm, the formative power of which was developed to the representation of Apollonian conditions. The music of Apollo was Doric architectonics in tones, but in merely suggested tones, such as those of the cithara. The very element which forms the essence of Dionysian music (and hence of music in general) is carefully excluded as un-Apollonian; namely, the thrilling power of the tone, the uniform stream of the melos, and the thoroughly incomparable world of harmony. In the Dionysian dithyramb man is incited to the highest exaltation of all his symbolic faculties; something never before experienced struggles for utterance—the annihilation of the veil of Mâyâ, Oneness as genius of the race, ay, of nature. The essence of nature is now to be expressed symbolically; a new world of symbols is required; for once the entire symbolism of the body, not only the symbolism of the lips, face, and speech, but the whole pantomime of dancing which sets all the members into rhythmical motion. Thereupon the other symbolic powers, those of music, in rhythmics, dynamics, and harmony, suddenly become impetuous. To comprehend this collective discharge of all the symbolic powers, a man must have already attained that height of self-abnegation, which wills to express itself symbolically through these powers: the Dithyrambic votary of Dionysus is therefore understood only by those like himself! With what astonishment must the Apollonian Greek have beheld him! With an astonishment, which was all the greater the more it was mingled with the shuddering suspicion that all this was in reality not so very foreign to him, yea, that, like unto a veil, his Apollonian consciousness only hid this Dionysian world from his view.

Much is disclosed in the above. But, at this point, we need to stop using the comparisons of sensation and idea and mythical being to Greek gods and Greek culture and start explaining what Nietzsche discloses in his essay with examples of how the same things he articulates play out in the individual, in the human psyche.

First, he speaks of a time when the Apollonian forces were predominant and the Dionysian forces were mostly restrained by the Apollonian forces. But then, returning to the Greek example, something happened to lessen the restraint provided by the Apollonian forces. The Dionysian forces, whom Nietzsche says were resident primarily within the barbaric people, found their way into Greece. When that happened, Doric music, for instance, which previously resembled the constant rhythm of waves lapping the shoreline, suddenly began to show a more tumultuous rhythm, perhaps with less consonant sounds and more dissonant sounds. Most extraordinary of all, the arousal of Dionysian forces within the predominantly Apollonian ancient Greece also gave rise for a desire to tear asunder the veil of Maya, which, according to Schopenhauer, whom Nietzsche studied devotedly, was something dream-like and definitely illusory that bespoke the entire span of knowledge about the world, perhaps meaning nature or even human nature. And more specifically, Nietzsche says that the destruction of the veil of Maya resulted in a state of genius, which he also called a very close proximity with inner nature. And as a further result of that destruction, entirely new forces of nature arose, and these were forces about which the beholder previously had no idea or experience. He goes on to say that any representation of these new forces, be they musical, for instance, or literary, would go totally unnoticed to someone who had not also experienced them. And finally, he notes that the ancient Greek would have been surprised to learn that these powerful

Dionysian forces had all along been a part of his inner nature and were only hidden to him by the Apollonian forces.

That is as good a summary as I can offer of the above paragraph. But it only becomes useful when we articulate the same chain of events as they play out within the human psyche.

Absent a Union, The Sensation and Ideation Realms Behave Antagonistically

This articulation becomes much more informative when we say that there are individuals in whom idea and Ego have become predominant over emotions and that there are individuals who use idea and Ego to restrain emotion. And, in fact, the Ego arises in the wake of the dismemberment of the wholesome Self *and* works as a stopgap to prevent those subliminal emotions that caused the dismemberment from entering consciousness. Thus, the Ego imparts an innate antipathy toward the emotions. In this way, we might rightly say that the Apollonian forces have become predominant over the Dionysian forces. Imagine the reaction of such an individual if, one day, the repressed Dionysian forces (subliminal and repressed demons, for instance) began to emerge. If the emergence was involuntary, which would make it actually impossible, the reaction would be sheer terror. But if the emergence was voluntary, willed, the emergence would amount to a celebration. And it would lead further to a desire to tear asunder the Ego in order to grant more freedom to the Dionysian forces, one's feelings. Another aspect of the transformation would be the addition of tone and rhythm to emotion, where previously they had been monotone due to the restraint placed on them. And would it not be possible that previously undiscovered passions, like a deeper surge of morale and strong surges of bravery, would appear on the horizon? Indeed, it would. And lastly, is it not also easy to understand how such an individual, who discovered true and stronger emotions laying beyond the veil of his Ego, just beneath the surface, would also be astonished as Nietzsche says the Greeks must have been astonished to discover the whole storm of Dionysian forces laying beyond the veil of Apollo, the veil of the repressive Ego, though, admittedly he calls it the veil of Maya?

The Dithyramb Is A Symbolic Representation Whose Decryption Requires Initiation

The other point I wish to make here is that, in Nietzsche's dithyrambic tragedy, it is not possible to understand a particular dithyramb that depicts a state of mind that is a direct result of a period of growth that has been depicted in the previous dithyrambs. The fact that, in the above cited text, he mentions that "man is incited to the highest exaltation of all his symbolic faculties" in the dithyramb is a curious note that bears significance on this point. And the point bears further resemblance to his mention of the fact that "the Dithyrambic votary of Dionysus is therefore understood only by those like himself!" Kaufmann translated this citation to say that the votary of Dionysus could not be understood except by an initiate. And, in fact, Zarathustra's Prologue does indeed provide a rite of initiation insofar as it requires the actor to first achieve a full devaluation of the Platonic idealization of a conceived Self (an entirely cerebral and dismembered vision that is rooted in thought rather than feeling) in order to begin the growth of the mythical Self.

I point out these resemblances because I believe that everything Nietzsche articulated in *The Birth of Tragedy* bears constant relevance on his composition of *Thus Spoke Zarathustra*, though a clearer and more direct articulation may have been too difficult for him. To that end, it is also worth noting that, in his second preface to *The Birth of Tragedy*, he bemoaned his articulation in terms relative to his studies of Schopenhauer and Greek culture rather than more direct terms that might have provided a clearer articulation.

3: The Role of Mythopoeia in Life

Whence Arises Mythopoeia?

In order to comprehend this, we must take down the artistic structure of the *Apollonian culture,* as it were, stone by stone, till we behold the foundations on which it rests. Here we observe first of all the glorious *Olympian* figures of the gods, standing on the gables of this structure, whose deeds, represented in far-shining reliefs, adorn its friezes. Though Apollo stands among them as an individual deity, side by side with others, and without claim to priority of rank, we must not suffer this fact to mislead us. The same impulse which embodied itself in Apollo has, in general, given birth to this whole Olympian world, and in this sense we may regard Apollo as the father thereof. What was the enormous

3: THE ROLE OF MYTHOPOEIA IN LIFE

> need from which proceeded such an illustrious group of Olympian beings?

The Greek gods were mythical beings. And by "myth," you must read my *Birth of Dionysia* as I am not going to repeat it here, as extensive an explanation as it is. But, in the above paragraph, he now moves to the origin of these mythical beings, their creation, which are entirely fictive, insofar as they exist solely in the mind. In any case, I *do not* mean myth as a false notion of cause. I mean myth as a fictive being in which we vest unwavering credulousness. The next question is whence myth arises. What is the artistic process by which mythopoeia arises and succeeds?

> Whosoever, with another religion in his heart, approaches these Olympians and seeks among them for moral elevation, even for sanctity, for incorporeal spiritualisation, for sympathetic looks of love, will soon be obliged to turn his back on them, discouraged and disappointed. Here nothing suggests asceticism, spirituality, or duty: here only an exuberant, even triumphant life speaks to us, in which everything existing is deified, whether good or bad. And so the spectator will perhaps stand quite bewildered before this fantastic exuberance of life, and ask himself what magic potion these madly merry men could have used for enjoying life, so that, wherever they turned their eyes, Helena, the ideal image of their own existence "floating in sweet

sensuality," smiled upon them. But to this spectator, already turning backwards, we must call out: "depart not hence, but hear rather what Greek folk-wisdom says of this same life, which with such inexplicable cheerfulness spreads out before thee." There is an ancient story that king Midas hunted in the forest a long time for the wise *Silenus,* the companion of Dionysus, without capturing him. When at last he fell into his hands, the king asked what was best of all and most desirable for man. Fixed and immovable, the demon remained silent; till at last, forced by the king, he broke out with shrill laughter into these words: "Oh, wretched race of a day, children of chance and misery, why do ye compel me to say to you what it were most expedient for you not to hear? What is best of all is for ever beyond your reach: not to be born, not to *be*, to be *nothing.* The second best for you, however, is soon to die."

Mythopoeia Fulfills a Need for Delight that Sustains Life

Toward an understanding of the process out of which the Greeks created their mythical beings, he points to suffering, as in the next cited sentence, and more specifically to knowledge that life, most essentially, is not worth living.

3: THE ROLE OF MYTHOPOEIA IN LIFE

> How is the Olympian world of deities related to this folk-wisdom? Even as the rapturous vision of the tortured martyr to his sufferings.

This sentence would have been better translated as "How is the Olympian world (of mythical beings) related to the knowledge that life is essentially not worth living? And the answer is: precisely as a rapturous vision that arises within the suffering martyr. Moreover, it is precisely out of his suffering that the vision arises. In other words, without the suffering, there would be no vision and no rapture.

If this insight is spot on, and I assure you, having experienced it, that it is, then we have begun to touch upon the value of human suffering in mythopoeia, specifically the mythopoeia of Self. More importantly, if there is value in suffering, then there is value in raising subliminal suffering from the subconscious into consciousness, which, of course, makes proto-tragedy, the tearing asunder of the veil of the Ego, the most valuable.

> Now the Olympian magic mountain opens, as it were, to our view and shows to us its roots. The Greek knew and felt the terrors and horrors of existence: to be able to live at all, he had to interpose the shining dream-birth of the Olympian world between himself and them. The excessive distrust of the titanic powers of nature, the Moira throning inexorably over all knowledge, the vulture of the great philanthropist Prometheus, the terrible fate of the wise

Œdipus, the family curse of the Atridæ which drove Orestes to matricide; in short, that entire philosophy of the sylvan god, with its mythical exemplars, which wrought the ruin of the melancholy Etruscans—was again and again surmounted anew by the Greeks through the artistic *middle world* of the Olympians, or at least veiled and withdrawn from sight. To be able to live, the Greeks had, from direst necessity, to create these gods: which process we may perhaps picture to ourselves in this manner: that out of the original Titan thearchy of terror the Olympian thearchy of joy was evolved, by slow transitions, through the Apollonian impulse to beauty, even as roses break forth from thorny bushes. How else could this so sensitive people, so vehement in its desires, so singularly qualified for *sufferings* have endured existence, if it had not been exhibited to them in their gods, surrounded with a higher glory? The same impulse which calls art into being, as the complement and consummation of existence, seducing to a continuation of life, caused also the Olympian world to arise, in which the Hellenic "will" held up before itself a transfiguring mirror. Thus do the gods justify the life of man, in that they themselves live it—the only satisfactory Theodicy! Existence under the bright sunshine of such gods is regarded as that

3: THE ROLE OF MYTHOPOEIA IN LIFE

> which is desirable in itself, and the real *grief* of the Homeric men has reference to parting from it, especially to early parting: so that we might now say of them, with a reversion of the Silenian wisdom, that "to die early is worst of all for them, the second worst is—some day to die at all." If once the lamentation is heard, it will ring out again, of the short-lived Achilles, of the leaf-like change and vicissitude of the human race, of the decay of the heroic age. It is not unworthy of the greatest hero to long for a continuation of life, ay, even as a day-labourer. So vehemently does the "will," at the Apollonian stage of development, long for this existence, so completely at one does the Homeric man feel himself with it, that the very lamentation becomes its song of praise.

I would point to the following single sentence as the most revealing in the whole paragraph above:

- "The same impulse which calls art into being, as the complement and consummation of existence, seducing to a continuation of life, caused also the Olympian world to arise, in which the Hellenic 'will' held up before itself a transfiguring mirror."

Notice again that he speaks of art in the creation of mythical beings, though, in the above instance, he speaks of it with reference to the creation of mythical divine beings. But the more important point is the creation of mythical being in the instance of human being, which is, in fact, entirely mythical with regard to Self. That is the most important aspect of his use of the word "art" in his Thalesian insight: art as it plays out within the human soul, the creation of something in the human mind that did not previously exist. Notice also that he says the will of the ancient Greek was reflected, as if in a transfiguring mirror, in his gods. This insight is most revealing if, again, we apply it to the human psyche.

Mythopoeia Empowers Man

To make my point, I must call on the reader's personal experience with his or her own suffering. It has been my experience that, in an effort to bring some one or other subliminal suffering into daylight, it is impossible, insuperable, *until* I see my Self in the demon. The very act of *filtering* the suffering through the eyes of Self literally transforms the suffering into something more bearable, indeed, more loveable, as if by a miracle. The mythical Self makes life bearable. The question is how does it do this. Nietzsche says it is due to illusion. The mythical Self is an illusion that does not exist; we create it. And there is no doubt that it is an illusion because all mythical beings are entirely fictive beings that exist only in the mind of the beholder. And, by nature of its illusoriness, it imparts a certain beauty to everything that is beheld through its eyes, so that the suffering becomes colored differently than when viewed merely as a foreign haunting passion. That is the miracle provided by illusory beauty. But what's more is that, in the envelopment of subliminal suffering by illusory Self, not only does the suffering become bearable, but the previously insuperable obstacle is overcome so that the will is *freed*. In that overcoming, the will and its freedom become reflected as well in the triumphant vision of Self, just as the Hellenic will and its freedom became reflected in the Greek gods. And I am not waxing poetic here; there is actually a lasting sense of freedom that literally animates out of the vision of Self in that triumph. The beauty of appearance and sophrosyne overcome the titan of horrific and exigent emotion. And the transformation is so profound that any sentiment toward the unworthiness of living is totally nullified and is itself transformed into its opposite: a very strong yearning toward life. But it is important to note that the need for the creation of mythical Self is precisely what called it into being, and that need is rooted most assuredly in the horror of existence, which also reveals the dual relationship between the Apollonian and Dionysian forces of human nature or, more simply, the mystery of art.

Mythical Self Cloaks Suffering in Ameliorative Naivete

In the next paragraph, Nietzsche notes that the illusoriness of mythical Self also instills a great measure of naivete, by which he means innocence, within the beholder, and the naivete stands in relation to his suffering.

> Here we must observe that this harmony which is so eagerly contemplated by modern man, in fact, this oneness of man with nature, to express which Schiller introduced the technical term "naïve," is by no means such a simple, naturally resulting and, as it were, inevitable condition, which *must* be found at the gate of every

culture leading to a paradise of man: this could be believed only by an age which sought to picture to itself Rousseau's Émile also as an artist, and imagined it had found in Homer such an artist Émile, reared at Nature's bosom. Wherever we meet with the "naïve" in art, it behoves us to recognise the highest effect of the Apollonian culture, which in the first place has always to overthrow some Titanic empire and slay monsters, and which, through powerful dazzling representations and pleasurable illusions, must have triumphed over a terrible depth of world-contemplation and a most keen susceptibility to suffering. But how seldom is the naïve—that complete absorption, in the beauty of appearance—attained! And hence how inexpressibly sublime is *Homer,* who, as unit being, bears the same relation to this Apollonian folk-culture as the unit dream-artist does to the dream-faculty of the people and of Nature in general. The Homeric "naïveté" can be comprehended only as the complete triumph of the Apollonian illusion: it is the same kind of illusion as Nature so frequently employs to compass her ends. The true goal is veiled by a phantasm: we stretch out our hands for the latter, while Nature attains the former through our illusion. In the Greeks the "will" desired to contemplate itself in the transfiguration of

3: THE ROLE OF MYTHOPOEIA IN LIFE

> the genius and the world of art; in order to glorify themselves, its creatures had to feel themselves worthy of glory; they had to behold themselves again in a higher sphere, without this consummate world of contemplation acting as an imperative or reproach. Such is the sphere of beauty, in which, as in a mirror, they saw their images, the Olympians. With this mirroring of beauty the Hellenic will combated its talent—correlative to the artistic—for suffering and for the wisdom of suffering: and, as a monument of its victory, Homer, the naïve artist, stands before us.

Notice that he says naivete derives from a complete absorption with the beauty of appearance or illusion. And that its attainment is strictly dependent upon the existence of its opposite, namely horrific suffering, such as we find repressed within the subconscious that is all at once exigent, moving, and minatory when it begins to emerge from the subconscious. And when he says that the illusoriness of mythical Self, as the true goal in suffering, "is veiled by a phantasm: we stretch out our hands for the latter, while Nature attains the former through our illusion," is it not possible to compare this to suffering man who willingly extends his hand to the frightening demon only to find himself transported in that reach into a higher and deeper sense of Self? Is that not a transfiguration a hundred times more meaningful to us than the transfiguration Nietzsche speaks of in the transfiguration the ancient Greeks found of themselves in their gods? Is that not the more grand and redemptive transfiguration we would all seek in life if only we thought it existed? Indeed.

4: Myth Heals and Enables Life

Mythical Being (Self) Arises Out of a Need Created by Suffering

> Concerning this naïve artist the analogy of dreams will enlighten us to some extent. When we realise to ourselves the dreamer, as, in the midst of the illusion of the dream-world and without disturbing it, he calls out to himself: "it is a dream, I will dream on"; when we must thence infer a deep inner joy in dream-contemplation; when, on the other hand, to be at all able to dream with this inner joy in contemplation, we must have completely forgotten the day and its terrible obtrusiveness, we may, under the direction of the dream-reading Apollo, interpret all these phenomena to ourselves somewhat as follows. Though it is certain that of the two halves of life, the waking and the dreaming, the former appeals to us as by far the more preferred, important, excellent and worthy

4: MYTH HEALS AND ENABLES LIFE

of being lived, indeed, as that which alone is lived: yet, with reference to that mysterious ground of our being of which we are the phenomenon, I should, paradoxical as it may seem, be inclined to maintain the very opposite estimate of the value of dream life. For the more clearly I perceive in nature those all-powerful art impulses, and in them a fervent longing for appearance, for redemption through appearance, the more I feel myself driven to the metaphysical assumption that the Verily-Existent and Primordial Unity, as the Eternally Suffering and Self-Contradictory, requires the rapturous vision, the joyful appearance, for its continuous salvation: which appearance we, who are completely wrapt in it and composed of it, must regard as the Verily Non-existent,—*i.e.,* as a perpetual unfolding in time, space and causality,—in other words, as empiric reality. If we therefore waive the consideration of our own "reality" for the present, if we conceive our empiric existence, and that of the world generally, as a representation of the Primordial Unity generated every moment, we shall then have to regard the dream as an *appearance of appearance,* hence as a still higher gratification of the primordial desire for appearance. It is for this same reason that the innermost heart of Nature experiences that indescribable joy in the naïve artist and in the naïve work of art, which is likewise only "an appearance of appearance." In a symbolic painting, *Raphael*, himself one of these immortal "naïve" ones, has represented to us this depotentiating of appearance to appearance, the primordial process of the naïve artist and at the same time of Apollonian culture. In his *Transfiguration,* the lower half, with the possessed boy, the despairing bearers, the helpless, terrified disciples, shows to us the reflection of eternal primordial pain, the sole basis of the world: the "appearance" here is the counter-appearance of eternal Contradiction, the father of things. Out of this appearance then arises, like an ambrosial vapour, a visionlike new world of appearances, of which those wrapt in the first appearance see nothing—a radiant floating in purest bliss and painless Contemplation beaming from wide-open eyes. Here there is presented to our view, in the highest symbolism of art, that Apollonian world of beauty and its substratum, the terrible wisdom of Silenus, and we comprehend, by intuition, their necessary interdependence. Apollo, however, again appears to us as the apotheosis of the *principium individuationis,* in which alone the perpetually attained end of the Primordial

4: MYTH HEALS AND ENABLES LIFE

> Unity, its redemption through appearance, is consummated: he shows us, with sublime attitudes, how the entire world of torment is necessary, that thereby the individual may be impelled to realise the redeeming vision, and then, sunk in contemplation thereof, quietly sit in his fluctuating barque, in the midst of the sea.

He is simply continuing to make the point that illusion and our absorption into illusion (i.e., the mythical Self) is what makes life worth living and that suffering is the necessary fundament out of which the need for and the will toward the creation of mythical being, which is art itself, arises. In other words, the extreme circumstance of exigent and minatory suffering creates a most profound need and that need is met by the creation of mythical Self, therewith prompting mythopoeia, which reveals a instinctual union between suffering and redemption. In the case of subindividuated man, who has already fallen out of "Schopenhauer's boat," the principium individuationis, and into the abyss, the effect of mythopoeia is to save him from that abyss and bring him back to a state of existence wherein he is raised above and separated from it (individuated out of it) along with the exhilarating transfiguration of spirit that accompanies that rescue.

But then he makes another interesting point.

He says that our dreams are a visionary representation of that which we experience during our waking hours, which itself is a visionary representation that becomes manifest through the perspective of Self. Therefore, our dreams are a visionary representation of a more fundamental visionary representation. And it is that compound visionariness that makes our dreams so delightful, thus confirming Nietzsche's argument that visionariness provides a profound delight in existence and that the delight is necessary in order to endure life's suffering.

> This apotheosis of individuation, if it be at all conceived as imperative and laying down precepts, knows but one law—the individual, *i.e.,* the observance of the boundaries of the individual, *measure* in the Hellenic sense. Apollo, as ethical deity, demands due proportion of his disciples, and, that this may be observed, he demands self-knowledge. And thus, parallel to the æsthetic necessity for beauty, there run the demands "know thyself" and "not too much," while presumption and undueness are regarded as the truly hostile demons of the non-Apollonian sphere, hence as characteristics of the pre-Apollonian age, that of the Titans, and of the extra-Apollonian world, that of the barbarians. Because of his Titan-like love for man, Prometheus had to be torn to pieces by vultures; because of his excessive wisdom, which solved the riddle of the Sphinx, Œdipus had to plunge into a bewildering vortex of monstrous crimes: thus did the Delphic god interpret the Grecian past.

4: MYTH HEALS AND ENABLES LIFE

Mythical Self Is the Principium Individuationis

The mythopoeia of Self, the creation of an idea and a sense of being that affords us the ability to interpret the inner world in which we are immersed and which provides us the redemption in appearance and illusion that makes life possible and worth living, results in a vision of being. And that vision of being, our Self, constitutes the principium individuationis. Mythical Self *individuates* us so that we become an entity separate from the entire realm of sensation and emotion in which we live immersed. As individuated entities, we become defined, henceforth existing by strictly defined limitations and boundaries that must never be violated, lest we become *sub-individuated*, as is evidenced in the devolution of myth from the Self to the Ego. Thus, we have the wise and ancient dictums "Know thyself" and "nothing in excess" arising out of the instinctual need to maintain those boundaries and limits. In contrast to the limit-respecting Apollonian forces, the titanic Dionysian forces move man naturally and exigently away from a strict observance of those limits and into a circumstance wherein those limits are breached. But, by the same token, titanic Dionysian forces lead to titanic desires and ambitions, which have their obvious value as well.

> So also the effects wrought by the *Dionysian* appeared "titanic" and "barbaric" to the Apollonian Greek: while at the same time he could not conceal from himself that he too was inwardly related to these overthrown Titans and heroes. Indeed, he had to recognise still more than this: his

entire existence, with all its beauty and moderation, rested on a hidden substratum of suffering and of knowledge, which was again disclosed to him by the Dionysian. And lo! Apollo could not live without Dionysus! The "titanic" and the "barbaric" were in the end not less necessary than the Apollonian. And now let us imagine to ourselves how the ecstatic tone of the Dionysian festival sounded in ever more luring and bewitching strains into this artificially confined world built on appearance and moderation, how in these strains all the *undueness* of nature, in joy, sorrow, and knowledge, even to the transpiercing shriek, became audible: let us ask ourselves what meaning could be attached to the psalmodising artist of Apollo, with the phantom harp-sound, as compared with this demonic folk-song! The muses of the arts of "appearance" paled before an art which, in its intoxication, spoke the truth, the wisdom of Silenus cried "woe! woe!" against the cheerful Olympians. The individual, with all his boundaries and due proportions, went under in the self-oblivion of the Dionysian states and forgot the Apollonian precepts. The *Undueness* revealed itself as truth, contradiction, the bliss born of pain, declared itself but of the heart of nature. And thus, wherever the Dionysian

> prevailed, the Apollonian was routed and annihilated. But it is quite as certain that, where the first assault was successfully withstood, the authority and majesty of the Delphic god exhibited itself as more rigid and menacing than ever. For I can only explain to myself the *Doric* state and Doric art as a permanent war-camp of the Apollonian: only by incessant opposition to the titanic-barbaric nature of the Dionysian was it possible for an art so defiantly-prim, so encompassed with bulwarks, a training so warlike and rigorous, a constitution so cruel and relentless, to last for any length of time.

Ancient Greek Culture Lived as an Embodiment of Nietzsche's Thalesian Insight

In the above, he states that the ancient Greeks, in whom the Apollonian forces had reached a level of development previously unknown and since never matched, abided most religiously by their dictums of self-knowledge and self-restraint in order to preserve themselves. But, at the same time, they knew better than anyone since that it was precisely the titanic emotion arising from within horrific suffering that gave rise to their visionary genius. They knew better than anyone since that what was required in life was *both* a highly developed realm of emotion as well as a highly developed realm of mind. They knew that the two necessarily go hand in hand. Thus, they experienced life as a musically rhythmed movement of extremes, where an excessively developed Dionysian side was eventually tamed by the Apollonian side and, intermittently, an excessively developed Apollonian side was eventually destroyed by the Dionysian side. And it was that very rare wisdom that gave birth to proto-tragedy, as we shall see shortly.

> Up to this point we have enlarged upon the observation made at the beginning of this essay: how the Dionysian and the Apollonian, in ever new births succeeding and mutually augmenting one another, controlled the Hellenic genius: how from out the age of "bronze," with its Titan struggles and rigorous folk-philosophy, the Homeric world develops under the fostering sway of the Apollonian impulse to beauty, how this "naïve" splendour is again overwhelmed by the inbursting flood of the Dionysian, and how against this new power the Apollonian rises to the austere majesty of Doric art and the Doric view of things. If, then, in this way, in the strife of these two hostile principles, the older Hellenic history falls into four great periods of art, we are now driven to inquire after the ulterior purpose of these unfoldings and processes, unless perchance we should regard the last-attained period, the period of Doric art, as the end and aim of these artistic impulses: and here the sublime and highly celebrated art-work of *Attic tragedy* and dramatic dithyramb presents itself to our view as the common goal of both these impulses, whose

4: MYTH HEALS AND ENABLES LIFE

> mysterious union, after many and long precursory struggles, found its glorious consummation in such a child,—which is at once Antigone and Cassandra.

Proto-Tragedy Is Symbiosis of the Two Realms of Sensation and Ideation

Nietzsche restates that, when Apollonian forces became threatened by surging Dionysian forces, the Apollonian forces would rebound with even greater strength, and that the two sides would remain eternally opposed to each other. Eventually, however, the two forces of human nature would join together, no longer eternally opposed but intermittently reconciling and taunting each other and, in that union, would beget proto-tragedy.

The essay now moves on to a discussion of the dithyramb and, eventually, dithyrambic drama as tragedy.

5: The Role of Art in Life

We now approach the real purpose of our investigation, which aims at acquiring a knowledge of the Dionyso-Apollonian genius and his art-work, or at least an anticipatory understanding of the mystery of the aforesaid union. Here we shall ask first of all where that new germ which subsequently developed into tragedy and dramatic dithyramb first makes itself perceptible in the Hellenic world. The ancients themselves supply the answer in symbolic form, when they place *Homer* and *Archilochus* as the forefathers and torch-bearers of Greek poetry side by side on gems, sculptures, etc., in the sure conviction that only these two thoroughly original compeers, from whom a stream of fire flows over the whole of Greek posterity, should be taken into consideration. Homer, the aged dreamer sunk in himself, the type of the Apollonian naïve artist, beholds now with astonishment the impassioned genius of the warlike votary of the muses, Archilochus, violently tossed to and fro on the billows of existence: and modern æsthetics could only add by way of interpretation, that here the "objective" artist is confronted by the first "subjective" artist. But this interpretation is of little service to us, because we know the subjective artist only as the poor artist, and in every type and elevation of art we demand specially and first of all the conquest of the Subjective, the redemption from the "ego" and the cessation of every individual will and desire; indeed, we find it impossible to believe in any truly artistic production, however insignificant, without objectivity, without pure, interestless contemplation. Hence our æsthetics must first solve the problem as to how the "lyrist" is possible as an artist: he who according to the experience of all ages continually says "I" and sings off to us the entire chromatic scale of his passions and desires. This very Archilochus appals us, alongside of Homer, by his cries of hatred and scorn, by the drunken outbursts of his desire. Is not just he then, who has been called the first subjective artist, the non-artist proper? But whence then the reverence which was shown to him—the poet—in very remarkable utterances by the Delphic oracle itself, the focus of "objective" art?

Art Speaks from the Belly of Being

Here, Nietzsche identifies Homer as an epic poet who is engaged in the creation of art as appearance that is intended to induce contemplation of beautiful images in the beholder, and he identifies Archilochus as a lyric poet who is engaged in the creation of art as passion that is intended to induce arousal of emotion in the beholder. And he speaks of the false appearance that Homer the epic poet is an objective artist, which is quite proper with regard to the aims of art, and that Archilochus is a subjective artist, which is quite improper because art is not art if it does not appeal to everyone and subjective art does not appeal to everyone insofar as, in the case of Archilochus, it depicts the passions of a single individual, namely Archilochus. Nietzsche points out specifically that good art must be devoid of anything that is egotistical or communicating a will or a desire that is original only to a particular individual. And in lyrical poetry, the artist is continually reciting the word "I" in his poetry, suggesting he speaks of himself in his art. Having said that, Nietzsche then makes a sharp turn and embarks on a roller coast ride of explanations that I believe few will follow, as below.

> *Schiller* has enlightened us concerning his poetic procedure by a psychological observation, inexplicable to himself, yet not apparently open to any objection. He acknowledges that as the preparatory state to the act of poetising he had not perhaps before him or within him a series of pictures with co-ordinate causality of thoughts, but rather a *musical mood* ("The perception

with me is at first without a clear and definite object; this forms itself later. A certain musical mood of mind precedes, and only after this does the poetical idea follow with me.") Add to this the most important phenomenon of all ancient lyric poetry, *the union,* regarded everywhere as natural, *of the lyrist with the musician,* their very identity, indeed,—compared with which our modern lyric poetry is like the statue of a god without a head,—and we may now, on the basis of our metaphysics of æsthetics set forth above, interpret the lyrist to ourselves as follows. As Dionysian artist he is in the first place become altogether one with the Primordial Unity, its pain and contradiction, and he produces the copy of this Primordial Unity as music, granting that music has been correctly termed a repetition and a recast of the world; but now, under the Apollonian dream-inspiration, this music again becomes visible to him as in a *symbolic dream-picture.* The formless and intangible reflection of the primordial pain in music, with its redemption in appearance, then generates a second mirroring as a concrete symbol or example. The artist has already surrendered his subjectivity in the Dionysian process: the picture which now shows to him his oneness with the heart of the world, is a dream-scene, which embodies the primordial contradiction and

> primordial pain, together with the primordial joy, of appearance. The "I" of the lyrist sounds therefore from the abyss of being: its "subjectivity," in the sense of the modern æsthetes, is a fiction. When Archilochus, the first lyrist of the Greeks, makes known both his mad love and his contempt to the daughters of Lycambes, it is not his passion which dances before us in orgiastic frenzy: we see Dionysus and the Mænads, we see the drunken reveller Archilochus sunk down to sleep—as Euripides depicts it in the Bacchæ, the sleep on the high Alpine pasture, in the noonday sun:—and now Apollo approaches and touches him with the laurel. The Dionyso-musical enchantment of the sleeper now emits, as it were, picture sparks, lyrical poems, which in their highest development are called tragedies and dramatic dithyrambs.

First, he says that the composition of poetry arises from a musical mood. Then he says that lyrical poetry has historically been identified as akin to music. And finally, he says that lyrical poetry arises from the Dionysian realm of human nature.

- That the lyricist is fused with the Primordial Unity, a Oneness with Nature;

- A Oneness with Nature bespeaks pain and contradiction;

5: THE ROLE OF ART IN LIFE

- The lyricist produces a representation of the pain and contradiction inherent in the Oneness with Nature *as music*;

- But then, under the influence of the Apollonian side of human nature, that musical representation is transformed into an image or vision that reverberates the same pain and contradiction.

- Most importantly, the vision or image of primordial pain and contradiction *redeems* that pain and contradiction.

Let us think simply and say that the Primordial Unity is simply an experience with one's own inner nature absent the prejudices of devolved egotistical being, or, to put it another way, to experience one's feelings absent any fear of or other antipathy toward them, to simply allow one's feelings to come forth freely, without any repression or mitigation or other distortion. To produce a representation of, for instance, a deep-seated pain, would be to articulate it, thereby acknowledging its reality and giving it free rein, transforming it from an unutterable and haunting disturbance into an articulable emotion, which would not be easy. But that articulation would be a representation of it. Upon achieving that articulation, something quite extraordinary happens: the beholder sees his Self in the pain. In other words, the pain becomes reverberated in the image of Self. It may not be easy for the reader to imagine that reverberation as a concept if he or she has never experienced it, which would entail overcoming dismemberment, at least temporarily. But that is, in fact, what happens. Sometimes, the order is reversed, so that the subject sees his Self in the pain first and then is able to articulate it, but it is all the same thing. In my own experience, subliminal and repressed pain seems insuperable and only becomes livable (or embodiable) after seeing one's Self in it. And that is because the illusory nature of mythical Self *redeems* the pain with the beauty of *appearance*. In such a way, the beauty of appearance makes life worth living. The beauty of appearance also invokes a yearning that translates to a yearning for life, in contrast to the pain that extinguishes any such longing.

Granted, all these insights are applied by Nietzsche to the composition of poetry, specifically dithyrambic poetry, but it is necessary first to understand them as phenomena that play out within us, which, hopefully, you now do.

Continuing with the second half of the above paragraph, Nietzsche then goes on to say that when the lyricist writes "I," it is not him personally about which he writes, but rather human nature in general, which Nietzsche references as speaking from the "abyss of being." The most important point to understand about the composition and interpretation of poetry is that when you read "I," it is not the poet who speaks but rather "you" or "all men" or "human nature" that speaks. This becomes very relevant when you read *Thus Spoke Zarathustra*, which is written entirely in the dithyramb and which speaks from the belly of being so that the speaking "I' in the dithyramb is the speaking belly of being, not the speaking individual.

Tragic "Music" as Will Prompts Mythopoeia as Reverberation

Lastly, in the paragraph above, he writes that "The Dionyso-musical enchantment of the sleeper now emits, as it were, picture sparks, lyrical poems, which in their highest development are called tragedies and dramatic dithyrambs."

5: THE ROLE OF ART IN LIFE

This goes to the point, upon which we will elaborate shortly, that the aim of the dithyramb as an art form is mythopoeia, the creation of a visionary image ("picture sparks") within the actor who undertakes the dithyrambic drama. However, remember also that, as we have revealed from Nietzsche's insights via this reiteration, myth represents the fulfillment of a most profound need arising out of a tension created by suffering. And since myth arises out of suffering, then the actor who undertakes the dithyrambic drama for the purpose of envisioning the myths that are taught therein must also undertake the same measure of suffering. And the "I" that suffers in the dithyrambic drama is a universal "I," but certainly not Nietzsche's "I."

> The plastic artist, as also the epic poet, who is related to him, is sunk in the pure contemplation of pictures. The Dionysian musician is, without any picture, himself just primordial pain and the primordial re-echoing thereof. The lyric genius is conscious of a world of pictures and symbols—growing out of the state of mystical self-abnegation and oneness,—which has a colouring causality and velocity quite different from that of the world of the plastic artist and epic poet. While the latter lives in these pictures, and only in them, with joyful satisfaction, and never grows tired of contemplating them with love, even in their minutest characters, while even the picture of the angry Achilles is to him but a picture, the angry expression of which he enjoys with the dream-joy in appearance—

so that, by this mirror of appearance, he is guarded against being unified and blending with his figures;—the pictures of the lyrist on the other hand are nothing but *his very* self and, as it were, only different projections of himself, on account of which he as the moving centre of this world is entitled to say "I": only of course this self is not the same as that of the waking, empirically real man, but the only verily existent and eternal self resting at the basis of things, by means of the images whereof the lyric genius sees through even to this basis of things. Now let us suppose that he beholds *himself* also among these images as non-genius, *i.e.,* his subject, the whole throng of subjective passions and impulses of the will directed to a definite object which appears real to him; if now it seems as if the lyric genius and the allied non-genius were one, and as if the former spoke that little word "I" of his own accord, this appearance will no longer be able to lead us astray, as it certainly led those astray who designated the lyrist as the subjective poet. In truth, Archilochus, the passionately inflamed, loving and hating man, is but a vision of the genius, who by this time is no longer Archilochus, but a genius of the world, who expresses his primordial pain symbolically in the figure of the man Archilochus: while the subjectively willing

5: THE ROLE OF ART IN LIFE

> and desiring man, Archilochus, can never at any time be a poet. It is by no means necessary, however, that the lyrist should see nothing but the phenomenon of the man Archilochus before him as a reflection of eternal being; and tragedy shows how far the visionary world of the lyrist may depart from this phenomenon, to which, of course, it is most intimately related.

The points we need to consider form the above are:

- The Apollonian artist, and specifically the epic poet, is engaged in the pure *contemplation* of visions, but the Dionysian artist, and specifically the dithyrambic poet, is engaged in the pure *experience* of emotion *in addition* to its reverberation in visions or images, which are a direct production of dithyrambic poetry.

- While the dithyrambic poet is immersed in the experience of emotions, and, as we shall see shortly, specifically ruth, he is also aware of an entire realm of visions arising out of that experience.

- In addition, the visions arising out of the dithyrambic poet's experience of emotion possess a vitality, an animation, and a more resplendent reality than what is reflected in the epic poet's visions; they bear a stronger significance, particularly to the emotions out of which they arise, and they reveal a meaning about the "abyss of being," the Dionysian side of life. That meaning, which presents itself as a reverberation or echo, is lacking in the epic poet's visions.

Schopenhauer, who did not shut his eyes to the difficulty presented by the lyrist in the philosophical contemplation of art, thought he had found a way out of it, on which, however, I cannot accompany him; while he alone, in his profound metaphysics of music, held in his hands the means whereby this difficulty could be definitely removed: as I believe I have removed it here in his spirit and to his honour. In contrast to our view, he describes the peculiar nature of song as follows[5] (*Welt als Wille und Vorstellung,* I. 295):—"It is the subject of the will, *i.e.,* his own volition, which fills the consciousness of the singer; often as an unbound and satisfied desire (joy), but still more often as a restricted desire (grief), always as an emotion, a passion, or an agitated frame of mind. Besides this, however, and along with it, by the sight of surrounding nature, the singer becomes conscious of himself as the subject of pure will-less knowing, the unbroken, blissful peace of which now appears, in contrast to the stress of desire, which is always restricted and always needy. The feeling of this contrast, this alternation, is really what the song as a whole expresses and what principally constitutes the lyrical state of

---

[5] *World as Will and Idea*, I. 323, 4th ed. of Haldane and Kemp's translation. Quoted with a few changes.

5: THE ROLE OF ART IN LIFE

> mind. In it pure knowing comes to us as it were to deliver us from desire and the stress thereof: we follow, but only for an instant; for desire, the remembrance of our personal ends, tears us anew from peaceful contemplation; yet ever again the next beautiful surrounding in which the pure will-less knowledge presents itself to us, allures us away from desire. Therefore, in song and in the lyrical mood, desire (the personal interest of the ends) and the pure perception of the surrounding which presents itself, are wonderfully mingled with each other; connections between them are sought for and imagined; the subjective disposition, the affection of the will, imparts its own hue to the contemplated surrounding, and conversely, the surroundings communicate the reflex of their colour to the will. The true song is the expression of the whole of this mingled and divided state of mind."

Nietzsche here summarizes Schopenhauer's understanding of the lyricist, though he does not agree with him, insofar as Schopenhauer saw the lyricist as a subjective artist, not an objective artist in the way that Nietzsche viewed Archilochus. But the point to grasp is that both Nietzsche and Schopenhauer saw an arousal of emotion in poetry that was then complemented or accompanied by a vision of beauty. Schopenhauer saw a release of and from the lyricist's emotion (his will) in that vision. Nietzsche saw a redemption of the lyricist's will in the vision.

> Who could fail to see in this description that lyric poetry is here characterised as an imperfectly attained art, which seldom and only as it were in leaps arrives at its goal, indeed, as a semi-art, the essence of which is said to consist in this, that desire and pure contemplation, *i.e.,* the unæsthetic and the æsthetic condition, are wonderfully mingled with each other? We maintain rather, that this entire antithesis, according to which, as according to some standard of value, Schopenhauer, too, still classifies the arts, the antithesis between the subjective and the objective, is quite out of place in æsthetics, inasmuch as the subject *i.e.,* the desiring individual who furthers his own egoistic ends, can be conceived only as the adversary, not as the origin of art. In so far as the subject is the artist, however, he has already been released from his individual will, and has become as it were the medium, through which the one verily existent Subject celebrates his redemption in appearance. For this one thing must above all be clear to us, to our humiliation *and* exaltation, that the entire comedy of art is not at all performed, say, for our betterment and culture, and that we are just as little the true authors of this art-

5: THE ROLE OF ART IN LIFE

> world: rather we may assume with regard to ourselves, that its true author uses us as pictures and artistic projections, and that we have our highest dignity in our significance as works of art—for only as an *æsthetic phenomenon* is existence and the world eternally *justified:*—while of course our consciousness of this our specific significance hardly differs from the kind of consciousness which the soldiers painted on canvas have of the battle represented thereon. Hence all our knowledge of art is at bottom quite illusory, because, as knowing persons we are not one and identical with the Being who, as the sole author and spectator of this comedy of art, prepares a perpetual entertainment for himself. Only in so far as the genius in the act of artistic production coalesces with this primordial artist of the world, does he get a glimpse of the eternal essence of art, for in this state he is, in a marvellous manner, like the weird picture of the fairy-tale which can at will turn its eyes and behold itself; he is now at once subject and object, at once poet, actor, and spectator.

Notice above that Nietzsche equates the unaesthetic with emotion or will and the aesthetic with vision or idea. And he says, as does Schopenhauer, that there is a certain mingling or interaction that plays out between the two, which goes directly to the notion of art arising out of the antagonistic relationship between the Dionysian and Apollonian forces. Notice also his assertion that lyrical poetry seldom reaches its end, which would be either a representation of the will or of a vision of the will, and, when it does, it succeeds only by a grand leap.

And take particular notice of his statement that "In so far as the subject is the artist, however, he has already been released from his individual will, and has become as it were the medium, through which the one verily existent Subject celebrates his redemption in appearance." When Nietzsche says "in so far as the subject is the artist," he contradicts Schopenhauer's assertion that the lyricist exclaims his own volition in his poetry and asserts, instead, that the "subject" is not a subject at all but rather has become the artist, the creator. What he seeks to create is a representation of the "abyss of being," the "Primal Unity," the communion of Self with emotion absent the prejudice of Ego. And to the extent that he succeeds, then he himself becomes the medium, the vehicle, the canvass, for that representation. However, that which he endeavors to create is a representation of an unvarnished communion with human nature, so, in that sense, he is also the subject of the representation, inasmuch as he himself possesses the human nature that he is trying to depict, but the subject is certainly not an egocentric participant in the instance of human nature that is being depicted.

All of this makes much more sense if we apply it to the actor who undertakes Nietzsche's dithyrambic drama, which is something I have already explained quite extensively in *The Birth of Dionysia* and will not do again here. The dithyrambs of *Thus Spoke Zarathustra*, all eighty-one of them, are representations of human nature, specifically human nature in the throes of conflict between conscience and passion as well as human nature in the redemptive *and visionary* victories that ensue after overcoming those conflicts. Every dithyramb ends with the words "Thus Spoke Zarathustra," but there is no character named Zarathustra. Zarathustra is the name given to the voice of the "abyss of being" that speaks to us of human nature and the process of growth, of life, that plays out within human being. And that voice speaks to us from out of an innermost communion with Self and emotion, from out of the belly of being, that is itself absent any distraction or prejudice or other confusion *whatsoever* — and certainly not from out of Nietzsche's egocentric being.

The Consummation of Life as an Aesthetic Phenomenon

What is most noteworthy about this particular passage is what Nietzsche did not say and only hinted at: "only as an *æsthetic phenomenon* is existence and the world eternally *justified*." As we previously noted, Nietzsche considers that which is aesthetic to be found only in the Apollonian realm, while that which is unaesthetic is found in the Dionysian realm. More specifically, that which is aesthetic is beauty and illusion, both of which impart redemption and healing, and it is the beauty and the healing that make the world eternally justified, that turn the wisdom of Silenus — about life not being worth living — on its head, so that the subject who achieves redemption and healing via image proclaims instead that life is most worthy of living.

And the single most aesthetic phenomenon from which derive the redemptive qualities of beauty and illusion is mythopoeia, the creation of myth. The creation of myth, whether it be a mythical being, as in Self, or a gateway myth, as in the idea of an eternally recurring world, is the art in

Nietzsche's Thalesian insight, as stated in the first sentence of his essay. But, incredibly, he never comes out with it, not explicitly. Instead, he spoke only of Greek art, which left everyone talking about Greek tragedy, in the same erroneous way that Thales' insight left everyone talking about "water."

Dithyrambic Drama as a Close Approximation of Art in Nature

Lastly, to finish up with the last paragraph of cited text, Nietzsche proclaims that mythopoeia is a natural phenomenon, not an invented one. He says "as knowing persons we are not one and identical with the Being who, as the sole author and spectator of this comedy of art, prepares a perpetual entertainment for himself." The "Being" may be God, although I doubt very much that is what he meant. Or it may be Heraclitus' great child of chance, which is a much more likely possibility. But quite simply, he means Nature. And he says that, through natural mythopoeia, Nature turns us ourselves into its works of art. And inasmuch as we are ourselves illusory works of art, the illusoriness distinguishes us from Nature itself. We are mere projections cast in the image of Nature, and, as images, our knowledge of the artistic process is therewith limited. We can get a close approximation of the process and we can employ that approximation in a copy of Nature, but we can never really achieve a wielding of the hand by which Nature itself makes its strokes. And I propose to you that is precisely what dithyrambic drama is: a spot-on approximation of the artistic process by which Nature plays out its comedy, the child's game of chance.

And finally, he says "Only in so far as the genius in the act of artistic production coalesces with this primordial artist of the world does he get a glimpse of the eternal essence of art, for in

5: THE ROLE OF ART IN LIFE

this state he is, in a marvelous manner, like the weird picture of the fairy-tale which can at will turn its eyes and behold itself; he is now at once subject and object, at once poet, actor, and spectator." Keeping in mind that it is dithyrambic drama we most wish to understand, we might reiterate Nietzsche's insight to say that only insofar as the dithyrambist succeeds in replicating the phenomena leading to mythopoeia will he also succeed in experiencing "the eternal essence of art." But so, too, will the actor undertaking the dithyrambic drama also experience the eternal essence of art. Indeed, one might rightly say that the actor who undertakes Nietzsche's dithyrambic drama is — at the same time — subject and object of the drama and both actor and spectator. Through dithyrambic drama, the actor himself becomes a work of art.

6: Theory of Dithyrambic Music

With reference to Archilochus, it has been established by critical research that he introduced the *folk-song* into literature, and, on account thereof, deserved, according to the general estimate of the Greeks, his unique position alongside of Homer. But what is this popular folk-song in contrast to the wholly Apollonian epos? What else but the *perpetuum vestigium* of a union of the Apollonian and the Dionysian? Its enormous diffusion among all peoples, still further enhanced by ever new births, testifies to the power of this artistic double impulse of nature: which leaves its vestiges in the popular song in like manner as the orgiastic movements of a people perpetuate themselves in its music. Indeed, one might also furnish historical proofs, that every period which is highly productive in popular songs has been most violently stirred by Dionysian currents, which we must always

6: THEORY OF DITHYRAMBIC MUSIC

> regard as the substratum and prerequisite of the popular song.

Dithyrambic Drama as an Admixture of Epic and Lyrical Poetry

In this paragraph, he states that in contrast with epic poetry, which engages strictly with image as its art form, folk-song, which he is no longer equating to lyrical poetry but as something unto itself, engages in both the Apollonian and the Dionysian, which is to say both emotion and vision (as idea and myth). What he is doing is making his way to the point that dithyrambic poetry, unlike epic poetry, which deals with image, and unlike lyrical poetry, which deals with passion, in fact, deals with both, though, at this point in the essay, he is merely equating the dithyramb with the folk song without explicitly defining the dithyramb.

> First of all, however, we regard the popular song as the musical mirror of the world, as the Original melody, which now seeks for itself a parallel dream-phenomenon and expresses it in poetry. *Melody is therefore primary and universal,* and as such may admit of several objectivations, in several texts. Likewise, in the naïve estimation of the people, it is regarded as by far the more important and necessary. Melody generates the poem out of itself by an ever-recurring process. *The strophic form of the popular song* points to the same phenomenon, which I always beheld with astonishment, till at

> last I found this explanation. Any one who in accordance with this theory examines a collection of popular songs, such as "Des Knaben Wunderhorn," will find innumerable instances of the perpetually productive melody scattering picture sparks all around: which in their variegation, their abrupt change, their mad precipitance, manifest a power quite unknown to the epic appearance and its steady flow. From the point of view of the epos, this unequal and irregular pictorial world of lyric poetry must be simply condemned: and the solemn epic rhapsodists of the Apollonian festivals in the age of Terpander have certainly done so.

First Mention of Dithyrambic Music

With this, Nietzsche now moves his focus to music, and, eventually, he will begin referencing something he calls dramatic music, which is not at all like audible, traditional music. It is a new concept, and it is not easy to grasp. But, for the time being, I would direct the reader's attention to his mention of a relationship between music and the creation of image. Next, he equates that which he calls music with will. And he begins to speak of a representation of will in language. And that is very significant because the dithyramb is a literary representation of the will and, as such, defines Nietzsche's new concept of "dithyrambic music" and his theory that dithyrambic music invokes mythopoeia, the creation of Self and other gateway ideas that enable the will. Lastly, notice in the above

6: Theory of Dithyrambic Music

that he once again mentions the creation of image out of "Original melody," which he calls "primary and universal."

> Accordingly, we observe that in the poetising of the popular song, language is strained to its utmost *to imitate music;* and hence a new world of poetry begins with Archilochus, which is fundamentally opposed to the Homeric. And in saying this we have pointed out the only possible relation between poetry and music, between word and tone: the word, the picture, the concept here seeks an expression analogous to music and now experiences in itself the power of music. In this sense we may discriminate between two main currents in the history of the language of the Greek people, according as their language imitated either the world of phenomena and of pictures, or the world of music. One has only to reflect seriously on the linguistic difference with regard to colour, syntactical structure, and vocabulary in Homer and Pindar, in order to comprehend the significance of this contrast; indeed, it becomes palpably clear to us that in the period between Homer and Pindar the *orgiastic flute tones of Olympus* must have sounded forth, which, in an age as late as Aristotle's, when music was infinitely more developed, transported people to drunken enthusiasm, and which, when their

influence was first felt, undoubtedly incited all the poetic means of expression of contemporaneous man to imitation. I here call attention to a familiar phenomenon of our own times, against which our æsthetics raises many objections. We again and again have occasion to observe how a symphony of Beethoven compels the individual hearers to use figurative speech, though the appearance presented by a collocation of the different pictorial world generated by a piece of music may be never so fantastically diversified and even contradictory. To practise its small wit on such compositions, and to overlook a phenomenon which is certainly worth explaining, is quite in keeping with this æsthetics. Indeed, even if the tone-poet has spoken in pictures concerning a composition, when for instance he designates a certain symphony as the "pastoral" symphony, or a passage therein as "the scene by the brook," or another as the "merry gathering of rustics," these are likewise only symbolical representations born out of music—and not perhaps the imitated objects of music—representations which can give us no information whatever concerning the *Dionysian* content of music, and which in fact have no distinctive value of their own alongside of other pictorical expressions. This process of a discharge of music in

> pictures we have now to transfer to some youthful, linguistically productive people, to get a notion as to how the strophic popular song originates, and how the entire faculty of speech is stimulated by this new principle of imitation of music.

- "... the word, the picture, the concept here seeks an expression analogous to music and now experiences in itself the power of music."
- "... according as their language imitated either the world of phenomena and of pictures, or the world of music."
- "This process of a discharge of music in pictures ..."
- "... by this new principle of imitation of music."

Music as Will

For the time being, until we get into a more detailed explanation of what Nietzsche means by "music," suffice it to say that he means will. However, will itself is merely a representation of "music" and does not reach into the depths of human nature they way "music" does. From the three bullets outlined above, the concept of something (anything) seeks to find its expression in "music," and, as we are about to see, finds it in will. With that, the concept attains a much deeper meaning than it would without the expression it finds of itself in will. For instance, consider a man who scans the horizon of his consciousness and realizes that there are subliminal emotions within him that lay beyond that horizon. He knows this, and his

DIONYSIA METAPHYSICA

concept of those emotions is that of haunting rumblings, demons. Eventually, he finds his way to see his Self in those subliminal emotions so that they are no longer mere foreign rumblings but a dimension of his being, wherein he becomes moved by them. And when that happens, then those emotions that were once foreign hauntings are now his emotions. With that, they become invested with his will. With that, the concept of demon now experiences itself in the power of the will and literally comes to life. And, inasmuch as those emotions become invested with his will, they attain a higher and deeper meaning. That is an example of the concept seeking an expression of itself in will and, in succeeding, also experiencing itself in the power of the will. And that is an example of how "music," or will, transforms the empty and hollow concept (of anything) into something that instead reflects the spirit and meaning of the will out of which it arose. But the reader must remember that Nietzsche continually uses the word "music" to mean will, and the reader must understand "will" when Nietzsche says "music."

Next, in the second bullet above, Nietzsche speaks of poetry as language that imitates either concepts or will, which, we now know, are two very different things, as per my example. In epic poetry, language clearly imitates or reflects concept, insofar as it presents itself expressly for the purpose of contemplating images. Later, he will go on to say that folk poetry or dithyrambic poetry is language that imitates will purely, absent any concept whatsoever. And the "pure" representation of will, which is dithyrambic music proper, is also void of any visions, though dithyrambic music produces image and vision *secondarily, as art*.

However, it is within the nature of concept that it seeks to find an expression of itself in will. Except that it is not so much that concept actively struggles with will to find a place for itself therein. It is more that will discharges itself in concept, thereby transforming concept into a dimension of the will. And the concept that arises from out of the depth of the will has a far greater depth and meaning than concept that sits alone outside the realm of the will. All of this goes to the creation of art from out of the Apollonian-Dionysian duality or, more specifically, the act of mythopoeia out of an interaction between sensation and ideation.

"Music" as Mythopoeia

Finally, in the fourth above bullet, Nietzsche speaks of a "new principle," wherein poetry seeks to imitate the creation of both will and concept, unlike epic poetry that deals only with concept and unlike lyrical poetry that deals only with passion. This "new principle" is Nietzsche's invention of dithyrambic poetry that deals in *both* concept or image and passion, but with concept or image being a naturally occurring discharge or creation of will — or, more simply, *art*. Whereas Schiller said that poetry starts with emotion, Nietzsche says that concept, and more importantly, much more importantly, myth — starts with will. Find a way to represent the will and you have found a way to represent, nay, *create*, image, concept, and myth.

> If, therefore, we may regard lyric poetry as the effulguration of music in pictures and concepts, we can now ask: "how does music *appear* in the mirror of symbolism and conception?" *It appears as will,* taking the word in the Schopenhauerian

sense, *i.e.,* as the antithesis of the æsthetic, purely contemplative, and passive frame of mind. Here, however, we must discriminate as sharply as possible between the concept of essentiality and the concept of phenominality; for music, according to its essence, cannot be will, because as such it would have to be wholly banished from the domain of art—for the will is the unæsthetic-in-itself;—yet it appears as will. For in order to express the phenomenon of music in pictures, the lyrist requires all the stirrings of passion, from the whispering of infant desire to the roaring of madness. Under the impulse to speak of music in Apollonian symbols, he conceives of all nature, and himself therein, only as the eternally willing, desiring, longing existence. But in so far as he interprets music by means of pictures, he himself rests in the quiet calm of Apollonian contemplation, however much all around him which he beholds through the medium of music is in a state of confused and violent motion. Indeed, when he beholds himself through this same medium, his own image appears to him in a state of unsatisfied feeling: his own willing, longing, moaning and rejoicing are to him symbols by which he interprets music. Such is the phenomenon of the lyrist: as Apollonian genius he interprets music through the

> image of the will, while he himself, completely released from the avidity of the will, is the pure, undimmed eye of day.

- "… we must discriminate as sharply as possible between the concept of essentiality and the concept of phenomenality…."
- "…he himself rests in the quiet calm of Apollonian contemplation, however much all around him which he beholds through the medium of music is in a state of confused and violent motion."
- "Such is the phenomenon of the lyrist: as Apollonian genius he interprets music through the image of the will…."

Reality vs. Actuality

The distinction between the concept of essentiality and the concept of phenomenality goes to the distinction between reality and actuality. That which we call reality is that which is reflected in the Self. Using the example I used above once again, when a man finally admits his subliminal emotions into his consciousness, they become a dimension of his being, which means they are transformed from foreign haunting rumblings into true emotions, into reality. In that transformation, the man might rightly say that his demons have become real; they have become an aspect of reality to the extent that he acknowledges reality. Whereas, previously, he denied the reality of these feelings, not because he thought they were not real but because he lacked the strength and the bravery to lend them the quality of reality. Yet, despite the denial of the quality of reality, they continued to haunt him nonetheless because, though they may not exist all the time in reality, they *do* exist all the time in actuality. That is the difference between reality and actuality. And who would deny that they deem reality the higher, truer domain of experience, when, in fact, the truer domain is actuality?

But what is reality? Reality is that which is reflected in the Self. The Self is pure image, pure Apollonian, and, in the same way, that which it reflects is pure image. But image is an illusion that does not exist except in the mind of its beholder. All that exists — actually — is that which is a part of the Dionysian realm, which is only pure sensation. And it is this actuality that Nietzsche refers to as "music." Thus, reality is a creation of art. Reality constitutes the aesthetic. And it is precisely for that reason that terrifying emotions that seem insuperable suddenly become tolerable when seen through the eyes of the Self.

Do not be confused by Nietzsche's choice of metaphor to allude to something that only his extraordinary vision of genius was able to see. That is the same mistake people make when they speak of Thales' insight into the essence of all things that "all is water." Nietzsche, at least, understood that statement to mean something else, according to what he wrote about it.

> And just as words and verse to the dramatist are only stammerings in a foreign language, to tell in it what he lived, what he saw, and what he can directly promulgate by gesture and music only, thus the expression of every deep philosophical intuition by means of dialectics and scientific reflection is, it is true, on the one hand the only means to communicate what has been seen, but on the

> other hand it is a paltry means, and at the bottom a metaphorical, absolutely inexact translation into a different sphere and language. Thus Thales saw the Unity of the "Existent," and when he wanted to communicate this idea he talked of water.

Nietzsche never said explicitly what he thought Thales meant, but, obviously, per the above, he took the word "water" as a metaphor. It is my opinion that Thales meant "all is becoming," not "all is water."

But in the same way, when Nietzsche speaks of the essence of all things as "music," he means something other than our common conception of audible music. In order to understand why he chose the metaphor "music" to describe what he perceived as the essence of all things (that is, the essence beyond all appearance), we will need to elucidate this further, and we will do so shortly when we come upon the quality of dissonance in music.

The Representation of "Music" in Metaphor

Lastly, I would point the reader to the last bullet in the above citation. The lyricist, unlike the dithyrambist, may indeed be engaged in the representation of passion, unlike the epic poet who is engaged in the pure contemplation of image and its beauty, but, still, the lyrical representation remains an image, though it be an image of the will. Shortly, we will move on to the point that dithyrambic poetry is a representation of actuality, which is why we may rightly call it dithyrambic music. This is a very important point that I wish to make very clear. Like the lyricist, the dithyrambist wants to communicate will, which

Nietzsche calls "music." To put it another way, the dithyrambist aims to communicate desire, for instance, not by saying "you must want this to happen," but rather by actually communicating the desire itself by presenting an embodiable representation of the desire, which, once embodied, literally moves the actor who achieved the embodiment to the same extent that any desire moves a subject who is beholden to the desire. In this way, the actor undertakes the drama and attains to the images and concepts and especially the myths *from within* via will (from within the music out of which the images naturally arise) rather than from without via concept. And, in such a way, those images and concepts and myths that are attained from within via will are endowed with a much higher meaning than if they were attained via concept. Moreover, repeating what Nietzsche said above about the dramatist wanting to communicate what he has himself already lived through and not being able to do it except in metaphor and gesture, making the metaphors obviously gesticulative and not literal then serves to point the actor more directly to the will that his metaphors are meant to represent. Except that, up until now, everyone has taken the dithyrambist's metaphors literally. He says himself that words are an "absolutely inexact translation into a different sphere and language." And has not every single reader of *Thus Spoke Zarathustra* been taken to a completely different sphere and language than what Nietzsche the dramatist intended, namely a story, which it is not?

> Our whole disquisition insists on this, that lyric poetry is dependent on the spirit of music just as music itself in its absolute sovereignty does not *require* the picture and the concept, but only *endures* them as

6: Theory of Dithyrambic Music

> accompaniments. The poems of the lyrist can express nothing which has not already been contained in the vast universality and absoluteness of the music which compelled him to use figurative speech. By no means is it possible for language adequately to render the cosmic symbolism of music, for the very reason that music stands in symbolic relation to the primordial contradiction and primordial pain in the heart of the Primordial Unity, and therefore symbolises a sphere which is above all appearance and before all phenomena. Rather should we say that all phenomena, compared with it, are but symbols: hence *language,* as the organ and symbol of phenomena, cannot at all disclose the innermost essence, of music; language can only be in superficial contact with music when it attempts to imitate music; while the profoundest significance of the latter cannot be brought one step nearer to us by all the eloquence of lyric poetry.

- "By no means is it possible for language adequately to render the cosmic symbolism of music...."

- "... hence *language,* as the organ and symbol of phenomena, cannot at all disclose the innermost essence, of music; language can only be in superficial contact with music when it attempts to imitate music...."

Therefore, when we read a dithyramb, it is very important to understand that the words we read are but a "superficial contact" with what is *actually* being communicated, which goes to the point that, in fact, those words are merely gestures that are meant to point us in a direction for us to look within ourselves for something comparable within ourselves, namely human will that is totally absent any concept except the concept that may arise later from within that will and only out of an embodiment of that will. In any case, the words of a dithyramb are in no way meant to be taken literally, and this simple point has been missed by everyone for more than a century since the drama was published.

7: Actuality vs. Reality

The Role of the Chorus in Tragedy

> We shall now have to avail ourselves of all the principles of art hitherto considered, in order to find our way through the labyrinth, as we must designate *the origin of Greek tragedy.* I shall not be charged with absurdity in saying that the problem of this origin has as yet not even been seriously stated, not to say solved, however often the fluttering tatters of ancient tradition have been sewed together in sundry combinations and torn asunder again. This tradition tells us in the most unequivocal terms, *that tragedy sprang from the tragic chorus,* and was originally only chorus and nothing but chorus: and hence we feel it our duty to look into the heart of this tragic chorus as being the real proto-drama, without in the least contenting ourselves with current art-phraseology—according to which the chorus is the ideal spectator, or represents the people in contrast to the regal

7: ACTUALITY VS. REALITY

> side of the scene. The latter explanatory notion, which sounds sublime to many a politician—that the immutable moral law was embodied by the democratic Athenians in the popular chorus, which always carries its point over the passionate excesses and extravagances of kings—may be ever so forcibly suggested by an observation of Aristotle: still it has no bearing on the original formation of tragedy, inasmuch as the entire antithesis of king and people, and, in general, the whole politico-social sphere, is excluded from the purely religious beginnings of tragedy; but, considering the well-known classical form of the chorus in Æschylus and Sophocles, we should even deem it blasphemy to speak here of the anticipation of a "constitutional representation of the people," from which blasphemy others have not shrunk, however. The ancient governments knew of no constitutional representation of the people *in praxi,* and it is to be hoped that they did not even so much as "anticipate" it in tragedy.

Nietzsche focuses on the tragic chorus as something that may reveal the origins of proto-tragedy. He then goes no to surmise about the role of the chorus and dismisses any notion that it played a geo-political role in something that he asserts had a religious origin. And we should regard the religious traits of proto-tragedy as the performance of miracles, as something that enables in the face of insuperable obstacles. We should anticipate an understanding of proto-tragedy as a healing art form that produced miraculous results in its healing properties.

Dithyrambic Drama as an Embodiable Representation of Human Will

> Much more celebrated than this political explanation of the chorus is the notion of A. W. Schlegel, who advises us to regard the chorus, in a manner, as the essence and extract of the crowd of spectators,—as the "ideal spectator." This view when compared with the historical tradition that tragedy was originally only chorus, reveals itself in its true character, as a crude, unscientific, yet brilliant assertion, which, however, has acquired its brilliancy only through its concentrated form of expression, through the truly Germanic bias in favour of whatever is called "ideal," and through our momentary astonishment. For we are indeed astonished the moment we compare our well-known theatrical public with this chorus, and ask ourselves if it could ever be possible to idealise something analogous to the Greek chorus out of such a public. We tacitly deny this, and now wonder as much at the boldness of Schlegel's assertion as at the totally different nature of the Greek public. For hitherto we always believed that the true spectator, be he who he may, had

7: ACTUALITY VS. REALITY

> always to remain conscious of having before him a work of art, and not an empiric reality: whereas the tragic chorus of the Greeks is compelled to recognise real beings in the figures of the stage. The chorus of the Oceanides really believes that it sees before it the Titan Prometheus, and considers itself as real as the god of the scene. And are we to own that he is the highest and purest type of spectator, who, like the Oceanides, regards Prometheus as real and present in body? And is it characteristic of the ideal spectator that he should run on the stage and free the god from his torments? We had believed in an æsthetic public, and considered the individual spectator the better qualified the more he was capable of viewing a work of art as art, that is, æsthetically; but now the Schlegelian expression has intimated to us, that the perfect ideal spectator does not at all suffer the world of the scenes to act æsthetically on him, but corporeo-empirically. Oh, these Greeks! we have sighed; they will upset our æsthetics! But once accustomed to it, we have reiterated the saying of Schlegel, as often as the subject of the chorus has been broached.

Next, he goes to discuss the possibility that the chorus represented a spectator and the other possibility that the chorus was a participant.

- "... hitherto we always believed that the true spectator, be he who he may, had always to remain conscious of having before him a work of art, and not an empiric reality: whereas the tragic chorus of the Greeks is compelled to recognise real beings in the figures of the stage."

- "And is it characteristic of the ideal spectator that he should run on the stage and free the god from his torments?"

- "We had believed in an æsthetic public, and considered the individual spectator the better qualified the more he was capable of viewing a work of art as art, that is, æsthetically; but now the Schlegelian expression has intimated to us, that the perfect ideal spectator does not at all suffer the world of the scenes to act æsthetically on him, but corporeo-empirically."

What I ask the reader here to consider is the possibility that a dramatic art form might somehow draw its spectators into itself so that they begin to undertake the drama themselves, rather than viewing before themselves a spectacle that is meant to impress something upon them. Because, as we are about to see, that is precisely the nature of dithyrambic drama, through which the reader, the spectator, himself becomes actor and, at the same time, both the subject matter about which the drama has been composed and the object of the drama, inasmuch as he achieves an embodiment of the human will represented therein, so that he himself, in the end, becomes a work of art. And how could a human being become a work of art? If you read my *Birth of Dionysia*, specifically the exegeses contained therein, you will see many ways that the actor becomes a work of art. But, generally speaking, it happens with the manifestation of beauty within his soul. That said, what is important to take away from the above three bulleted citations is that the dithyrambic drama is a veritable representation of human nature and human will, to the extent that the dithyrambist achieved the closest possible approximation of that nature and that will, and that the reader is meant to become the drama's actor corporally and empirically *by embodying the will that is represented.*

We are accustomed to think of drama as a spectacle. But dithyrambic drama does not present a spectacle.

The Tragic Chorus a Wall Against Ho-Hum, Egotistical Reality

> But the tradition which is so explicit here speaks against Schlegel: the chorus as such, without the stage,—the primitive form of tragedy,—and the chorus of ideal spectators do not harmonise. What kind of art would that be which was extracted from the concept of the spectator, and whereof we are to regard the "spectator as such" as the true form? The spectator without the play is something absurd. We fear that the birth of tragedy can be explained neither by the high esteem for the moral intelligence of the multitude nor by the concept of the spectator without the play; and we regard the problem as too deep to be even so much as touched by such superficial modes of contemplation. An infinitely more valuable insight into the signification of the chorus had already been

> displayed by Schiller in the celebrated Preface to his Bride of Messina, where he regarded the chorus as a living wall which tragedy draws round herself to guard her from contact with the world of reality, and to preserve her ideal domain and poetical freedom.

- "... the chorus [is] a living wall which tragedy draws round herself to guard her from contact with the world of reality...."

After much discussion and speculation about the role of the chorus within tragedy, Nietzsche draws his conclusion and says it was a "wall." What is important to understand here is not Nietzsche's account of Greek tragedy but rather that what he *sees* in Greek tragedy is what we will *find* in his dithyrambic tragedy. And what we find in his tragedy is that the metaphorical structure of Nietzsche's dithyrambs provides a wall surrounding his drama. And that "wall" is bolstered by his construction of a deliberately false appearance of a story that is also canonical, as in the dithyrambs entitled Of Marriage and Children, Of the State, Of the Friend, and others that seem to depict the travels of Zarathustra. *But what is on the other side of the wall,* beyond the false appearance of a story and beyond the false appearance of a book of canon?

The Tragic Chorus as an Ideal Domain

> It is with this, his chief weapon, that Schiller combats the ordinary conception of the natural, the illusion ordinarily required in

7: ACTUALITY VS. REALITY

> dramatic poetry. He contends that while indeed the day on the stage is merely artificial, the architecture only symbolical, and the metrical dialogue purely ideal in character, nevertheless an erroneous view still prevails in the main: that it is not enough to tolerate merely as a poetical license *that* which is in reality the essence of all poetry. The introduction of the chorus is, he says, the decisive step by which war is declared openly and honestly against all naturalism in art.—It is, methinks, for disparaging this mode of contemplation that our would-be superior age has coined the disdainful catchword "pseudo-idealism." I fear, however, that we on the other hand with our present worship of the natural and the real have landed at the nadir of all idealism, namely in the region of cabinets of wax-figures. An art indeed exists also here, as in certain novels much in vogue at present: but let no one pester us with the claim that by this art the Schiller-Goethian "Pseudo-idealism" has been vanquished.

That which exists on the other side of the wall that protects tragedy is an ideal domain, and it is ideal in the sense that naturalism exists within it. But it is a state of naturalism that exists unto itself but which we rarely experience and, therefore, do not understand. It is the chaotic world that exists within subindividuated, egocentric, and suffering man but beyond his Ego — within his Self, wherein resides also a close proximity with emotion. And that is the world, the Dionysian world, that is depicted in Nietzsche's dithyrambs. It is a world of actuality out of which reality arises, and it arises as a creation of art and will. And it is a creation of art that heals man and makes life for him worth living. And "the wall" of metaphor keeps all Ego — with its extreme limitations and its extreme prejudices — out.

> It is indeed an "ideal" domain, as Schiller rightly perceived, upon—which the Greek satyric chorus, the chorus of primitive tragedy, was wont to walk, a domain raised far above the actual path of mortals. The Greek framed for this chorus the suspended scaffolding of a fictitious *natural state* and placed thereon fictitious *natural beings*. It is on this foundation that tragedy grew up, and so it could of course dispense from the very first with a painful portrayal of reality. Yet it is not an arbitrary world placed by fancy betwixt heaven and earth; rather is it a world possessing the same reality and trustworthiness that Olympus with its dwellers possessed for the believing Hellene. The satyr, as being the Dionysian chorist, lives in a religiously acknowledged reality under the sanction of the myth and cult. That tragedy begins with him, that the Dionysian wisdom of tragedy speaks through him, is just as surprising a phenomenon to us as, in general, the derivation of tragedy from the chorus. Perhaps we shall get a starting-point for our

7: ACTUALITY VS. REALITY

> inquiry, if I put forward the proposition that the satyr, the fictitious natural being, is to the man of culture what Dionysian music is to civilisation. Concerning this latter, Richard Wagner says that it is neutralised by music even as lamplight by daylight. In like manner, I believe, the Greek man of culture felt himself neutralised in the presence of the satyric chorus: and this is the most immediate effect of the Dionysian tragedy, that the state and society, and, in general, the gaps between man and man give way to an overwhelming feeling of oneness, which leads back to the heart of nature. The metaphysical comfort,—with which, as I have here intimated, every true tragedy dismisses us—that, in spite of the perpetual change of phenomena, life at bottom is indestructibly powerful and pleasurable, this comfort appears with corporeal lucidity as the satyric chorus, as the chorus of natural beings, who live ineradicable as it were behind all civilisation, and who, in spite of the ceaseless change of generations and the history of nations, remain for ever the same.

- "... a domain raised far above the actual path of mortals."

As the individual undertaking Nietzsche's dithyrambic tragedy begins to delineate his Self amidst the chaos within him, he feels as if raised up to a higher reality.

- "... a fictitious *natural state* and placed thereon fictitious *natural beings* .... It is on this foundation that tragedy grew up...."

The Tragic Chorus as Aborning Reality

The fictitious natural state is reality, the view of the world through the eyes of illusory Self, which rises up out of the world of actuality as art. It is not a view of, for instance, the raw and crass actuality of the horrific and painful haunting demons that linger with minatory exigency within the subconscious but of the articulable reality present in the beauty and healing of the illusory Self that incorporates the subconscious demons into itself as emotion, as a dimension of Self.

As we will see shortly, Nietzsche traced the origin of the proto-tragic phenomenon specifically to dissonance, the accumulation of power that maintains its drive toward a further accumulation by intermittently negating that accumulation while at the same time expanding the base of nutrients on which the drive toward power accrues. In other words, as the dithyrambic actor delineates his Self, he experiences an accumulation of the power that Self-apprehension bestows on him, and that drive toward a further accumulation cannot proceed further except by destroying that vision of Self, which itself constitutes the proto-tragic phenomenon. In destroying existing Self, the actor is able to redraw and extend the horizon, the limits of individuation, to see further into the depths, wherein he finds deeper emotions and, subsequently, a deeper Self. And the whole process starts anew, leading to another tragic collapse of the existing Self and the subsequent mythopoeia of another, different (but original), and deeper Self.

7: ACTUALITY VS. REALITY

But none of this is articulated by Nietzsche in the above citation, though it is important to understand the elevation that Self-discovery imparts (as self-empowerment) because it is that elevation that defines the higher reality that is found in "the satyr chorus."

- "... it could of course dispense from the very first with a painful portrayal of reality. Yet it is not an arbitrary world placed by fancy betwixt heaven and earth; rather is it a world possessing the same reality and trustworthiness that Olympus with its dwellers possessed for the believing Hellene."

The dithyramb is an accurate portrayal of reality. But more importantly, it is not an invention of any one person's fancy; it is an accurate portrayal of actuality, juxtaposed with anticipatory hope alongside the reality that rises up out of that actuality as art.

- "The satyr, as being the Dionysian chorist, lives in a religiously acknowledged reality under the sanction of the myth and cult."

Here, he defines the tragic chorus as a reality higher than that of ho-hum, everyday reality or the supposed reality of cultural man, which is something akin to the reality of a man immersed in egotism. The higher reality of tragic man, in contrast to that of cultural man, is sanctioned by the presence of true, deep, and original Self. Thus, rich with the cloaking veil of Self and not the cloaking veil of Ego, it is founded on illusory myth inasmuch as it is defined by Self and the perspective provided by Self. Nietzsche has not yet reached a discussion of myth in this essay, but he will shortly, and then we shall see quite clearly the role that myth plays in proto-tragedy.

- "... tragedy begins with him ..."
- "... the satyr, the fictitious natural being, is to the man of culture what Dionysian music is to civilisation."

There are people who pride themselves on their sense of culture, but, for those people, that which they call "culture" is nothing more than appearance, a fancy dress that they use to impress themselves and their neighbors. In contrast, there are more genuine people, who, one might say, possess an overbearing rule of integrity that precludes self-aggrandizement. And it is those genuine people who are more likely to possess the more strict manner of honesty that is required to find one's Self. It is for those people that dramatic tragedy is intended.

In Comparison, The Satyr Is to Tragedy as the Idyllic Shepherd Is to Opera

The curious caricature of the satyr, half-man and half-beast is a representation of the *type* of man for whom tragedy, as a religious self-healing art form, is intended. Nietzsche sees the half-beast nature as a more honest and unpretentious nature that is absent the character of the presumptuous Ego. I, on the other hand, see it as a nature in which Self has been destroyed and subsequently devolved into an unwholesome and unmanageable nature in which the fine balance between emotion and idea has run amok. Thus, I see it as primed for the discovery of Self, which is the whole aim of the art and healing process of proto-tragedy.

7: ACTUALITY VS. REALITY

- "… Richard Wagner [or rather Nietzsche] says that [so-called cultured or civilized man] is neutralised by [Dionysian] music even as lamplight by daylight. In like manner, I believe, the Greek man of culture felt himself neutralised in the presence of the satyric chorus: and this is the most immediate effect of the Dionysian tragedy, that the state and society, and, in general, the gaps between man and man give way to an overwhelming feeling of oneness, which leads back to the heart of nature."

In dramatic tragedy, the actor throws off his cultural airs and rejoices in the actuality (or reality) in which he finds himself immersed once he becomes engaged with the drama.

Art as Savior from Nausea

> With this chorus the deep-minded Hellene, who is so singularly qualified for the most delicate and severe suffering, consoles himself:—he who has glanced with piercing eye into the very heart of the terrible destructive processes of so-called universal history, as also into the cruelty of nature, and is in danger of longing for a Buddhistic negation of the will. Art saves him, and through art life saves him—for herself.

- "…in danger of longing for a Buddhistic negation of the will."

- "Art saves him, and through art life saves him—for herself."

DIONYSIA METAPHYSICA

Now he approaches the matter of precisely how the dithyrambic actor himself becomes a work of art, and, in doing so, he also shows how the will-to-power becomes manifest in human being as art.

He refers to the nausea of will that occurs when the discovery of the deepest subliminal suffering is met by a profound lethargy that results in an equally profound inability to act upon that which is found and raised. What is important to note here is that, while proto-tragedy is a good and redemptive experience, with the shattering of the limits of consciousness, there does occur with it a profound malady, which is precisely this lethargic impotency of will.

This nausea that occurs as a lethargic inaction of the will can be difficult to conceptualize. And, without the reader experiencing proto-tragedy and the subsequent fathoming of the subconscious, a deducible conception is the only option for understanding it. Toward that deduction, think of the zest and gusto an individual feels at the prospect of undertaking a difficult task, not always but sometimes. The discovery of a deeper sense of Self is an exhilarating experience that opens up an entire horizon of possibilities, and the hope and sudden empowerment of that moment of discovery would certainly impart a zest and gusto to the beholder with regard to an undertaking of the new possibilities. But that is not what happens. What happens instead is that the actor loses sight of his newfound vision and returns to the ho-hum everyday reality he knew beforehand. And in that forlorn return, the actor loses all zest and gusto. A lethargy invades his soul that is something like a nausea one might unexpectedly feel sitting down in anticipation to a delicious meal. The nausea that Nietzsche describes in the lethargy that results from proto-tragedy is an appropriate description in the sense that the zest and gusto one

7: ACTUALITY VS. REALITY

sometimes feels in life is suddenly replaced with an unexpected repulsion or at least an aversion.

Nausea invades the actor's soul or, more precisely, his willingness to act, when he plumbs the deepest part of his being and discovers titanic subliminal suffering. By raising that repressed suffering into the most brilliant consciousness, he also discovers his deeper Self. And that vision of deeper Self is highly exhilarating. But when the actor returns from that deeper and more brilliant reality he found in the subconscious to the everyday ho-hum reality he knew previously, he is overwhelmed by disgust with life. And that disgust induces a lethargy within the will that places the will in danger of a fatal resignation. Art saves suffering man from this nausea and its fatal resignation with the beauty and yearning for life that exudes from the sudden appearance of illusory Self *and the hope, most especially the hope,* that he may permanently reclaim that deeper Self, provided he is willing to create it or build it.

> For we must know that in the rapture of the Dionysian state, with its annihilation of the ordinary bounds and limits of existence, there is a *lethargic* element, wherein all personal experiences of the past are submerged. It is by this gulf of oblivion that the everyday world and the world of Dionysian reality are separated from each other. But as soon as this everyday reality rises again in consciousness, it is felt as such, and nauseates us; an ascetic will-paralysing mood is the fruit of these states. In this sense the Dionysian man may be said

DIONYSIA METAPHYSICA

to resemble Hamlet: both have for once seen into the true nature of things, —they have *perceived,* but they are loath to act; for their action cannot change the eternal nature of things; they regard it as shameful or ridiculous that one should require of them to set aright the time which is out of joint. Knowledge kills action, action requires the veil of illusion—it is this lesson which Hamlet teaches, and not the cheap wisdom of John-a-Dreams who from too much reflection, as it were from a surplus of possibilities, does not arrive at action at all. Not reflection, no!—true knowledge, insight into appalling truth, preponderates over all motives inciting to action, in Hamlet as well as in the Dionysian man. No comfort avails any longer; his longing goes beyond a world after death, beyond the gods themselves; existence with its glittering reflection in the gods, or in an immortal other world is abjured. In the consciousness of the truth he has perceived, man now sees everywhere only the awfulness or the absurdity of existence, he now understands the symbolism in the fate of Ophelia, he now discerns the wisdom of the sylvan god Silenus: and loathing seizes him.

- "Knowledge kills action, action requires the veil of illusion...."

7: ACTUALITY VS. REALITY

- "For we must know that in the rapture of the Dionysian state, with its annihilation of the ordinary bounds and limits of existence, there is a *lethargic* element, wherein all personal experiences of the past are submerged."

Knowledge of the suffering that resides "wherein all personal experiences of the past are submerged," which is the subconscious, kills all hope of any action that might come as a remedy to that suffering. What is necessary in this state of profound nausea and lethargy is to overcome the "gulf of oblivion" that separates the deeper and highly exhilarating reality from the ho-hum everyday reality. And it is precisely proto-tragedy that will overcome the chasm. That is the miracle, the religious role in life, of tragedy.

- "It is by this gulf of oblivion that the everyday world and the world of Dionysian reality are separated from each other."

The gulf of oblivion is the dismemberment that results from titanic suffering, giving rise to the Ego, which itself exists as a stopgap to prevent any perception of subliminal suffering, i.e., the subconscious.

- "But as soon as this everyday reality rises again in consciousness, it is felt as such, and nauseates us; an ascetic will-paralysing mood is the fruit of these states."

An individual who succeeds in raising the subconscious into consciousness but then loses his grip and returns to a state of dismemberment comes to loathe his dismembered existence.

DIONYSIA METAPHYSICA

And this is precisely the loathing that is mentioned in Zarathustra's Prologue, when he says the greatest moment you can experience is when you feel contempt for your egotistical existence because that contempt will then lead to a collapse of the Ego, which is the proto-tragic phenomenon.

- "... they have *perceived,* but they are loath to act; for their action cannot change the eternal nature of things; they regard it as shameful or ridiculous that one should require of them to set aright the time which is out of joint."

- "... true knowledge, insight into appalling truth, preponderates over all motives inciting to action, in Hamlet as well as in the Dionysian man."

What is lacking in the perception of subliminal suffering and its raising into consciousness is the lion's voice, the will to battle that enormous weight (the camel).

> Here, in this extremest danger of the will, *art* approaches, as a saving and healing enchantress; she alone is able to transform these nauseating reflections on the awfulness or absurdity of existence into representations wherewith it is possible to live: these are the representations of the *sublime* as the artistic subjugation of the awful, and the *comic* as the artistic delivery from the nausea of the absurd. The satyric chorus of dithyramb is the saving deed of Greek art; the paroxysms described above

7: ACTUALITY VS. REALITY

> spent their force in the intermediary world of these Dionysian followers.

- "Here, in this extremest danger of the will, *art* approaches, as a saving and healing enchantress...."

- "... she alone is able to transform these nauseating reflections on the awfulness or absurdity of existence into representations wherewith it is possible to live...."

- "... these are the representations of the *sublime* as the artistic subjugation of the awful, and the *comic* as the artistic delivery from the nausea of the absurd."

This goes to Nietzsche's discovery of the overman, which is different from the supra-Self. The most extreme danger is not the lethargy that nullifies the will; it is the encounter with that which killed the original Self. You can read about it in the dithyramb entitled The Ugliest Man, specifically in the encounter with the subliminal suffering that Zarathustra identifies when he exclaims "you are the murderer of God." In that extreme moment with that most extreme suffering that originally, in a more primordial time, killed the Self, the will *is blocked*, utterly unable to move forward. And what happens? The suffering individual "*laughs*." And the word "laughs" here is a gesticulative metaphor.

In another dithyramb, entitled Of the Vision and the Riddle, Zarathustra comes upon a man lying dead, having choked on a snake that crawled down his throat. And he exhorts the dead man to bite off the head of the snake. And when the dead man does indeed bite off the head, he springs up, resurrected and renewed in a most extraordinary way. In his resurrection, he is no longer a man. Now he is transformed, surrounded with light, and *laughing.*

I have wondered long and hard, for many years, about Nietzsche's choice for the metaphor he used to point the actor toward the instinct that is called upon when he encounters his worst subliminal suffering. What is it about laughter, I wondered, that resembles this particular instinct? I saw very little. So, I searched *Human, All Too Human* and *The Gay Science*, and, still, I found nothing.

But here, in the next to last sentence of the seventh section of *The Birth of Tragedy*, he refers to this profound healing and redemptive transformation *as comic.* He saw comedy in this resurrection. Obviously, I do not mean comedy in the modern sense, just as I have never meant tragedy in the modern sense. And this would be a good time to point out that Nietzsche did not close the horizon for the next philosophical genius who comes along looking for a mighty task. Nietzsche achieved much that had never before been achieved, with his work on tragedy. But he said himself that the mystery of comedy still lay unsolved, thereby inviting someone to do with it what he did with tragedy. The same questions we asked about tragedy, namely its meaning and role in life, apply to comedy as well. This task remains open for the worthy task master. And if there would be anything I might add to the mystery of comedy, I would say to look for its origin in the transformation of suffering into a lightness of being, a weightlessness in being. Begin your search in Nietzsche's over-Self. I believe it is out of that astounding accumulation of self-empowerment that comedy arose and the mystery of its origin and meaning may be found.

And just what did Nietzsche discover in this redemption of the worst suffering that he named it over-Self? I have discussed this transformation quite extensively in *The Birth of Dionysia*

7: ACTUALITY VS. REALITY

and I would direct the reader there for any elaboration, but, suffice it to say, for our discussion here, that it arises as a shifting of the center of the gravity of being from within the principium individuationis to above it. And it arises from within the deepest part of the abyss into which subindividuated man falls via abyssal suffering; in other words, *from its opposite*.

Proto-tragedy is redemptive, but it leads to nausea with life. That nausea is rooted in the actor's lack of faith that the deeper Self he envisioned deep within his subconscious is, in fact, reclaimable. Proto-tragedy presents the very real possibility that it is.

Nietzsche says that the illusion of Self is the one and perhaps only thing that has the power to overcome this nausea. But it then becomes life's work to reclaim the buried Self, to build it up, to raise it up from the dead. And it happens incrementally, one grade of Self at a time, according to the actor's ability to brave each step forward. And every step along the way requires destruction of the previously raised Self, which is the proto-tragic phenomenon, because the view of the horizon, which is defined by Self, must continually be broadened in order to see deeper into the subconscious. That is the work of life. And it proceeds upon a desire for Self. And insofar as a desire for Self leads to self-empowerment, life proceeds upon a will to power. But the nausea with life, which extends into the action required by life, must also be continually overcome. Thus, in his dithyrambs, Zarathustra teaches love of Self. And there are numerous other dithyrambs that teach numerous other steps and movements that assist life.

8: Theory of Dithyrambic Drama

The Meaning of the Tragic Satyr

The satyr, like the idyllic shepherd of our more recent time, is the offspring of a longing after the Primitive and the Natural; but mark with what firmness and fearlessness the Greek embraced the man of the woods, and again, how coyly and mawkishly the modern man dallied with the flattering picture of a tender, flute-playing, soft-natured shepherd! Nature, on which as yet no knowledge has been at work, which maintains unbroken barriers to culture—this is what the Greek saw in his satyr, which still was not on this account supposed to coincide with the ape. On the contrary: it was the archetype of man, the embodiment of his highest and strongest emotions, as the enthusiastic reveller enraptured By the proximity of his god, as the fellow-suffering companion in whom the suffering of the god repeats itself, as the herald of wisdom speaking from the very depths of nature, as the emblem of the sexual omnipotence of nature, which the Greek was wont to contemplate with reverential awe. The satyr was something sublime and godlike: he could not but appear so, especially to the sad and wearied eye of the Dionysian man. He would have been offended by our spurious tricked-up shepherd, while his eye dwelt with sublime satisfaction on the naked and unstuntedly magnificent characters of nature: here the illusion of culture was brushed away from the archetype of man; here the true man, the bearded satyr, revealed himself, who shouts joyfully to his god. Before him the cultured man shrank to a lying caricature. Schiller is right also with reference to these beginnings of tragic art: the chorus is a living bulwark against the onsets of reality, because it—the satyric chorus—portrays existence more truthfully, more realistically, more perfectly than the cultured man who ordinarily considers himself as the only reality. The sphere of poetry does not lie outside the world, like some fantastic impossibility of a poet's imagination: it seeks to be the very opposite, the unvarnished expression of truth, and must for this very reason cast aside the false finery of that supposed reality of the cultured man. The contrast between this intrinsic truth of nature and the falsehood of culture, which poses as the only reality, is similar to that existing between the eternal kernel of things, the thing in itself, and the collective world of phenomena. And even as tragedy, with its metaphysical comfort, points to the eternal life of this kernel of existence, notwithstanding the perpetual dissolution of phenomena, so the symbolism of the satyric chorus already expresses figuratively this primordial relation between the thing in itself and phenomenon. The idyllic shepherd of the modern man is but a copy of the sum of the illusions of culture which he calls nature; the Dionysian Greek desires truth and nature in their most potent form;—he sees himself metamorphosed into the satyr.

- "The satyr, like the idyllic shepherd of our more recent time, is the offspring of a longing after the Primitive and the Natural...."

The satyr is subindividuated man, which would include every single human being. Insofar as every human being, as an individuated being, has limits and boundaries, and insofar as life on this Earth is haphazard and random, those limits and boundaries are inevitably violated, thereby rendering every human being subindividuated. The only difference among us is the extent of subindividuation. But the satyr represents the subindividuated man who *recognizes* his unfortunate lot and seeks salvation in a reunion with his lost Self.

The Chorus Walls Off the Worlds of Ego and Self

- "... the chorus is a living bulwark against the onsets of reality, because it—the satyric chorus—portrays existence more truthfully, more realistically, more perfectly than the cultured man who ordinarily considers himself as the only reality."

As I have said, for Nietzsche, the tragic chorus was a wall that kept out egotistical man, which is a subindividuated man who is not committed to finding his long-lost Self. He is lost and has not yet vowed to find his way. On the other side of the wall, which he will surmount only when he has learned to disregard his Ego, is *actuality*, out of which reality will arise upon mythopoeia, which is the vision part of the drama.

The Dithyramb is an Embodiable Representation

- "The sphere of poetry does not lie outside the world, like some fantastic impossibility of a poet's imagination: it seeks to be the very opposite, the unvarnished expression of truth, and must for this very reason cast aside the false finery of that supposed reality of the cultured man."

Never forget, while reading Nietzsche's dithyrambs, that each and every one of them is a finely detailed representation of actuality, what you would call reality. There is nothing in them that is begotten of any individual's egocentric mind, nothing. Everything that is depicted can be found in human nature, though it is possible that it may only be found in a higher human nature, if there is such a thing, and I have still not decided that there is. Obviously, some people do not have certain instincts, but is that because they are not capable of those instincts or is that because they do not listen to themselves with sufficient attention?

- "The contrast between this intrinsic truth of nature and the falsehood of culture, which poses as the only reality, is similar to that existing between the eternal kernel of things, the thing in itself, and the collective world of phenomena."

Indeed, the contrast between the actuality that is depicted in Nietzsche's dithyrambs and the so-called reality of everyday life is striking. The so-called reality of everyday life, which is a reality that has devolved under the prejudices of egotistical being, is a gross distortion of how things really or actually are *above* in the higher domain where Self reigns supreme.

> The revelling crowd of the votaries of Dionysus rejoices, swayed by such moods and perceptions, the power of which transforms them before their own eyes, so that they imagine they behold themselves as reconstituted genii of nature, as satyrs. The later constitution of the tragic chorus is the artistic imitation of this natural phenomenon, which of course required a separation of the Dionysian spectators from the enchanted Dionysians. However, we must never lose sight of the fact that the public of the Attic tragedy rediscovered

itself in the chorus of the orchestra, that there was in reality no antithesis of public and chorus: for all was but one great sublime chorus of dancing and singing satyrs, or of such as allowed themselves to be represented by the satyrs. The Schlegelian observation must here reveal itself to us in a deeper sense. The chorus is the "ideal spectator"[6] in so far as it is the only *beholder*,[7] the beholder of the visionary world of the scene. A public of spectators, as known to us, was unknown to the Greeks. In their theatres the terraced structure of the spectators' space rising in concentric arcs enabled every one, in the strictest sense, to *overlook* the entire world of culture around him, and in surfeited contemplation to imagine himself a chorist. According to this view, then, we may call the chorus in its primitive stage in proto-tragedy, a self-mirroring of the Dionysian man: a phenomenon which may be best exemplified by the process of the actor, who, if he be truly gifted, sees hovering before his eyes with almost tangible perceptibility the character he is to represent. The satyric chorus is first of all a vision of the Dionysian throng, just as the world of the stage is, in turn, a vision of the

---

[6] Zuschauer.
[7] Schauer.

> satyric chorus: the power of this vision is great enough to render the eye dull and insensible to the impression of "reality," to the presence of the cultured men occupying the tiers of seats on every side. The form of the Greek theatre reminds one of a lonesome mountain-valley: the architecture of the scene appears like a luminous cloud-picture which the Bacchants swarming on the mountains behold from the heights, as the splendid encirclement in the midst of which the image of Dionysus is revealed to them.

- "The chorus is the "ideal spectator" in so far as it is the only *beholder,* the beholder of the visionary world of the scene."

The Dithyramb Is Communicative as Passion and Dischargeable as Vision

And so, too, is there a visionary world within the dithyrambic tragedy. It is the vision of reality being created out of mythopoeia. It is the vision of Self growing brighter and more pronounced as the actor delves ever deeper into the subconscious, incorporating it into consciousness, and finding his deeper Self in its depth. But this visionary world is not explained; it must be created. In such a way, anyone who has not entered into the drama and learned to live through it, enact it, is blind to that visionary world. *He simply never sees it.* Thus, the dithyrambic drama is incomprehensible except to those who have achieved an initiation into it, via the Prologue.

8: THEORY OF DITHYRAMBIC DRAMA

Owing to our learned conception of the elementary artistic processes, this artistic proto-phenomenon, which is here introduced to explain the tragic chorus, is almost shocking: while nothing can be more certain than that the poet is a poet only in that he beholds himself surrounded by forms which live and act before him, into the innermost being of which his glance penetrates. By reason of a strange defeat in our capacities, we modern men are apt to represent to ourselves the æsthetic proto-phenomenon as too complex and abstract. For the true poet the metaphor is not a rhetorical figure, but a vicarious image which actually hovers before him in place of a concept. The character is not for him an aggregate composed of a studied collection of particular traits, but an irrepressibly live person appearing before his eyes, and differing only from the corresponding vision of the painter by its ever continued life and action. Why is it that Homer sketches much more vividly[8] than all the other poets? Because he contemplates[9] much more. We talk so abstractly about poetry, because we are all wont to be bad poets. At bottom the æsthetic phenomenon is simple: let a man but have

---

[8] Anschaulicher.
[9] Anschaut.

> the faculty of perpetually seeing a lively play and of constantly living surrounded by hosts of spirits, then he is a poet: let him but feel the impulse to transform himself and to talk from out the bodies and souls of others, then he is a dramatist.

- "For the true poet the metaphor is not a rhetorical figure, but a vicarious image which actually hovers before him in place of a concept. The character is not for him an aggregate composed of a studied collection of particular traits, but an irrepressibly live person appearing before his eyes...."

I cannot over-emphasize the fact that the dithyramb is a highly veritable depiction of actuality or what you would call reality, except that it is the reality in which you will find Self immersed, which is a higher reality, even down to the smallest detail.

- "... let him but feel the impulse to transform himself and to talk from out the bodies and souls of others, then he is a dramatist."

And given the highly veritable depiction that the dithyramb presents, in order to bring it to life, it is necessary to embody it. Every dithyramb is a depiction of will and its conflicts. And the actor is required to embody that depiction in such a way that the will that is depicted *moves him* as would his own will because it is out of that will that the higher reality he so desperately seeks will arise — as his own creation, as art.

8: Theory of Dithyrambic Drama

The Concept of Dithyrambic Transport

> The Dionysian excitement is able to impart to a whole mass of men this artistic faculty of seeing themselves surrounded by such a host of spirits, with whom they know themselves to be inwardly one. This function of the tragic chorus is the *dramatic* proto-phenomenon: to see one's self transformed before one's self, and then to act as if one had really entered into another body, into another character. This function stands at the beginning of the development of the drama. Here we have something different from the rhapsodist, who does not blend with his pictures, but only sees them, like the painter, with contemplative eye outside of him; here we actually have a surrender of the individual by his entering into another nature. Moreover. this phenomenon appears in the form of an epidemic: a whole throng feels itself metamorphosed in this wise. Hence it is that the dithyramb is essentially different from every other variety of the choric song. The virgins, who with laurel twigs in their hands solemnly proceed to the temple of Apollo and sing a processional hymn, remain what they are and retain their civic names: the dithyrambic chorus is a chorus of transformed beings, whose civic past and social rank are totally forgotten: they have

> become the timeless servants of their god that live aloof from all the spheres of society. Every other variety of the choric lyric of the Hellenes is but an enormous enhancement of the Apollonian unit-singer: while in the dithyramb we have before us a community of unconscious actors, who mutually regard themselves as transformed among one another.

- "... the *dramatic* proto-phenomenon: to see one's self transformed before one's self, and then to act as if one had really entered into another body, into another character."

He brings attention to what he calls the dramatic proto-phenomenon but which I call dithyrambic transport.

As I have said repeatedly, that which is depicted in the dithyramb is entirely Dionysian, by which I mean emotion, a state of mind arising out of a conflict between will and conscience or simply a particular passion, be it a passion for or against something. Insofar as the state of mind or passion is depicted in gesticulative metaphor, the actor must find that which the metaphor points to in order to render the metaphor. And in the course of finding that to which the gesticulative metaphor points, the actor then embodies that state of mind or passion in such a way that he may either cultivate it or mitigate it. The process of looking for and eventually finding within oneself the passion or state of mind that is depicted in the dithyramb constitutes what I call dithyrambic transport and which Nietzsche calls the dramatic proto-phenomenon.

8: Theory of Dithyrambic Drama

The effect of dithyrambic transport is embodiment of a will that did not necessarily arise within the actor of his own volition. He has been "walked" into the will. And insofar as the dithyrambist composed the drama that is driven along by that will, it might be said that the actor is entering into the soul of the dithyrambist. Except that, in Nietzsche's case, the will he depicts is the will to power, which is a will to one's Self, and it is one's Self one finds in the end, not Nietzsche's Self, obviously.

> This enchantment is the prerequisite of all dramatic art. In this enchantment the Dionysian reveller sees himself as a satyr, *and as satyr he in turn beholds the god,* that is, in his transformation he sees a new vision outside him as the Apollonian consummation of his state. With this new vision the drama is complete.

Via dithyrambic transport, the actor enters into the will that is represented in the dithyramb, and, as he becomes moved by that will, he sees a vision. The vision, which is the Apollonian complement to the Dionysian realm, is one's Self. And it is the vision of one's Self that completes the dithyrambic drama, except it doesn't — because the drama is a tragedy. Eventually, the vision collapses into a deeper depth of perceived emotion, out of which rises a more brilliant vision of Self, and even then, thanks to tragedy, the whole process starts over again. And that recurring process of growth, which is life itself as it becomes manifest within human being, goes to Nietzsche's idea of the supra-Self, always the next Self and never the current Self, which is a myth, an idea of the world that makes it both comprehensible and manageable and that also gives the will its maximum freedom and meaning.

Myth as only One Aim of Dithyrambic Drama

> According to this view, we must understand Greek tragedy as the Dionysian chorus, which always disburdens itself anew in an Apollonian world of pictures. The choric parts, therefore, with which tragedy is interlaced, are in a manner the mother-womb of the entire so-called dialogue, that is, of the whole stage-world, of the drama proper. In several successive outbursts does this primordial basis of tragedy beam forth the vision of the drama, which is a dream-phenomenon throughout, and, as such, epic in character: on the other hand, however, as objectivation of a Dionysian state, it does not represent the Apollonian redemption in appearance, but, conversely, the dissolution of the individual and his unification with primordial existence. Accordingly, the drama is the Apollonian embodiment of Dionysian perceptions and influences, and is thereby separated from the epic as by an immense gap.

- "In several successive outbursts does this primordial basis of tragedy beam forth the vision of the drama, which is a dream-phenomenon throughout, and, as such, epic in character...."

8: THEORY OF DITHYRAMBIC DRAMA

Throughout this essay thus far, Nietzsche has written extensively about the Apollonian realm as a realm of visions and how it is the complement to the Dionysian realm, acting as its governor in many regards but also as its discharge. This is the first time he writes of the visions emanating from the Apollonian realm (1) as a discharge or unburdening of the Dionysian influences upon it and (2) *as being successive* or continual, repetitive. This phenomenon of continual visions goes directly to Nietzsche's discovery of the supra-Self, an ever-brightening sense of Self arising out of an ever-widening and ever-deepening scope of consciousness of the subliminal emotion. And the phenomenon of successive visions succeeds only if the actor is not beguiled into a complacency with a brilliant contemplation of beauty, which is a real danger.

- "... on the other hand, however, as objectivation of a Dionysian state, it does not represent the Apollonian redemption in appearance, but, conversely, the dissolution of the individual and his unification with primordial existence."

The Tragic Wisdom that Drives Continual Mythopoeia

Regarding the statement that "it [the tragic vision] does not represent the Apollonian redemption in appearance," this is a misleading translation. Kaufmann translates it more accurately as it does not represent "the Apollonian redemption through mere appearance," the keyword being "mere." The visions that the dithyrambic actor beholds in Nietzsche's drama are, indeed, very redemptive — in fact, wholly redemptive — but they are also much more. They also teach the actor that, in order to achieve even brighter and more redemptive visions, he or she must let go of the existing vision of Self. He must let the tragic vision, the vision of Self that arises from within the proto-tragic phenomenon, fall asunder, in order to behold the deeper substratum of subliminal emotions out of which that ever-brighter vision of Self, which is the supra-Self, will arise. That is tragic wisdom, wisdom that arises only out of the phenomenon of proto-tragedy: that all life requires some measure of death and disintegration. *And that wisdom* distinguishes the Apollonian vision that arises out of the Dionsyian substratum from the mere epic with a gap that is quite measurable and quite distinct.

The myth is an Apollonian embodiment of the world, but it is an idea of the world that also reflects the will of the world, which is its Dionysian substratum.

The Chorus as Reality

> The *chorus* of Greek tragedy, the symbol of the mass of the people moved by Dionysian excitement, is thus fully explained by our conception of it as here set forth. Whereas, being accustomed to the position of a chorus on the modern stage, especially an operatic chorus, we could never comprehend why the tragic chorus of the Greeks should be older, more primitive, indeed, more important than the "action" proper,—as has been so plainly declared by the voice of tradition; whereas, furthermore, we could not reconcile with this traditional paramount importance and primitiveness

the fact of the chorus' being composed only of humble, ministering beings; indeed, at first only of goatlike satyrs; whereas, finally, the orchestra before the scene was always a riddle to us; we have learned to comprehend at length that the scene, together with the action, was fundamentally and originally conceived only as a *vision,* that the only reality is just the chorus, which of itself generates the vision and speaks thereof with the entire symbolism of dancing, tone, and word. This chorus beholds in the vision its lord and master Dionysus, and is thus for ever the *serving* chorus: it sees how he, the god, suffers and glorifies himself, and therefore does not itself *act*. But though its attitude towards the god is throughout the attitude of ministration, this is nevertheless the highest expression, the Dionysian expression of *Nature,* and therefore, like Nature herself, the chorus utters oracles and wise sayings when transported with enthusiasm: as *fellow-sufferer* it is also the *sage* proclaiming truth from out the heart of Nature. Thus, then, originates the fantastic figure, which seems so shocking, of the wise and enthusiastic satyr, who is at the same time "the dumb man" in contrast to the god: the image of Nature and her strongest impulses, yea, the symbol of Nature, and at the same time the herald of

> her art and wisdom: musician, poet, dancer, and visionary in one person.

- "... we have learned to comprehend at length that the scene, together with the action, was fundamentally and originally conceived only as a *vision,* that the only reality is just the chorus, which of itself generates the vision and speaks thereof with the entire symbolism of dancing, tone, and word."

In a similar way, we may rightly say that the words comprising the dithyramb are meaningless outside the "mood," the passion to which they point as a gesticulation. Nor would it make any sense to *explain* via concept the Übermensch or any other *idea* arising out of the dithyramb *because* they arise only out of the passions, the will, that creates the reality of which they are a constitution, *as a part of that will*. Without the will, the ideas and the visions are barely existent. True, we could conceive, but what good would that do without the instincts that are a part of them? What is needed instead of a conception is an apprehension. What is needed is the attainment of instinct.

In dithyrambic drama, the words with which they are composed, which are specifically gesticulative metaphors, communicate a willfulness. And it is only through an embodiment of that willfulness that the vision of Self becomes apparent. The reality that is comprised by the will is the only reality that the actor may ever hope to attain.

- "... as *fellow-sufferer* it is also the *sage* proclaiming truth from out the heart of Nature."

This is not the only instance where Nietzsche speaks of the dithyramb as a representation of suffering, particularly a

8: Theory of Dithyrambic Drama

representation of a god's ruth, which is to say that dithyrambic tragedy requires the presence of a tremendous ruling need within its actor, specifically the need to find his Self. And I have already elucidated that fact at the outset of Nietzsche's definition of the chorus.

Tragic Mythopoeia as Supra-Self

> Agreeably to this view, and agreeably to tradition, *Dionysus,* the proper stage-hero and focus of vision, is not at first actually present in the oldest period of tragedy, but is only imagined as present: *i.e.,* tragedy is originally only "chorus" and not "drama." Later on the attempt is made to exhibit the god as real and to display the visionary figure together with its glorifying encirclement before the eyes of all; it is here that the "drama" in the narrow sense of the term begins. To the dithyrambic chorus is now assigned the task of exciting the minds of the hearers to such a pitch of Dionysian frenzy, that, when the tragic hero appears on the stage, they do not behold in him, say, the unshapely masked man, but a visionary figure, born as it were of their own ecstasy. Let us picture Admetes thinking in profound meditation of his lately departed wife Alcestis, and quite consuming himself in spiritual contemplation thereof—when suddenly the veiled figure of a woman resembling her in form and gait is led

towards him: let us picture his sudden trembling anxiety, his agitated comparisons, his instinctive conviction—and we shall have an analogon to the sensation with which the spectator, excited to Dionysian frenzy, saw the god approaching on the stage, a god with whose sufferings he had already become identified. He involuntarily transferred the entire picture of the god, fluttering magically before his soul, to this masked figure and resolved its reality as it were into a phantasmal unreality. This is the Apollonian dream-state, in which the world of day is veiled, and a new world, clearer, more intelligible, more striking than the former, and nevertheless more shadowy, is ever born anew in perpetual change before our eyes. We accordingly recognise in tragedy a thorough-going stylistic contrast: the language, colour, flexibility and dynamics of the dialogue fall apart in the Dionysian lyrics of the chorus on the one hand, and in the Apollonian dream-world of the scene on the other, into entirely separate spheres of expression. The Apollonian appearances, in which Dionysus objectifies himself, are no longer "ein ewiges Meer, ein wechselnd Weben, ein glühend Leben,"[10] as is the music of the chorus, they are no

---

[10] An eternal sea, A weaving, flowing, Life, all glowing. Faust, trans. of Bayard Taylor.—TR.

8: THEORY OF DITHYRAMBIC DRAMA

> longer the forces merely felt, but not condensed into a picture, by which the inspired votary of Dionysus divines the proximity of his god: the clearness and firmness of epic form now speak to him from the scene, Dionysus now no longer speaks through forces, but as an epic hero, almost in the language of Homer.

- "This is the Apollonian dream-state, in which the world of day is veiled, and a new world, clearer, more intelligible, more striking than the former, and nevertheless more shadowy, is ever born anew in perpetual change before our eyes."

This would make much more sense if it was articulated as the actor discovering his deeper Self in the drama, which is precisely what happens. As the actor delves ever more deeply into his subliminal emotions, driven by a will to power, which is defined by the empowerment his vision of Self bestows, he discovers a new world (the child from the dithyramb entitled Of the Three Metamorphoses), which is much more intelligible, more brilliant, more striking, *more naive*, than what he beheld previously under the prejudicial guise of Ego. And, yes, it is more shadowy because the Self is an illusion, as is everything that is Apollonian (i.e., fictive). And the illusory Self imparts beauty and joy upon that which becomes a part of it, thus coloring it. And also, it is not the first vision of Self that appears which the actor's will so eagerly anticipates. Rather, it is the succession of visions of Self that he truly seeks, and that is the supra-Self, "ever born anew in perpetual change."

- "The Apollonian appearances, in which Dionysus objectifies himself, are no longer "ein ewiges Meer, ein wechselnd Weben, ein glühend Leben," as is the music of the chorus, they are no longer the forces merely felt, but not condensed into a picture, by which the inspired votary of Dionysus divines the proximity of his god: the clearness and firmness of epic form now speak to him from the scene, Dionysus now no longer speaks through forces, but as an epic hero, almost in the language of Homer."

This goes to the previous point that the Apollonian visions of Self that arise within the actor's mind as a result of his fathoming and incorporating the Dionysian substratum of subliminal emotions *are not mere appearance*. There is much more to them than mere appearance. They bestow wisdom as well, and they speak with a clarity and certainty that is most pronounced, especially in comparison with the muted, confused, and sometimes superfluous speech of egotistical thought. Whereas previously, before the actor beholds an apprehension of his Self, the only reality he hears in the dithyramb is the representation of will, then, with his newfound vision, in which his will has become vested, reality now speaks to him through vision and will *simultaneously*. And the creation of that vision as well as the will through which it was achieved represent what is heroic in the drama.

9: Genius as an Expansion of the Limits of Individuation via Tragedy

Mythical Self as a Healing Mirror of the World

> Whatever rises to the surface in the dialogue of the Apollonian part of Greek tragedy, appears simple, transparent, beautiful. In this sense the dialogue is a copy of the Hellene, whose nature reveals itself in the dance, because in the dance the greatest energy is merely potential, but betrays itself nevertheless in flexible and vivacious movements. The language of the Sophoclean heroes, for instance, surprises us by its Apollonian precision and clearness, so that we at once imagine we see into the innermost recesses of their being, and marvel not a little that the way to these

9: GENIUS AS AN EXPANSION OF THE LIMITS OF INDIVIDUATION VIA TRAGEDY

recesses is so short. But if for the moment we disregard the character of the hero which rises to the surface and grows visible—and which at bottom is nothing but the light-picture cast on a dark wall, that is, appearance through and through,—if rather we enter into the myth which projects itself in these bright mirrorings, we shall of a sudden experience a phenomenon which bears a reverse relation to one familiar in optics. When, after a vigorous effort to gaze into the sun, we turn away blinded, we have dark-coloured spots before our eyes as restoratives, so to speak; while, on the contrary, those light-picture phenomena of the Sophoclean hero,—in short, the Apollonian of the mask,—are the necessary productions of a glance into the secret and terrible things of nature, as it were shining spots to heal the eye which dire night has seared. Only in this sense can we hope to be able to grasp the true meaning of the serious and significant notion of "Greek cheerfulness"; while of course we encounter the misunderstood notion of this cheerfulness, as resulting from a state of unendangered comfort, on all the ways and paths of the present time.

- "… if for the moment we disregard the character of the hero which rises to the surface and grows visible—and which at bottom is nothing but the light-picture cast on

a dark wall, that is, appearance through and through,—
if rather we enter into the myth which projects itself in
these bright mirrorings, we shall of a sudden
experience a phenomenon which bears a reverse
relation to one familiar in optics."

This is the first time he mentions the word "myth," and, yet, it is myth that is the whole aim of dithyrambic drama. In other words, the reason that an actor would undertake a dithyrambic drama is to "see" the myth that it teaches. Any by "see," I mean apprehend. Only as an apprehension, which speaks to the actor's instincts, does the myth become a part of the actor's soul.

Still, despite the importance of "myth," he drops the word only nonchalantly. Myth and its fictive cousin, idea, are the elements within the Apollonian realm that arise out of the dithyrambic drama *as its art*, its creation. Do take note that, in the above citation, he equates "myth" with the "bright mirrorings" of the Apollonian visions.

- "When, after a vigorous effort to gaze into the sun, we turn away blinded, we have dark-coloured spots before our eyes as restoratives, so to speak; while, on the contrary, those light-picture phenomena of the Sophoclean hero,—in short, the Apollonian of the mask,—are the necessary productions of a glance into the secret and terrible things of nature, as it were shining spots to heal the eye which dire night has seared."

Evolution of Mythical Self Via Life

Simply put, when the actor, in the course of undertaking Nietzsche's dithyrambic tragedy, fathoms previously unfathomable subliminal emotions, he will *see* his Self more clearly because each time he takes a step further into his subconscious, the mythopoeic instinct will kick in and generate an image of Self whose brilliance will stand in direct relation to the depth he has succeeded in plumbing. As his ability to fathom more deeply increases, so, too, will his image of Self increase in brilliance. This step-by-step process of growth leads to the development of the supra-Self, which the actor must continually surpass in order to find the deepest supra-Self. In such a way, the numerous and consecutive visions of supra-Self are "the shining spots" that are meant to "heal the eye which dire need has seared."

An Analysis of Sophoclean Tragedy

> The most sorrowful figure of the Greek stage, the hapless *Œdipus,* was understood by Sophocles as the noble man, who in spite of his wisdom was destined to error and misery, but nevertheless through his extraordinary sufferings ultimately exerted a magical, wholesome influence on all around him, which continues effective even after his death. The noble man does not sin; this is what the thoughtful poet wishes to tell us: all laws, all natural order, yea, the moral world itself, may be destroyed through his

action, but through this very action a higher magic circle of influences is brought into play, which establish a new world on the ruins of the old that has been overthrown. This is what the poet, in so far as he is at the same time a religious thinker, wishes to tell us: as poet, he shows us first of all a wonderfully complicated legal mystery, which the judge slowly unravels, link by link, to his own destruction. The truly Hellenic delight at this dialectical loosening is so great, that a touch of surpassing cheerfulness is thereby communicated to the entire play, which everywhere blunts the edge of the horrible presuppositions of the procedure. In the "Œdipus at Colonus" we find the same cheerfulness, elevated, however, to an infinite transfiguration: in contrast to the aged king, subjected to an excess of misery, and exposed solely as a *sufferer* to all that befalls him, we have here a supermundane cheerfulness, which descends from a divine sphere and intimates to us that in his purely passive attitude the hero attains his highest activity, the influence of which extends far beyond his life, while his earlier conscious musing and striving led him only to passivity. Thus, then, the legal knot of the fable of Œdipus, which to mortal eyes appears indissolubly entangled, is slowly unravelled—and the profoundest human joy comes upon us in

9: GENIUS AS AN EXPANSION OF THE LIMITS OF INDIVIDUATION VIA TRAGEDY

the presence of this divine counterpart of dialectics. If this explanation does justice to the poet, it may still be asked whether the substance of the myth is thereby exhausted; and here it turns out that the entire conception of the poet is nothing but the light-picture which healing nature holds up to us after a glance into the abyss. Œdipus, the murderer of his father, the husband of his mother, Œdipus, the interpreter of the riddle of the Sphinx! What does the mysterious triad of these deeds of destiny tell us? There is a primitive popular belief, especially in Persia, that a wise Magian can be born only of incest: which we have forthwith to interpret to ourselves with reference to the riddle-solving and mother-marrying Œdipus, to the effect that when the boundary of the present and future, the rigid law of individuation and, in general, the intrinsic spell of nature, are broken by prophetic and magical powers, an extraordinary counter-naturalness—as, in this case, incest—must have preceded as a cause; for how else could one force nature to surrender her secrets but by victoriously opposing her, *i.e.,* by means of the Unnatural? It is this intuition which I see imprinted in the awful triad of the destiny of Œdipus: the very man who solves the riddle of nature—that double-constituted

> Sphinx—must also, as the murderer of his father and husband of his mother, break the holiest laws of nature. Indeed, it seems as if the myth sought to whisper into our ears that wisdom, especially Dionysian wisdom, is an unnatural abomination, and that whoever, through his knowledge, plunges nature into an abyss of annihilation, must also experience the dissolution of nature in himself. "The sharpness of wisdom turns round upon the sage: wisdom is a crime against nature": such terrible expressions does the myth call out to us: but the Hellenic poet touches like a sunbeam the sublime and formidable Memnonian statue of the myth, so that it suddenly begins to sound—in Sophoclean melodies.

First and foremost, the above is an analysis of Sophoclean tragedy, and neither I nor Nietzsche subscribe to Sophocles' theory of tragedy. It is my firm belief that, in the beginning, original tragedy, or proto-tragedy, was a rite of passage that played out individually and within the soul. It was not a theatrical spectacle in any manner. Moreover, any attempt to morally interpret tragedy will most definitely result in an incorrect understanding of its role and its process.

Here is a summary of Nietzsche's analysis of Sophoclean tragedy as it appears in Oedipus.

- The individual to whom the tragedy happens is a noble individual.

9: GENIUS AS AN EXPANSION OF THE LIMITS OF INDIVIDUATION VIA TRAGEDY

- The tragic individual is also wise, but he is destined to a tragic fate and his wisdom has no effect on that fate.

- Neither is the tragic individual sinful.

- The entire order of things (in and around him), including the order of moral matters, will fall asunder as a result of tragedy.

- Interestingly, a new order will arise on the ruins of the destruction wrought by tragedy.

- The poet who composed the tragedy presents a complex mystery whose unravelling, piece by piece, leads to the tragedy and also arouses a certain delight in the spectator.

- In fact, that delight mitigates the horror of tragedy.

- More importantly, there is an influence on the infliction of tragedy and its effect upon the tragically fallen from a higher order, perhaps from God but most certainly from beyond the individual and his Ego.

- It is also from within that higher order that the delight in tragedy originates, thereby rendering the delight titanic.

- Lastly, note that the tragically fallen individual is passive to the tragedy that happens to him, perhaps resigned to it but certainly not resistant to it, and that all his conscious striving prior to the tragedy actually led him into the passivity in which he welcomes the tragedy that befalls him.

- In order for delight in tragedy to succeed, the tragic circumstances from which the unravelling proceeds must first appear to be totally unsolvable.

- In the case of the Oedipus tragedies, Oedipus himself was an unusually wise individual and the accumulation of extreme wisdom was a direct result of an earlier crime, which, in his instance, was birth from incest.

- In the case of Oedipus, according to Nietzsche, crime results in extreme wisdom by opposing Nature with something that is unnatural, thereby compelling Nature to give up her secrets. Without opposing and compelling Nature, wisdom would not be so forthcoming.

- By opposing Nature, the individual who so opposes must himself be destroyed, and that is the gist of the "myth" that Sophoclean tragedy teaches. In short, "wisdom is a crime against Nature."

The two other points I wish to highlight from the above summary of Sophoclean tragedy are (1) Nietzsche's mention of an association between crime and genius and (2) the violation of the limits and boundaries of individuation involved in the play of tragedy, on which I will elaborate shortly but not now.

An Analysis of Aeschylean Tragedy

Next, Nietzsche goes on to summarize Aeschylean tragedy, which is different from Sophoclean tragedy in that Sophoclean tragedy depicts a passive hero, whose resignation leads directly

9: GENIUS AS AN EXPANSION OF THE LIMITS OF INDIVIDUATION VIA TRAGEDY

to the glory of tragedy, and Aeschylean tragedy depicts an active hero, whose actions lead directly to the occurrence of the tragedy.

> With the glory of passivity I now contrast the glory of activity which illuminates the *Prometheus* of Æschylus. That which Æschylus the thinker had to tell us here, but which as a poet he only allows us to surmise by his symbolic picture, the youthful Goethe succeeded in disclosing to us in the daring words of his Prometheus:—
>
> "Hier sitz' ich, forme Menschen
> Nach meinem Bilde,
> Ein Geschlecht, das mir gleich sei,
> Zu leiden, zu weinen,
> Zu geniessen und zu freuen sich,
> Und dein nicht zu achten,
> Wie ich!"11
>
> Man, elevating himself to the rank of the Titans, acquires his culture by his own

---

[11] "Here sit I, forming mankind
In my image,
A race resembling me,—
To sorrow and to weep,
To taste, to hold, to enjoy,
And not have need of thee,
As I!"
(Translation in Hæckel's History of the Evolution of Man.)

efforts, and compels the gods to unite with him, because in his self-sufficient wisdom he has their existence and their limits in his hand. What is most wonderful, however, in this Promethean form, which according to its fundamental conception is the specific hymn of impiety, is the profound Æschylean yearning for *justice*: the untold sorrow of the bold "single-handed being" on the one hand, and the divine need, ay, the foreboding of a twilight of the gods, on the other, the power of these two worlds of suffering constraining to reconciliation, to metaphysical oneness—all this suggests most forcibly the central and main position of the Æschylean view of things, which sees Moira as eternal justice enthroned above gods and men. In view of the astonishing boldness with which Æschylus places the Olympian world on his scales of justice, it must be remembered that the deep-minded Greek had an immovably firm substratum of metaphysical thought in his mysteries, and that all his sceptical paroxysms could be discharged upon the Olympians. With reference to these deities, the Greek artist, in particular, had an obscure feeling as to mutual dependency: and it is just in the Prometheus of Æschylus that this feeling is symbolised. The Titanic artist found in himself the daring belief that he could create men and at least destroy Olympian deities:

namely, by his superior wisdom, for which, to be sure, he had to atone by eternal suffering. The splendid "can-ing" of the great genius, bought too cheaply even at the price of eternal suffering, the stern pride of the *artist*: this is the essence and soul of Æschylean poetry, while Sophocles in his Œdipus preludingly strikes up the victory-song of the *saint*. But even this interpretation which Æschylus has given to the myth does not fathom its astounding depth of terror; the fact is rather that the artist's delight in unfolding, the cheerfulness of artistic creating bidding defiance to all calamity, is but a shining stellar and nebular image reflected in a black sea of sadness. The tale of Prometheus is an original possession of the entire Aryan family of races, and documentary evidence of their capacity for the profoundly tragic; indeed, it is not improbable that this myth has the same characteristic significance for the Aryan race that the myth of the fall of man has for the Semitic, and that there is a relationship between the two myths like that of brother and sister. The presupposition of the Promethean myth is the transcendent value which a naïve humanity attach to *fire* as the true palladium of every ascending culture: that man, however, should dispose at will of this fire, and should not receive it only as a gift from heaven, as the igniting lightning or the warming solar flame, appeared to the contemplative primordial men as crime and robbery of the divine nature. And thus the first philosophical problem at once causes a painful, irreconcilable antagonism between man and God, and puts as it were a mass of rock at the gate of every culture. The best and highest that men can acquire they obtain by a crime, and must now in their turn take upon themselves its consequences, namely the whole flood of sufferings and sorrows with which the offended celestials *must* visit the nobly aspiring race of man: a bitter reflection, which, by the *dignity* it confers on crime, contrasts strangely with the Semitic myth of the fall of man, in which curiosity, beguilement, seducibility, wantonness,—in short, a whole series of pre-eminently feminine passions,—were regarded as the origin of evil. What distinguishes the Aryan representation is the sublime view of *active sin* as the properly Promethean virtue, which suggests at the same time the ethical basis of pessimistic tragedy as the *justification* of human evil—of human guilt as well as of the suffering incurred thereby. The misery in the essence of things—which the contemplative Aryan is not disposed to explain away—the antagonism in the heart of the world, manifests itself to him as a medley of different worlds, for instance, a Divine and a human world, each of which is in the right individually, but as a separate existence alongside of another has to suffer for its individuation. With the heroic effort made by the individual for universality, in his attempt to pass beyond the bounds of individuation and become the *one* universal being, he experiences in himself the primordial contradiction concealed in the essence of things, *i.e.,* he trespasses and suffers. Accordingly crime[12] is understood by the Aryans to be a man, sin[13] by the Semites a woman; as also, the original crime is committed by man, the original sin by woman. Besides, the witches' chorus says:

"Wir nehmen das nicht so genau:
Mit tausend Schritten macht's die Frau;
Doch wie sie auch sich eilen kann
Mit einem Sprunge macht's der Mann."[14]

---

[12] *Der* Frevel.
[13] *Die* Sünde.
[14] We do not measure with such care:
Woman in thousand steps is there,
But howsoe'er she hasten may.
Man in one leap has cleared the way.
Faust, trans. of Bayard Taylor.—TR.

The Origin of Aeschylean Tragedy in the Natural Imposition of Justice

The crux of Aeschylean tragedy, according to Nietzsche, is the titanic will of man encroaching upon the divine will (with the theft of fire, which has always been regarded as a gift to man from the gods), and, in that trespass, though man may indeed obtain what he seeks in the heights, he is doomed to eternal suffering for the crime of trespassing, which does not mean that the titanic effort was unworthy or evil. He attributes the titanic will of man to unlimited ambition born of his Dionysian nature, and he attributes the indissoluble sovereignty of the divine to the Apollonian nature of man. Most importantly, he credits both contesting entities with an indisputable right to a full existence; the point being that a world full of individuated entities, with their limits and boundaries, is doomed to suffer, due to their individuated nature and the nature of the world, in which encroachment is inherent and inevitable. Lastly, he highlights Aeschylus' high regard for the imposition of justice, without regard for morality but only as a natural phenomenon, as the origin of the tragedy. Were it not for the natural inclination to impose justice, there would be no tragedy.

Greek Suffering as Folly and Semitic Suffering as Sin

In an interesting side note, in the second half of the above paragraph, he characterizes the belief regarding the "cause" of suffering as held by two different cultures of people. On the one hand, he states that the Greeks attributed suffering to their inadvertent or deliberate disregard of the limits of individuation.

9: GENIUS AS AN EXPANSION OF THE LIMITS OF INDIVIDUATION VIA TRAGEDY

In other words, a man has limits and, if he exceeds his limits, he is liable to either punishment or self-destruction. But then he states that the Semitic people attributed suffering exclusively to punishment, either by God or by fellow man and always as a result of sinning, whereas the Greeks attributed suffering to folly. In short, one theory of the origin of suffering may be called active, the Greek, and the other passive, the Semitic.

Genius as Transcendence of the Limits of Individuation

Lastly, I would like to point out that inherent in the fundamental Dionysian nature is the will to transcend the limits of individuation and "become one" with nature. And the reason I point it out is because it leads to supra-individuation, which we commonly call "genius." Genius exists beyond the limits of individuation. And it for that reason that the extraordinary individual whom we regard as a genius is an individual who is capable of so much more than ordinary individuals — because both his passions and his ability to think lie beyond the limits that are imposed by individuation upon ordinary individuals.

> He who understands this innermost core of the tale of Prometheus—namely the necessity of crime imposed on the titanically striving individual—will at once be conscious of the un-Apollonian nature of this pessimistic representation: for Apollo seeks to pacify individual beings precisely by drawing boundary lines between them, and by again and again calling attention

thereto, with his requirements of self-knowledge and due proportion, as the holiest laws of the universe. In order, however, to prevent the form from congealing to Egyptian rigidity and coldness in consequence of this Apollonian tendency, in order to prevent the extinction of the motion of the entire lake in the effort to prescribe to the individual wave its path and compass, the high tide of the Dionysian tendency destroyed from time to time all the little circles in which the one-sided Apollonian "will" sought to confine the Hellenic world. The suddenly swelling tide of the Dionysian then takes the separate little wave-mountains of individuals on its back, just as the brother of Prometheus, the Titan Atlas, does with the earth. This Titanic impulse, to become as it were the Atlas of all individuals, and to carry them on broad shoulders higher and higher, farther and farther, is what the Promethean and the Dionysian have in common. In this respect the Æschylean Prometheus is a Dionysian mask, while, in the afore-mentioned profound yearning for justice, Æschylus betrays to the intelligent observer his paternal descent from Apollo, the god of individuation and of the boundaries of justice. And so the double-being of the Æschylean Prometheus, his conjoint Dionysian and Apollonian nature, might be

9: Genius as an Expansion of the Limits of Individuation via Tragedy

> thus expressed in an abstract formula: "Whatever exists is alike just and unjust, and equally justified in both."
> Das ist deine Welt! Das heisst eine Welt![15]

The above last paragraph of this chapter becomes much more interesting if we apply it more palpably and more plausibly to human nature, which we will now do.

- "Apollo seeks to pacify individual beings precisely by drawing boundary lines between them, and by again and again calling attention thereto, with his requirements of self-knowledge and due proportion, as the holiest laws of the universe."

Tragedy as a Reunion with the "One Universal Being," Beyond Individuation

The Self also pacifies the individual by drawing boundary lines around itself and by urging the beholding individual to heed the laws of self-knowledge and "nothing in excess" so that he may thereby abide by the boundaries and limits that are drawn by Self.

- "In order, however, to prevent the form from congealing to Egyptian rigidity and coldness in consequence of this Apollonian tendency ... the high tide of the Dionysian tendency destroyed from time to time all the little circles in which the one-sided

---

[15] This is thy world, and what a world!—*Faust*.

Apollonian "will" sought to confine the Hellenic world."

But, in circumstances where titanic subliminal emotion becomes minatory, the boundaries of Self become more like a fortress, which, in turn, transform the threatened individual into something like a statute that is devoid of animation or emotion. An individual who feels threatened by his subconscious may also become excessively ideational inasmuch as he uses his ideas to quell his emotions. With regard to achieving proto-tragedy, what is needed is to defeat that fortress and allow emotion to come forward because doing so will restore a deeper Self, which itself would provide a much deeper and more lasting comfort than anything excessive ideation might provide.

- "The suddenly swelling tide of the Dionysian then takes the separate little wave-mountains of individuals on its back, just as the brother of Prometheus, the Titan Atlas, does with the earth. This Titanic impulse, to become as it were the Atlas of all individuals, and to carry them on broad shoulders higher and higher, farther and farther, is what the Promethean and the Dionysian have in common."

Insofar as those deeper emotions reveal a deeper Self, the destruction of the fortress of boundaries and ideas erected against them is a very good thing, clearly. That which is Dionysian, by which I mean specifically all emotions, therewith "carries" the tragic individual toward a closer proximity with his inner nature, with "the one universal being," both in a deeper sense, wherein he senses deeper feelings, but also in a higher sense, wherein he beholds a higher sense of Self. The descriptor

9: GENIUS AS AN EXPANSION OF THE LIMITS OF INDIVIDUATION VIA TRAGEDY

"one" in the phrase "the one universal being" is a reference to the absence of individuation, which is the delineation and distinction of being amidst the swirl of emotion that is imparted by the Apollonian Self, so that to become one with the "one universal being" is to disregard the limits and boundaries of individuation and to therewith experience deeper emotions and a broader scope of percipience. But that broader percipience and deeper experience in more animated emotions simultaneously leads to a more brilliant vision of Self as the mythopoeic instinct becomes triggered by the movement that inheres in the deeper emotions. Thus, in the interplay between the Apollonian and Dionysian realms, between emotion and idea, we see movement in two directions, inwardly (into deeper emotion) and upwardly (into the delineating and edifying mythopoeia of Self). And seeing one's deeper Self in the deeper emotions is the art that is created in the interplay. Insofar as it is fundamentally emotion at play in this evolution, it is in that sense that the Dionysian realm may rightly be compared to Aeschylus' Atlas because it is the Dionysian realm that lifts up the individual and carries him on higher. And it is significant to note that, in his dithyrambs, Nietzsche uses the metaphor of "the camel" to communicate the need for the actor to learn to plumb the depth of his feelings and to carry the weight of those deeper feelings in order to find the deeper sense of Self that is reflected in them.

- "... in the afore-mentioned profound yearning for justice, Æschylus betrays to the intelligent observer his paternal descent from Apollo, the god of individuation and of the boundaries of justice."

The Atlantean drive to subsume more and more of the subconscious also constitutes a profound drive toward justice insofar as the deeper Self that is revealed in the perception of deeper emotions imparts comfort to the one who strives in a way that only the Apollonian Self can do, i.e., *with illusion* and the beauty that illusion imparts. Simply put, without the sense of Self, repressed humiliation or repressed fear *appear* titanic, foreign, and absolutely insurmountable. But as soon as the individual senses his Self, his deeper Self, in those titans, they become a dimension of his being; they are transformed from strange and muted rumblings into articulable and very specific dilemmas that are also suddenly manageable, or at least interpretable. The haunted individual sees nothing in the face of the subconscious; he simply runs and hides. But the enlightened individual says "I am frightened" or "I am ashamed," and he *bears* his fear or his humiliation." Insofar as he does indeed feel better when he allows himself to be moved by that which haunts him, there is justice; there is a certain and very tangible victory in that moment. Or, as Zarathustra would say, "Shared injustice is half justice," insofar as the difficult emotions are borne by the deeper Self.

10: Important Concepts

Genius as Attainment of "One Universal Being"

It is an indisputable tradition that Greek tragedy in its earliest form had for its theme only the sufferings of Dionysus, and that for some time the only stage-hero therein was simply Dionysus himself. With the same confidence, however, we can maintain that not until Euripides did Dionysus cease to be the tragic hero, and that in fact all the celebrated figures of the Greek stage— Prometheus, Œdipus, etc.—are but masks of this original hero, Dionysus. The presence of a god behind all these masks is the one essential cause of the typical "ideality," so oft exciting wonder, of these celebrated figures. Some one, I know not whom, has maintained that all individuals are comic as individuals and are consequently un-tragic: from whence it might be inferred that the Greeks in general *could* not endure individuals on the tragic stage. And they really seem to have had these sentiments: as, in general, it is to be observed that the Platonic discrimination and valuation of the "idea" in contrast to the "eidolon," the image, is deeply rooted in the Hellenic being. Availing ourselves of Plato's terminology, however, we should have to speak of the tragic figures of the Hellenic stage somewhat as follows. The one truly real Dionysus appears in a multiplicity of forms, in the mask of a fighting hero and entangled, as it were, in the net of an individual will. As the visibly appearing god now talks and acts, he resembles an erring, striving, suffering individual: and that, in general, he *appears* with such epic precision and clearness, is due to the dream-reading Apollo, who reads to the chorus its Dionysian state through this symbolic appearance. In reality, however, this hero is the suffering Dionysus of the mysteries, a god experiencing in himself the sufferings of individuation, of whom wonderful myths tell that as a boy he was dismembered by the Titans and has been worshipped in this state as Zagreus:[16] whereby is intimated that this dismemberment, the properly Dionysian *suffering,* is like a transformation into air, water, earth, and fire, that we must

---

[16] See article by Mr. Arthur Symons in *The Academy*, 30th August 1902.

therefore regard the state of individuation as the source and primal cause of all suffering, as something objectionable in itself. From the smile of this Dionysus sprang the Olympian gods, from his tears sprang man. In his existence as a dismembered god, Dionysus has the dual nature of a cruel barbarised demon, and a mild pacific ruler. But the hope of the epopts looked for a new birth of Dionysus, which we have now to conceive of in anticipation as the end of individuation: it was for this coming third Dionysus that the stormy jubilation-hymns of the epopts resounded. And it is only this hope that sheds a ray of joy upon the features of a world torn asunder and shattered into individuals: as is symbolised in the myth by Demeter sunk in eternal sadness, who *rejoices* again only when told that she may *once more* give birth to Dionysus In the views of things here given we already have all the elements of a profound and pessimistic contemplation of the world, and along with these we have the *mystery doctrine of tragedy*: the fundamental knowledge of the oneness of all existing things, the consideration of individuation as the primal cause of evil, and art as the joyous hope that the spell of individuation may be broken, as the augury of a restored oneness.

10: Important Concepts

- "It is an indisputable tradition that Greek tragedy in its earliest form had for its theme only the sufferings of Dionysus...."

- "As the visibly appearing god now talks and acts, he resembles an erring, striving, suffering individual...."

What makes these two points interesting to note is that dithyrambic drama, too, has as its theme the suffering of the individual and only the individual, but in a universal way, insofar as everyone suffers, for instance, humiliation, fear, and pain, whose effects are profoundly transformative and run very deep. The actor who undertakes the drama finds within it only his Self and that which his Self is suffering. The whole point of the drama is to show the actor a way out of that suffering, to free up the will that has become blocked by the suffering, so that the will triumphs in whatever resolution proceeds. And the only way to find a way out of suffering is by developing the will, specifically the will to power, which itself is a will toward the apprehension of a deeper Self that further empowers the actor. The angst of the will in the grip of the suffering must be realized in order to triumph over that grip. Or, to put it another way, there can be no release without a tension. It is also very important for the actor to understand *where* he is going with every exit, with every overcoming. As I explained in *The Birth of Dionysia*, on the one hand, it leads to his supra-Self, but, in the end, it leads to the over-Self via the springboard that suffering provides. It is that springboard, when sufficiently made taut and harnessed, which only happens when the actor reaches the deepest supra-Self, that lifts the actor above the principium individuationis, which is a state of being that lies beyond all the limits and boundaries that are set by the PI, which is what we call "genius." It is only in this state of genius, this state beyond all individuation, that the actor may rightly be said to have achieved a state of "oneness" with nature. And the single qualifying criteria for that "oneness" is the transcendence of the limits of individuation, a transcendence of the reliance on the belief in Self.

- "In reality, however, this hero is the suffering Dionysus of the mysteries, a god experiencing in himself the sufferings of individuation, of whom wonderful myths tell that as a boy he was dismembered by the Titans and has been worshipped in this state as Zagreus: whereby is intimated that this dismemberment, the properly Dionysian *suffering,* is like a transformation into air, water, earth, and fire, that we must therefore regard the state of individuation as the source and primal cause of all suffering, as something objectionable in itself."

- "But the hope of the epopts looked for a new birth of Dionysus, which we have now to conceive of in anticipation as the end of individuation...."

A Yearning for Oneness with Nature Beyond Individuation as Will to Power

In order to understand the value and significance of individuation, or belief in Self, it is necessary to evaluate its worth from two perspectives: from the perspective of both sickness and health. An individual who has suffered and subsequently disintegrated into a subindividuated state desperately needs individuation. The best thing for him would

10: IMPORTANT CONCEPTS

be to find his Self and become individuated with clearly defined limits. But in the process of doing that, the actor learns the will to power, and the will to power teaches him that Self-definition, or individuation, empowers him, such that he develops, literally, a lust for power; he wants to become more empowered. (See the Three Evil Things in *Thus Spoke Zarathustra*.) And that lust for power keeps the actor moving along the line of its growth to a point wherein he reaches a state of extraordinary health wherein he learns that a deeper sense of Self begets a more brilliant vision of Self, and he becomes even more empowered. But the only way he can achieve a deeper sense of Self is by moving beyond the limits defined by his existing sense of Self and particularly the limited percipience it defines. Individuation maintains itself by drawing boundaries around itself, and one of those boundaries is a restricted view upon the entire realm of emotion, which is the Dionysian realm. But, insofar as Self is defined by feelings, the will to become ever more empowered requires looking beyond the limits of Self to find a deeper Self in deeper feelings. And in his pursuit of empowerment, as he continually grows beyond the limits of existing Self to a deeper Self, then he discovers the glory of freedom from the limits of individuation *generally*. Thus, the will to power teaches him the glory of freedom, not just freedom from the yoke of suffering, but freedom as well from the limits of individuation. But it is not strictly the goal of achieving oneness with nature that is the highest meaning of life, its ultimate goal, but rather escape from the limits of individuation, which, indeed, results in an absolute oneness with nature. But it is the freedom which results from that escape that instigates the yearning, not a desire for oneness with nature. And it is that yearning that constitutes the will to power.

- "... the *mystery doctrine of tragedy*: the fundamental knowledge of the oneness of all existing things, the consideration of individuation as the primal cause of evil, and art as the joyous hope that the spell of individuation may be broken, as the augury of a restored oneness."

It should be obvious that, if the supra-Self is the goal of the will to power, which it is, and, if the ultimate goal is the *deepest* supra-Self, which it is, then every grade of being that is met along the way must be destroyed to make way for the next Self. And it is this fact of life that makes proto-tragedy such a vital and integral aspect of life.

The All-Important Takeaway from *The Birth of Tragedy*

> It has already been intimated that the Homeric epos is the poem of Olympian culture, wherewith this culture has sung its own song of triumph over the terrors of the war of the Titans. Under the predominating influence of tragic poetry, these Homeric myths are now reproduced anew, and show by this metempsychosis that meantime the Olympian culture also has been vanquished by a still deeper view of things. The haughty Titan Prometheus has announced to his Olympian tormentor that the extremest danger will one day menace his rule, unless he ally with him betimes. In Æschylus we perceive the terrified Zeus, apprehensive of

his end, in alliance with the Titan. Thus, the former age of the Titans is subsequently brought from Tartarus once more to the light of day. The philosophy of wild and naked nature beholds with the undissembled mien of truth the myths of the Homeric world as they dance past: they turn pale, they tremble before the lightning glance of this goddess—till the powerful fist[17] of the Dionysian artist forces them into the service of the new deity. Dionysian truth takes over the entire domain of myth as symbolism of *its* knowledge, which it makes known partly in the public cult of tragedy and partly in the secret celebration of the dramatic mysteries, always, however, in the old mythical garb. What was the power, which freed Prometheus from his vultures and transformed the myth into a vehicle of Dionysian wisdom? It is the Heracleian power of music: which, having reached its highest manifestness in tragedy, can invest myths with a new and most profound significance, which we have already had occasion to characterise as the most powerful faculty of music. For it is the fate of every myth to insinuate itself into the narrow limits of some alleged historical reality, and to be treated by some later generation as a solitary fact with historical

---

[17] Die mächtige Faust.—Cf. *Faust*, Chorus of Spirits.—TR.

claims: and the Greeks were already fairly on the way to restamp the whole of their mythical juvenile dream sagaciously and arbitrarily into a historico-pragmatical *juvenile history*. For this is the manner in which religions are wont to die out: when of course under the stern, intelligent eyes of an orthodox dogmatism, the mythical presuppositions of a religion are systematised as a completed sum of historical events, and when one begins apprehensively to defend the credibility of the myth, while at the same time opposing all continuation of their natural vitality and luxuriance; when, accordingly, the feeling for myth dies out, and its place is taken by the claim of religion to historical foundations. This dying myth was now seized by the new-born genius of Dionysian music, in whose hands it bloomed once more, with such colours as it had never yet displayed, with a fragrance that awakened a longing anticipation of a metaphysical world. After this final effulgence it collapses, its leaves wither, and soon the scoffing Lucians of antiquity catch at the discoloured and faded flowers which the winds carry off in every direction. Through tragedy the myth attains its profoundest significance, its most expressive form; it rises once more like a wounded hero, and the whole surplus of

> vitality, together with the philosophical calmness of the Dying, burns in its eyes with a last powerful gleam.

- "Dionysian truth takes over the entire domain of myth as symbolism of *its* knowledge, which it makes known partly in the public cult of tragedy and partly in the secret celebration of the dramatic mysteries...."

The ideas to be understood here are what is Dionysian truth, what is the domain of myth, and how does Dionysian truth take over the domain of myth?

Myth and music and the creation of myth (as art) out of music are the three most important teaching concepts that a pupil can take away from *The Birth of Tragedy*.

I have explained what is meant by "myth" and "music" and "Dionysian" extensively in *The Birth of Dionysia*, and I encourage the reader to read those explanations. Therefore, I will not expend the same lengthy effort in this essay, but I will summarize what I have said previously.

A Practical Definition of "Dionysian" and "Apollonian"

That which he regards as Dionysian within human nature is everything that is indicated by facial gesture and tone of voice, which is emotion and particularly an inner state of passion. That which is indicated by Apollonian is everything in human nature that is comprised of idea and anything that is essentially ideational, including a state of mind. And there is a stark difference in those two aspects of human nature: emotion is physical and idea is fictive. Being fictive, that which is

Apollonian in human nature is indicated by nothing, except maybe action, in the way that the Dionysian side is revealed in facial gesture and tone of voice. Myth, however, has both physical (or emotional) and fictive (or ideational) traits.

A Practical Definition of Living Myth

In order to understand myth, it is necessary to understand that there are both living myths and dead myths. All the ancient Greek gods are dead myths. But, during their day, they were living myths. And by living myths, I mean that which is perceived as reality. Telling an ancient Greek that there was no such thing as any god would have been the same thing as telling him there was no such thing as the sun or the earth or the rock laying on the ground; it would have been laughable and just crazy.

Self as Assimilative Living Myth

Another instance of living myth is that which we call Self. With regard to Self, the beholder senses the arousal of sensation within himself and instinctively postulates a being as its cause, which we call Self. The predication of "cause" to an observed "effect" is innate within human nature and human thought. In that postulation, which arises from out of an instinct within us, the "cause" is entirely fictive; it exists within the mind of the beholder, and it is something that he himself *creates*. In other words, it is an idea, unlike the sensation he perceives, which is physical. Moreover, in the postulation of the idea of Self, sensation then becomes *assimilated* into Self *as emotion*. In other words, outside the postulation of Self, sensations are perceived as mere rumblings, as phenomena arising from within the body but in the same way that acid reflux is a phenomenon of the body, not as something like a willful exertion by which he moves a limb. However, when he attributes sensations like fear to his Self, then the sensation becomes assimilated into Self as a dimension of his being, as an emotion. And that attribution constitutes an assimilation insofar as he then exclaims "I am frightened." With that attribution and that assimilation and that articulation, he *knows*. The sensation therewith becomes an emotion and that emotion fills his being with the animation inherent in the emotion and moves him thusly. In that assimilation, mythical Self, which constitutes a sense of being, is transformed because it then becomes moved by that driving sensation. In such a way, the two realms of Dionysian and Apollonian are merged. In such a way, myth becomes a symbol of Dionysian truth. But neither realm sheds its inherent traits in the merger. Self, which is largely an Apollonian construction, maintains its ideational traits, such as constancy, restraint, and governance. But it also then assimilates Dionysian traits, specifically animation and excess, *and gains the wisdom that inheres* in the sensations arising from deep within the body, of which there is much. In such a way does the Apollonian realm become a symbol of the Dionysian realm. And thus, we observe a fundamental contradiction within mythical Self, the playing-out of which comprises the very process of living that we call life, insofar as the mythical Self *grows* only by incorporating sensation into itself.

It is a fundamental fact that emotion communicates knowledge of human nature to the individual that is entirely different, if not richer, from the knowledge communicated by idea or even Self. At its simplest. Self communicates self-restraint, while emotion communicates, among other things, yearning, for instance. And yearning is an essential trait of the will to power.

- "What was the power, which freed Prometheus from his vultures and transformed the myth into a vehicle of Dionysian wisdom? It is the Heracleian power of music: which, having reached its highest manifestness in tragedy, can invest myths with a new and most profound significance...."

Now we come to the idea of music, which at this point is undefined, and the idea that music transforms myth, especially the myth that arises from tragedy and the myth that arises from mysticism. Indeed, what does he mean by mysticism?

A Definition of "Music"

By "music," he does not mean audible music. What is necessary here, in order to understand Nietzsche's notion of music, is to understand the difference between reality and actuality.

Everything within us that is perceived through the perspective of Self, via myth, is perceived as reality. But not everything is perceived through the perspective of Self. The Self, by its very nature, is a constructed idea of *being* with very individual limits and boundaries. It grows according to its ability to incorporate more and more of sensation (the inner world) into itself as a dimension of itself, all the while abiding by very strict limits and boundaries.

10: IMPORTANT CONCEPTS

Actuality vs. Reality and Mysticism

Consider an individual with an underlying fear that he or she cannot brave. Insofar as that fear has not been incorporated into his being, it is not a part of his consciousness, it is not an emotion, and it is not a part of reality. Now, you might say that the mere fact that the fear exists within him makes it a part of reality. But that is inaccurate. The only qualifying criterion for what constitutes reality is attribution of the phenomena to Self so that it is assimilated into being and assumes the Veil of Maya. All that exists as reality exists only within the domain of being, the domain of myth, or Self. Everything that exists outside of reality is actuality. And actuality is categorically absent anything that is ideational, which means it is entirely sensational. Moreover, there are indeed phenomena that occur within the realm of sensation, which, being outside of the purview of reality, are outside our range of perception. Those phenomena that occur within actuality but outside of reality comprises that which we call mysticism. The events occur and their "effect" or benefit rise to the surface, but their occurrence itself is beyond the reach of our percipience. For instance, the overcoming of a fear results in a change in behavior as a result of the release of the stress, such as the sudden cessation of a nervous habit. The overcoming itself may be willful and observed, and the effect of the stress release may become observable, but what happens inside of us via that overcoming is totally invisible and unobservable to us. That is mysticism.

Actuality as "Music"

And everything that exists outside of reality and only in actuality is what Nietzsche calls "music." Since the Apollonian realm is entirely fictive and the Dionysian realm is entirely physical, all that exists in actuality is the Dionysian realm, and, again, everything that is revealed in facial gesture and tone of voice comprises the Dionysian realm. *Why* he calls it "music" is a question I will answer later in this essay when we come to something he wrote that reveals the answer directly.

Mythical Assimilation as an Aesthetic Phenomenon

Lastly, it is important to note that, insofar as "reality" is founded upon the mythical Self, and insofar as the mythical Self is an illusion, then, reality, too, is an illusion. But it is an illusion without which the human species cannot live. Without the illusion of being that is imposed upon a world which is wholly a world of becoming and which it is categorically absent any form of being, it is not possible for man even to think. But more importantly, illusion is the one and only quality about the Apollonian realm that *heals* suffering man. The attribution of fear to Self, in place of its existence as a mere haunting rumbling from within the subconscious, whereby it becomes a dimension of being, an emotion, makes the fear bearable. Indeed, this is the sense in which Nietzsche says life is only possible as an aesthetic phenomenon.

- "For it is the fate of every myth to insinuate itself into the narrow limits of some alleged historical reality, and to be treated by some later generation as a solitary fact with historical claims...."

- "For this is the manner in which religions are wont to die out: when of course under the stern, intelligent eyes of an orthodox dogmatism, the mythical presuppositions of a religion are systematised as a completed sum of historical events, and when one begins apprehensively to defend the credibility of the myth, while at the same time opposing all continuation of their natural vitality and luxuriance; when, accordingly, the feeling for myth dies out, and its place is taken by the claim of religion to historical foundations."

A Second Form of Myth: Gateway Myth

Not all myths are ideas of fictive beings. Some are ideas that provide a gateway for the will to proceed forward. For instance, science is a gateway myth that postulates (1) the world is knowable and (2) the world can be "fixed." Without those two postulations — and the postulation that all knowledge is worth attainment regardless of its use, science would not be possible. Thus, some myths are gateway myths, which I discuss more extensively in *The Birth of Dionysia*.

Dying Myth Entrenches Itself in an Historical Foundation

When a myth begins to die, something very interesting happens. Take for instance, the myth we call "God." If I told you to go out and find just one instance of something in this world that has always existed and will always exist without end, which is the very definition of being, you would find only one: God. That which we call "God" is a mythical being. And in our day, we are witnessing the death of this myth. In its death throes, adherents strive to give the myth an historical foundation in order to prolong its credibility. For instance, in an argument with an adherent about the worthiness of a belief in God, the adherent will argue that the belief has held firm and worthy for two thousand years, referring to Christianity but meaning "God." The myth no longer draws belief by its own power, so the draw is transferred to an historical foundation *as a reason for belief*. In the wake of a dying myth, nihilism takes hold. And nowhere is there more evidence of nihilism than in fundamental Islamists who go about destroying icons of other religious beliefs for the purpose of bolstering their own and especially their history, as if *their history* was all that ever existed. All value is transferred to the history. *Fundamentalism* is evidence of despair that itself is due to a dying myth.

- "Through tragedy the myth attains its profoundest significance...."

The Growth of Mythical Self via the Assimilation of Sensation

Quite simply, when the Self collapses via proto-tragedy, its limits and boundaries also give way and the principium individuationis readjusts itself to a greater depth of perception. In that readjustment, emotion achieves a more pronounced tone whereby the beholden individual hears the body speaking to him more clearly and more loudly. Simultaneously, a new vision of Self, the supra-Self, arises in the wake of the collapse of the former Self, given the new tone and the mythopoeic instinct that is triggered by that new tone. And the new supra-Self then endeavors to assimilate the louder and more pronounced bodily sensations into itself. In doing so, those sensations then become

10: Important Concepts

emotions, a dimension of Self, and the mythical Self itself then becomes clearer and more pronounced, and, with the assimilation, more endowed. In such a way, the Dionysian realm taunts the Apollonian realm to greater production. And then, in turn, through dissonance, whereby the accumulation of power *instinctively* begins to yearn for more power, the Apollonian realm (the new Self) eventually taunts the Dionysian realm to a greater production, so that the whole process begins anew and the individual seeks an even deeper arousal and assimilation of subliminal emotion.

The Dithyramb as Actuality and "Music"

> What meantest thou, oh impious Euripides, in seeking once more to enthral this dying one? It died under thy ruthless hands: and then thou madest use of counterfeit, masked myth, which like the ape of Heracles could only trick itself out in the old finery. And as myth died in thy hands, so also died the genius of music; though thou couldst covetously plunder all the gardens of music—thou didst only realise a counterfeit, masked music. And because thou hast forsaken Dionysus. Apollo hath also forsaken thee; rout up all the passions from their haunts and conjure them into thy sphere, sharpen and polish a sophistical dialectics for the speeches of thy heroes—thy very heroes have only counterfeit, masked passions, and speak only counterfeit, masked music.

DIONYSIA METAPHYSICA

The above paragraph goes to the point that tragedy arises only out of music. And by music, Nietzsche meant actuality, which lies beyond and outside the scope of reality. Reality arises via the *interpretation* of actuality. The Self senses movement (as sensation) within the body and then endeavors to assimilate that sensation into itself as an attribute of Self, as an emotion. And only when that assimilation and attribution succeed does the sensation then become a part of reality. But the sensation itself exists outside of reality. *And everything circumstantial, secondary, and tangential to that sensation also exists outside of reality.* With regard to the dithyramb, which endeavors to create myth (or Self) within its actor, that creation requires an *accurate* depiction of actuality, which must include all the circumstantial, secondary, and tangential elements of whatever sensation or emotion will trigger the mythopoeic instinct and, therewith, the myth. And Nietzsche calls the dull and comprehensive depiction of actuality "music." If one of the elements pertaining to the existence of the sensation (and, therefore, its triggered myth) is missing, what is depicted is not "music."

Speaking strictly with regard to the dithyramb, or the new dithyramb in which Nietzsche composed, and making no reference to the ancient dithyramb, insofar as the actor is required to achieve a plausible embodiment of the "music" that is depicted, by which I mean the actuality, then the dithyramb must be an accurate depiction of that actuality. Otherwise, a plausible embodiment is precluded. I should point out that you, the reader, would understand this more readily if I substituted the word "actuality" with the word "reality" and said that the dithyramb must be an accurate depiction of reality. But it is not reality that the dithyramb depicts. The dithyramb depicts actuality, which Nietzsche called "music." Once mythopoeia happens and the Self is apprehended through that mythopoeia, that is when "reality" appears. And the appearance of reality comes as a creation, an Apollonian creation, an entirely fictive creation, arising out of the mythical Self. The myth is the central and most fundamental creation. So, in an indirect way, yes, the dithyramb depicts reality, but only as its creation. The dithyramb depicts something much deeper than reality, its essence, which is actuality.

The Errors of Euripides

In the above cited paragraph, Nietzsche claims that Euripides misunderstood proto-tragedy on two points. One, he claims Euripides misunderstood the value and necessity of "music" with regard to the creation of myth. Two, Euripides failed to understand the profound delight that man derives from proto-tragedy, which derives from the collapse of the Ego toward a reunion with the deeper Self, or oneness with nature. And three, most importantly, Euripides moved proto-tragedy to the theater, wherein it became the modern tragedy that still exists today, and transformed it from a rite of passage that is integral to the process of life that plays out within the human soul to a purely theatrical spectacle.

In the first instance, today, when someone sits down to write a story, they can write out whatever plot they can imagine. And they can create whatever dialogue they wish in order to create whatever characters they wish, all toward executing the plot they have conjured up. It is all a work of fancy, of imagination. Fancy, creative imagination, and conjuring have no place whatsoever in the composition of the dithyramb, whose sole purpose is to create myth within its actor, not to map out a plot.

In the second instance, the only way you will understand the value of proto-tragedy is to experience it. And the only way you will experience it is by undertaking Nietzsche's dithyrambic tragedy. I assure you that, if you undertake it, you will discover *and embody* a deeper Self, which can only be done by shedding your old Self, your Ego. And when you do that, you will understand the value of proto-tragedy and the role it plays within the process of growth that leads to your discovery of Self. Knowledge of the value of proto-tragedy is wisdom of the rarest achievement, which the small ancient Greek civilization possessed and then lost. It is not uncommon for wisdom, especially rare wisdom, to elude us. And in Euripides' tragedies, we see that loss for the first time. For more than two thousand years, wisdom of the value of proto-tragedy has been lost to us, and it is only now that we have regained it. But in Euripides, we see the initial loss. And in that initial loss, we see tragedy entirely transformed. And in its new form, it has been moved onto the stage, where it may indeed provide a wondrous spectacle but absolutely nothing of its redemptive nature imparting itself to the individual.

11: The Failure of Modern Tragedy

Greek tragedy had a fate different from that of all her older sister arts: she died by suicide, in consequence of an irreconcilable conflict; accordingly she died tragically, while they all passed away very calmly and beautifully in ripe old age. For if it be in accordance with a happy state of things to depart this life without a struggle, leaving behind a fair posterity, the closing period of these older arts exhibits such a happy state of things: slowly they sink out of sight, and before their dying eyes already stand their fairer progeny, who impatiently lift up their heads with courageous mien. The death of Greek tragedy, on the other hand, left an immense void, deeply felt everywhere. Even as certain Greek sailors in the time of Tiberius once heard upon a lonesome island the thrilling cry, "great Pan is dead": so now as it were sorrowful wailing sounded through the Hellenic world: "Tragedy is dead! Poetry itself has perished with her!

11: THE FAILURE OF MODERN TRAGEDY

> Begone, begone, ye stunted, emaciated epigones! Begone to Hades, that ye may for once eat your fill of the crumbs of your former masters!"

Dithyrambic Poetry as Dithyrambic Music

In this passage, Nietzsche loudly proclaims the extraordinary value of proto-tragedy to life and to art and he defines its loss as a most profound loss to humanity. Notice also that he specifically mentions the fact that poetry was harmed by the loss of proto-tragedy. And that is because the loss of proto-tragedy also led to the loss of composing with "music," by which, again, I mean actuality but which you probably understand as reality. The beauty of poetry lies more in its poignancy that in its rhyme. And poetry that has been composed as "music" is far more poignant than anything which has not been composed in music. There are numerous instances within *Thus Spoke Zarathustra* when poetic articulations about the deepest, innermost nature of human being and the conflicts within, and especially those moments that see beyond the conflicts, present some of the most beautiful and poignant poetry you will ever find anywhere.

> But when after all a new Art blossomed forth which revered tragedy as her ancestress and mistress, it was observed with horror that she did indeed bear the features of her mother, but those very features the latter had exhibited in her long death-struggle. It was *Euripides* who fought this death-struggle of tragedy; the later art is

known as the *New Attic Comedy*. In it the degenerate form of tragedy lived on as a monument of the most painful and violent death of tragedy proper.

This connection between the two serves to explain the passionate attachment to Euripides evinced by the poets of the New Comedy, and hence we are no longer surprised at the wish of Philemon, who would have got himself hanged at once, with the sole design of being able to visit Euripides in the lower regions: if only he could be assured generally that the deceased still had his wits. But if we desire, as briefly as possible, and without professing to say aught exhaustive on the subject, to characterise what Euripides has in common with Menander and Philemon, and what appealed to them so strongly as worthy of imitation: it will suffice to say that the *spectator* was brought upon the stage by Euripides. He who has perceived the material of which the Promethean tragic writers prior to Euripides formed their heroes, and how remote from their purpose it was to bring the true mask of reality on the stage, will also know what to make of the wholly divergent tendency of Euripides. Through him the commonplace individual forced his way from the spectators' benches to the stage itself; the mirror in which formerly only great and bold traits found

11: THE FAILURE OF MODERN TRAGEDY

expression now showed the painful exactness that conscientiously reproduces even the abortive lines of nature. Odysseus, the typical Hellene of the Old Art, sank, in the hands of the new poets, to the figure of the Græculus, who, as the good-naturedly cunning domestic slave, stands henceforth in the centre of dramatic interest. What Euripides takes credit for in the Aristophanean "Frogs," namely, that by his household remedies he freed tragic art from its pompous corpulency, is apparent above all in his tragic heroes. The spectator now virtually saw and heard his double on the Euripidean stage, and rejoiced that he could talk so well. But this joy was not all: one even learned of Euripides how to speak: he prides himself upon this in his contest with Æschylus: how the people have learned from him how to observe, debate, and draw conclusions according to the rules of art and with the cleverest sophistications. In general it may be said that through this revolution of the popular language he made the New Comedy possible. For it was henceforth no longer a secret, how—and with what saws—the commonplace could represent and express itself on the stage. Civic mediocrity, on which Euripides built all his political hopes, was now suffered to speak, while heretofore the demigod in tragedy and the drunken satyr, or demiman, in comedy,

> had determined the character of the language. And so the Aristophanean Euripides prides himself on having portrayed the common, familiar, everyday life and dealings of the people, concerning which all are qualified to pass judgment. If now the entire populace philosophises, manages land and goods with unheard-of circumspection, and conducts law-suits, he takes all the credit to himself, and glories in the splendid results of the wisdom with which he inoculated the rabble.

Euripi-dean Tragedy and Everyday Reality

In place of actuality being depicted in the realm of proto-tragedy, with Euripides, reality was depicted. But it was not the higher reality resulting from a higher and more comprehensive Self, or myth, but rather the common and stark reality with which everyone is familiar in their daily lives, which is how modern tragedy exists today.

> It was to a populace prepared and enlightened in this manner that the New Comedy could now address itself, of which Euripides had become as it were the chorus-master; only that in this case the chorus of spectators had to be trained. As soon as this chorus was trained to sing in the Euripidean key, there arose that chesslike variety of the drama, the New Comedy, with its perpetual triumphs of cunning and artfulness. But

11: THE FAILURE OF MODERN TRAGEDY

Euripides—the chorus-master—was praised incessantly: indeed, people would have killed themselves in order to learn yet more from him, had they not known that tragic poets were quite as dead as tragedy. But with it the Hellene had surrendered the belief in his immortality; not only the belief in an ideal past, but also the belief in an ideal future. The saying taken from the well-known epitaph, "as an old man, frivolous and capricious," applies also to aged Hellenism. The passing moment, wit, levity, and caprice, are its highest deities; the fifth class, that of the slaves, now attains to power, at least in sentiment: and if we can still speak at all of "Greek cheerfulness," it is the cheerfulness of the slave who has nothing of consequence to answer for, nothing great to strive for, and cannot value anything of the past or future higher than the present. It was this semblance of "Greek cheerfulness" which so revolted the deep-minded and formidable natures of the first four centuries of Christianity: this womanish flight from earnestness and terror, this cowardly contentedness with easy pleasure, was not only contemptible to them, but seemed to be a specifically anti-Christian sentiment. And we must ascribe it to its influence that the conception of Greek antiquity, which lived on for centuries, preserved with almost enduring persistency

> that peculiar hectic colour of cheerfulness—as if there had never been a Sixth Century with its birth of tragedy, its Mysteries, its Pythagoras and Heraclitus, indeed as if the art-works of that great period did not at all exist, which in fact—each by itself—can in no wise be explained as having sprung from the soil of such a decrepit and slavish love of existence and cheerfulness, and point to an altogether different conception of things as their source.

- "But with it the Hellene had surrendered the belief in his immortality; not only the belief in an ideal past, but also the belief in an ideal future."

- "The saying taken from the well-known epitaph, 'as an old man, frivolous and capricious,' applies also to aged Hellenism."

- "The passing moment, wit, levity, and caprice, are its highest deities...."

- "... and if we can still speak at all of 'Greek cheerfulness,' it is the cheerfulness of the slave who has nothing of consequence to answer for, nothing great to strive for, and cannot value anything of the past or future higher than the present."

- "It was this semblance of 'Greek cheerfulness' ... this womanish flight from earnestness and terror, this cowardly contentedness with easy pleasure,"

11: THE FAILURE OF MODERN TRAGEDY

Inherent in the souls of those who subscribe to proto-tragedy is a belief in a better future, an eventual attainment of oneness with Nature. Nietzsche describes this faith as "Greek cheerfulness." Euripides' tragedies replaced this redemptory cheerfulness with a contended indulgence in easy pleasure and the moment. Remember that, at the outset of this essay, Nietzsche spoke of proto-tragedy arising out of a need for terror and that necessarily leads to a better existence, a better and higher reality, which goes to the very heart of his theory that tragedy derived as dissonance from within a vast accumulation of power. But Euripides' tragedies delivered a complacent indulgence with common reality, not a cataclysm that refreshed a complacency resulting from power.

> The assertion made a moment ago, that Euripides introduced the spectator on the stage to qualify him the better to pass judgment on the drama, will make it appear as if the old tragic art was always in a false relation to the spectator: and one would be tempted to extol the radical tendency of Euripides to bring about an adequate relation between art-work and public as an advance on Sophocles. But, as things are, "public" is merely a word, and not at all a homogeneous and constant quantity. Why should the artist be under obligations to accommodate himself to a power whose strength is merely in numbers? And if by virtue of his endowments and aspirations he feels himself superior to every one of these spectators, how could he feel greater respect

for the collective expression of all these subordinate capacities than for the relatively highest-endowed individual spectator? In truth, if ever a Greek artist treated his public throughout a long life with presumptuousness and self-sufficiency, it was Euripides, who, even when the masses threw themselves at his feet, with sublime defiance made an open assault on his own tendency, the very tendency with which he had triumphed over the masses. If this genius had had the slightest reverence for the pandemonium of the public, he would have broken down long before the middle of his career beneath the weighty blows of his own failures. These considerations here make it obvious that our formula—namely, that Euripides brought the spectator upon the stage, in order to make him truly competent to pass judgment—was but a provisional one, and that we must seek for a deeper understanding of his tendency. Conversely, it is undoubtedly well known that Æschylus and Sophocles, during all their lives, indeed, far beyond their lives, enjoyed the full favour of the people, and that therefore in the case of these predecessors of Euripides the idea of a false relation between art-work and public was altogether excluded. What was it that thus forcibly diverted this highly gifted artist, so incessantly impelled to production, from the

> path over which shone the sun of the greatest names in poetry and the cloudless heaven of popular favour? What strange consideration for the spectator led him to defy, the spectator? How could he, owing to too much respect for the public —disrespect the public?

- "Why should the artist be under obligations to accommodate himself to a power whose strength is merely in numbers? And if by virtue of his endowments and aspirations he feels himself superior to every one of these spectators, how could he feel greater respect for the collective expression of all these subordinate capacities than for the relatively highest-endowed individual spectator?"

Euripides Chose an Audience of Mass

What is interesting to note here is that Nietzsche discerned a difference in an audience of many and an audience of a few, specifically in the abilities of its members. In choosing an audience for *Thus Spoke Zarathustra*, he obviously took this discernment into serious consideration, and, in fact, addressed himself to a very few.

> Euripides—and this is the solution of the riddle just propounded—felt himself, as a poet, undoubtedly superior to the masses, but not to two of his spectators: he brought the masses upon the stage; these two spectators he revered as the only competent

judges and masters of his art: in compliance with their directions and admonitions, he transferred the entire world of sentiments, passions, and experiences, hitherto present at every festival representation as the invisible chorus on the spectators' benches, into the souls of his stage-heroes; he yielded to their demands when he also sought for these new characters the new word and the new tone; in their voices alone he heard the conclusive verdict on his work, as also the cheering promise of triumph when he found himself condemned as usual by the justice of the public.

Of these two, spectators the one is— Euripides himself, Euripides *as thinker,* not as poet. It might be said of him, that his unusually large fund of critical ability, as in the case of Lessing, if it did not create, at least constantly fructified a productively artistic collateral impulse. With this faculty, with all the clearness and dexterity of his critical thought, Euripides had sat in the theatre and striven to recognise in the masterpieces of his great predecessors, as in faded paintings, feature and feature, line and line. And here had happened to him what one initiated in the deeper arcana of Æschylean tragedy must needs have expected: he observed something incommensurable in every feature and in every line, a certain deceptive distinctness and at the same time an enigmatic profundity, yea an infinitude, of background. Even the clearest figure had always a comet's tail attached to it, which seemed to suggest the uncertain and the inexplicable. The same twilight shrouded the structure of the drama, especially the significance of the chorus. And how doubtful seemed the solution of the ethical problems to his mind! How questionable the treatment of the myths! How unequal the distribution of happiness and misfortune! Even in the language of the Old Tragedy there was much that was objectionable to him, or at least enigmatical; he found especially too much pomp for simple affairs, too many tropes and immense things for the plainness of the characters. Thus he sat restlessly pondering in the theatre, and as a spectator he acknowledged to himself that he did not understand his great predecessors. If, however, he thought the understanding the root proper of all enjoyment and productivity, he had to inquire and look about to see whether any one else thought as he did, and also acknowledged this incommensurability. But most people, and among them the best individuals, had only a distrustful smile for him, while none could explain why the great masters were still in the right in face of his scruples and objections. And in this painful

> condition he found *that other spectator,* who did not comprehend, and therefore did not esteem, tragedy. In alliance with him he could venture, from amid his lonesomeness, to begin the prodigious struggle against the art of Æschylus and Sophocles—not with polemic writings, but as a dramatic poet, who opposed *his own* conception of tragedy to the traditional one.

Euripides Applied Scientific Thought to Tragedy

Euripides, who was more of a thinker than he was a poet, did not understand tragedy, and, coincidentally, neither did Socrates. Thus, Euripides allied with Socrates, an even greater thinker than he, and undertook an overhaul of Aeschylean tragedy according to the norms laid out by Socrates.

12: Tragedy, Myth. and Will

> Before we name this other spectator, let us pause here a moment in order to recall our own impression, as previously described, of the discordant and incommensurable elements in the nature of Æschylean tragedy. Let us think of our own astonishment at the *chorus* and the *tragic hero* of that type of tragedy, neither of which we could reconcile with our practices any more than with tradition—till we rediscovered this duplexity itself as the origin and essence of Greek tragedy, as the expression of two interwoven artistic impulses, *the Apollonian and the Dionysian.*

Proto-Tragedy as the Production of Myth

Nietzsche restates his theory that proto-tragedy derives from the antagonism arising out of the dual relationship existing between the Apollonian realm and the Dionysian realm of human nature, between ideation and sensation. In other words, emotion (or the Dionysian realm) triggers the mythopoeic instinct, which, in turn, produces fictive visions (the Apollonian realm), either as mythical beings (Self) or as gateway ideas by which the will is allowed to move forward. Given the nature of the individuated being that is created by Self, with its limits and boundaries, both with regard to percipience (nothing is visible beyond the horizon, beyond the limits of reality) and to the measured and restricted freedom allotted to emotion, proto-tragedy destroys those limits and boundaries, therewith providing a oneness with Nature and allowing further growth that necessarily leads to ever expanding limits of percipience and ever greater passions, e.g., the genius. And most importantly, proto-tragedy, as dithyrambic drama, which is the only art form that avails tragedy to man, is written in "musical" form, what you might call reality, and definitely not imaginative or conjured, common, everyday reality.

> To separate this primitive and all-powerful Dionysian element from tragedy, and to build up a new and purified form of tragedy on the basis of a non-Dionysian art, morality, and conception of things—such is the tendency of Euripides which now reveals itself to us in a clear light.

Euripides Uprooted of Myth from Proto-Tragedy

Euripides drastically changed the art of tragedy by removing its musical foundation and bringing morality and quotidian reality into it.

DIONYSIA METAPHYSICA

In a myth composed in the eve of his life, Euripides himself most urgently propounded to his contemporaries the question as to the value and signification of this tendency. Is the Dionysian entitled to exist at all? Should it not be forcibly rooted out of the Hellenic soil? Certainly, the poet tells us, if only it were possible: but the god Dionysus is too powerful; his most intelligent adversary—like Pentheus in the "Bacchæ"—is unwittingly enchanted by him, and in this enchantment meets his fate. The judgment of the two old sages, Cadmus and Tiresias, seems to be also the judgment of the aged poet: that the reflection of the wisest individuals does not overthrow old popular traditions, nor the perpetually propagating worship of Dionysus, that in fact it behoves us to display at least a diplomatically cautious concern in the presence of such strange forces: where however it is always possible that the god may take offence at such lukewarm participation, and finally change the diplomat—in this case Cadmus—into a dragon. This is what a poet tells us, who opposed Dionysus with heroic valour throughout a long life—in order finally to wind up his career with a glorification of his adversary, and with suicide, like one staggering from giddiness, who, in order to escape the horrible vertigo he can no longer

12: TRAGEDY, MYTH, AND WILL

> endure, casts himself from a tower. This tragedy—the Bacchæ—is a protest against the practicability of his own tendency; alas, and it has already been put into practice! The surprising thing had happened: when the poet recanted, his tendency had already conquered. Dionysus had already been scared from the tragic stage, and in fact by a demonic power which spoke through Euripides. Even Euripides was, in a certain sense, only a mask: the deity that spoke through him was neither Dionysus nor Apollo, but an altogether new-born demon, called *Socrates*. This is the new antithesis: the Dionysian and the Socratic, and the artwork of Greek tragedy was wrecked on it. What if even Euripides now seeks to comfort us by his recantation? It is of no avail: the most magnificent temple lies in ruins. What avails the lamentation of the destroyer, and his confession that it was the most beautiful of all temples? And even that Euripides has been changed into a dragon as a punishment by the art-critics of all ages—who could be content with this wretched compensation?

- "Even Euripides was, in a certain sense, only a mask: the deity that spoke through him was neither Dionysus nor Apollo, but an altogether new-born demon, called *Socrates*. This is the new antithesis: the

Dionysian and the Socratic, and the art-work of Greek tragedy was wrecked on it."

The art of tragedy was destroyed by Socrates' teaching, which was science, dialectic, logic, anti-mysticism, consciousness, and knowledge for the sake of knowledge. Euripides was merely a precursor, an omen of what eventually arrived in full force in the person of Socrates.

> Let us now approach this *Socratic* tendency with which Euripides combated and vanquished Æschylean tragedy.
>
> We must now ask ourselves, what could be the ulterior aim of the Euripidean design, which, in the highest ideality of its execution, would found drama exclusively on the non-Dionysian? What other form of drama could there be, if it was not to be born of the womb of music, in the mysterious twilight of the Dionysian? Only *the dramatised epos:* in which Apollonian domain of art the *tragic* effect is of course unattainable. It does not depend on the subject-matter of the events here represented; indeed, I venture to assert that it would have been impossible for Goethe in his projected "Nausikaa" to have rendered tragically effective the suicide of the idyllic being with which he intended to complete the fifth act; so extraordinary is the power of the epic-Apollonian representation, that it charms, before our eyes, the most terrible

12: Tragedy, Myth. and Will

> things by the joy in appearance and in redemption through appearance. The poet of the dramatised epos cannot completely blend with his pictures any more than the epic rhapsodist. He is still just the calm, unmoved embodiment of Contemplation whose wide eyes see the picture *before* them. The actor in this dramatised epos still remains intrinsically rhapsodist: the consecration of inner dreaming is on all his actions, so that he is never wholly an actor.

- "We must now ask ourselves, what could be the ulterior aim of the Euripidean design, which, in the highest ideality of its execution, would found drama exclusively on the non-Dionysian? What other form of drama could there be, if it was not to be born of the womb of music, in the mysterious twilight of the Dionysian? Only *the dramatised epos*...."

Proto-Tragedy Is Rooted in Passion, Not Epic Concept

The dramatized epic is the only form of drama with which we moderns are familiar. The only other art form with which to draw a distinction, at least with regard to tragedy, is dithyrambic drama. And until you experience the art of the dithyramb, you will only ever understand drama as the dramatized epic.

- > The poet of the dramatised epos cannot completely blend with his pictures any more

> than the epic rhapsodist. He is still just the calm, unmoved embodiment of Contemplation whose wide eyes see the picture *before* them. The actor in this dramatised epos still remains intrinsically rhapsodist: the consecration of inner dreaming is on all his actions, so that he is never wholly an actor.

The key words here are "completely blend," which goes to the idea that dithyrambic music requires the actor to achieve a plausible embodiment of the passion, the emotion, the state of mind that is depicted. As I explained in *The Birth of Dionysia*, the dithyramb is composed in gesticulative metaphor. And the metaphors *point* the actor toward an inner pathos with both generalized and detailed gestures that the actor must then find within himself and embody. And only when he achieves that embodiment will he then become moved by that inner pathos, and movement is required for the drama to be completed. *There is nothing in a dramatized epic that is embodiable in this same manner.* All that is required by a dramatized epic is contemplation and the production of concept. That contemplation may indeed arouse certain emotions within the spectator, but it is the contemplation that comprises the primary, if only, interpretation in the epic, which is wholly an Apollonian art form, one of concept and image, unlike Dionysian, which is one of feeling.

12: Tragedy, Myth, and Will

The Production of Myth Requires Embodiment, Not Mere Contemplation

Notice in the above very last statement, Nietzsche defines "actor" by stating that it is not defined by contemplation of vision, image, idea, or concept. What he does not say, but which I can tell you is the case, is that the actor is defined by his ability to achieve a plausible embodiment of the inner pathos that is depicted by the dithyramb. And the reason that embodiment defines him as an actor is that the embodiment then drives him along the course of the drama, provided he finds a way beyond the conflictive state of mind that is represented by the dithyramb. And that "way" is usually provided by vision, image, idea, and concept, which frees up the will. That is the beauty of the dithyramb: it depicts the actuality, the music, in the form of pathos, strictly, out of which the ethos arises *as an act of will*, provided the actor achieves the embodiment, is moved by the pathos *in his will*, and then consummates the will by finding a way, via the Apollonian realm, for the will to move forward. Nothing like this happens in the epic, which involves merely the contemplation of concept or image and the beauty of the image.

> How, then, is the Euripidean play related to this ideal of the Apollonian drama? Just as the younger rhapsodist is related to the solemn rhapsodist of the old time. The former describes his own character in the Platonic "Ion" as follows: "When I am saying anything sad, my eyes fill with tears; when, however, what I am saying is awful and terrible, then my hair stands on end through fear, and my heart leaps." Here we

no longer observe anything of the epic absorption in appearance, or of the unemotional coolness of the true actor, who precisely in his highest activity is wholly appearance and joy in appearance. Euripides is the actor with leaping heart, with hair standing on end; as Socratic thinker he designs the plan, as passionate actor he executes it. Neither in the designing nor in the execution is he an artist pure and simple. And so the Euripidean drama is a thing both cool and fiery, equally capable of freezing and burning; it is impossible for it to attain the Apollonian, effect of the epos, while, on the other hand, it has severed itself as much as possible from Dionysian elements, and now, in order to act at all, it requires new stimulants, which can no longer lie within the sphere of the two unique art-impulses, the Apollonian and the Dionysian. The stimulants are cool, paradoxical *thoughts*, in place of Apollonian intuitions—and fiery *passions*—in place Dionysean ecstasies; and in fact, thoughts and passions very realistically copied, and not at all steeped in the ether of art.

- "… in order to act at all, it requires new stimulants, which can no longer lie within the sphere of the two unique art-impulses, the Apollonian and the Dionysian. The stimulants are cool, paradoxical *thoughts*, in place of Apollonian intuitions—and fiery *passions*—in place Dionysean ecstasies; and in fact, thoughts and passions very realistically copied, and not at all steeped in the ether of art."

In the above, he is speaking of the dramatic epic. And when he speaks of the ability to act, consider what I just told you about the definition of action. Insofar as the epic depicts nothing that can be embodied and instead depicts only that which can be contemplated, and insofar as the dramatic epic still considers itself a drama, what, then, constitutes action in the dramatic epic? The answer is that action can be found only in paradoxical thought. The spectator is led into a paradox, which is mostly a cerebral paradox but may also deepen into an emotional paradox, but which is resolved *via thought*, whereas, in the dithyramb, the difficulty is resolved by willful action.

What should be forming in the mind of the reader here is that the dithyrambic actor, in contrast with the epic spectator, himself becomes a work of art via willful action inasmuch as both the Dionysian realm and the Apollonian realm grow throughout the course of the dithyrambic drama. With the tragic collapse of the limits of individuation, the actor's ability to fathom ever deeper emotions brings him into conflict with the contradiction that is innate in those emotions, and those conflicts, in turn, increase his ability to develop idea with which to overcome the conflicts.

Notice also in the above that Nietzsche speaks of the dramatic epic "realistically" copying the thoughts and passions comprising the paradox that is presented in the drama but that none of them, as copies instead of gestures pointing to the real thing, ever attain to or fully plumb the actuality that is depicted, in contrast, in the dithyramb.

> Accordingly, if we have perceived this much, that Euripides did not succeed in establishing the drama exclusively on the Apollonian, but that rather his non-Dionysian inclinations deviated into a naturalistic and inartistic tendency, we shall now be able to approach nearer to the character *æsthetic Socratism.* supreme law of which reads about as follows: "to be beautiful everything must be intelligible," as the parallel to the Socratic proposition, "only the knowing is one virtuous." With this canon in his hands Euripides measured all the separate elements of the drama, and rectified them according to his principle: the language, the characters, the dramaturgic structure, and the choric music. The poetic deficiency and retrogression, which we are so often wont to impute to Euripides in comparison with Sophoclean tragedy, is for the most part the product of this penetrating critical process, this daring intelligibility. The Euripidian *prologue* may serve us as an example of the productivity of this, rationalistic method. Nothing could be more opposed to the technique of our stage than the prologue in the drama of Euripides. For a single person to appear at the outset of the play telling us who he is, what precedes the

> action, what has happened thus far, yea, what will happen in the course of the play, would be designated by a modern playwright as a wanton and unpardonable abandonment of the effect of suspense. Everything that is about to happen is known beforehand; who then cares to wait for it actually to happen? — considering, moreover, that here there is not by any means the exciting relation of a predicting dream to a reality taking place later on.

- "... Euripides did not succeed in establishing the drama exclusively on the Apollonian, but that rather his non-Dionysian inclinations deviated into a naturalistic and inartistic tendency...."

Tragedy and the Role of the Prologue

By "naturalistic and inartistic," we might surmise that he means naturalistic insofar as the pathoses depicted in Euripides' tragedy is a good copy of actuality, but it is also inartistic insofar as the link between myth and actuality is missing. The trigger between mythopoeia and the Dionysian realm eluded Euripides.

I think the most important point to note here is Nietzsche's claim that Euripides was influenced by Socrates' aesthetics, which, according to Nietzsche, taught that beauty had to be intelligible and comprehensible, not mystical, and that the pursuit of knowledge merely for the sake of knowledge was virtuous.

Then, Nietzsche moves on to discuss Euripides' use of the prologue, in which everything that is about to happen in the drama is disclosed to the spectator, a move that Nietzsche claims destroys the element of suspense.

In fact, Nietzsche's use of the prologue assumed an integral role in his dithyrambic tragedy *as a rite of initiation.* No one who undertakes the drama can reach the starting point without first living through Zarathustra's Prologue, which, among other things, is most importantly a complete devaluation of the Identity of Thought and Being, thus clearing the way for the proposition that Being (or Self) arises as myth not from thought but from emotion.

> Euripides speculated quite differently. The effect of tragedy never depended on epic suspense, on the fascinating uncertainty as to what is to happen now and afterwards: but rather on the great rhetoro-lyric scenes in which the passion and dialectics of the chief hero swelled to a broad and mighty stream. Everything was arranged for pathos, not for action: and whatever was not arranged for pathos was regarded as objectionable. But what interferes most with the hearer's pleasurable satisfaction in such scenes is a missing link, a gap in the texture of the previous history. So long as the spectator has to divine the meaning of this or that person, or the presuppositions of this or that conflict of inclinations and intentions, his complete absorption in the doings and sufferings of the chief persons is impossible, as is likewise breathless fellow-feeling and fellow-fearing. The Æschyleo-

Sophoclean tragedy employed the most ingenious devices in the first scenes to place in the hands of the spectator as if by chance all the threads requisite for understanding the whole: a trait in which that noble artistry is approved, which as it were masks the *inevitably* formal, and causes it to appear as something accidental. But nevertheless Euripides thought he observed that during these first scenes the spectator was in a strange state of anxiety to make out the problem of the previous history, so that the poetic beauties and pathos of the exposition were lost to him. Accordingly he placed the prologue even before the exposition, and put it in the mouth of a person who could be trusted: some deity had often as it were to guarantee the particulars of the tragedy to the public and remove every doubt as to the reality of the myth: as in the case of Descartes, who could only prove the reality of the empiric world by an appeal to the truthfulness of God and His inability to utter falsehood. Euripides makes use of the same divine truthfulness once more at the close of his drama, in order to ensure to the public the future of his heroes; this is the task of the notorious *deus ex machina*. Between the preliminary and the additional epic spectacle there is the dramatico-lyric present, the "drama" proper.

DIONYSIA METAPHYSICA

- "So long as the spectator has to divine the meaning of this or that person, or the presuppositions of this or that conflict of inclinations and intentions, his complete absorption in the doings and sufferings of the chief persons is impossible, as is likewise breathless fellow-feeling and fellow-fearing."

Euripides used the Prologue to inform the spectator of those things that were important to know so as not to become distracted by not knowing, so that the spectator could immerse himself fully in those moments wherein an experience of pathos was necessary. And Euripides used a trusted source, such as a god, as the mouthpiece through which the spectator learned of these necessary things. Another example of the use of a god as a trusted source is the deus ex machina, whereby an inexplicable and unexpected event unfolds as an event that necessarily completes the drama. In contrast, Aeschylus and Sophocles used the prologue to setup the supposedly accidental, later events that became necessary to complete the tragedy that happened in the end.

> Thus Euripides as a poet echoes above all his own conscious knowledge; and it is precisely on this account that he occupies such a notable position in the history of Greek art. With reference to his critico-productive activity, he must often have felt that he ought to actualise in the drama the words at the beginning of the essay of Anaxagoras: "In the beginning all things were mixed together; then came the understanding and created order." And if

Anaxagoras with his "νοῦς" seemed like the first sober person among nothing but drunken philosophers, Euripides may also have conceived his relation to the other tragic poets under a similar figure. As long as the sole ruler and disposer of the universe, the νοῦς, was still excluded from artistic activity, things were all mixed together in a chaotic, primitive mess;—it is thus Euripides was obliged to think, it is thus he was obliged to condemn the "drunken" poets as the first "sober" one among them. What Sophocles said of Æschylus, that he did what was right, though unconsciously, was surely not in the mind of Euripides: who would have admitted only thus much, that Æschylus, *because* he wrought unconsciously, did what was wrong. So also the divine Plato speaks for the most part only ironically of the creative faculty of the poet, in so far as it is not conscious insight, and places it on a par with the gift of the soothsayer and dream-interpreter; insinuating that the poet is incapable of composing until he has become unconscious and reason has deserted him. Like Plato, Euripides undertook to show to the world the reverse of the "unintelligent" poet; his æsthetic principle that "to be beautiful everything must be known" is, as I have said, the parallel to the Socratic "to be good everything must be known." Accordingly we may regard Euripides as the poet of æsthetic Socratism. Socrates, however, was that *second spectator* who did not comprehend and therefore did not esteem the Old Tragedy; in alliance with him Euripides ventured to be the herald of a new artistic activity. If, then, the Old Tragedy was here destroyed, it follows that æsthetic Socratism was the murderous principle; but in so far as the struggle is directed against the Dionysian element in the old art, we recognise in Socrates the opponent of Dionysus, the new Orpheus who rebels against Dionysus; and although destined to be torn to pieces by the Mænads of the Athenian court, yet puts to flight the overpowerful god himself, who, when he fled from Lycurgus, the king of Edoni, sought refuge in the depths of the ocean—namely, in the mystical flood of a secret cult which gradually overspread the earth.

Tragedy and Mysticism

The whole point of Nietzsche's disquisition into the influence of Socratic aestheticism on Euripides and tragedy comes down to the role that mysticism plays in tragedy and the fact that Euripides, under that influence, banned mysticism from tragedy. But exactly what is mysticism? It is the advance of the drama, both in the drive and in the manifestations, under circumstances that are unknown, simply put. Moreover, the

12: TRAGEDY, MYTH, AND WILL

realm of actuality is not entirely perceptible, and events occur within it that are also not perceptible. For Euripides, everything that plays out in tragedy must be knowable and known. But in dithyrambic tragedy, that is not the case. For instance, following the collapse of the Self and before the emergence of the supra-Self, subliminal emotions begin to rise into consciousness about which the actor has no prior knowledge whatsoever and certainly no articulable knowledge. Does that mean the drama should halt until the actor finds his articulation? No. What is important is to raise the emotion, regardless of the actor's ability to articulate it. Upon its emergence, an articulation will come more easily. But making an early articulation a prerequisite for the emergence is a mistake.

And there are other instances where mysticism plays a vital role in tragedy. Regarding the Apollonian realm of vision, idea, and concept, everything is unknown until the actor enters into the emotional conflict out of which the Apollonian aspects become visible via a resolution of that conflict. As I have said repeatedly, idea arises as a solution by which the will moves forward through a conflict. And vision, as Self, for instance, arises after only a very long struggle with an intense conflict of conscience and passion. But both idea and vision are the fruit of the drama; they are the creation in the artistic process. They are a product of the actor's will, his struggle, which, in dithyrambic tragedy, is the drama proper. And they are categorically unknown to him outside of that drama or before its completion. Thus, the entire drama is steeped in mysticism, the unknown. For Euripides, according to Nietzsche, this was not all acceptable — but that is because Euripides sought to tell a story, an Apollonian epic of idea and concept. His goal was not to present a drama that the spectator was meant to undertake as actor, although he did use pathos to draw the spectator into the ruth. Still, the pathoses he used were "inartistic" copies, not meant to trigger mythopoeia, and it is for that reason that dithyrambic poetry is so much more poignant.

13: An Analysis of The Failure of Western Thought in Science

> That Socrates stood in close relationship to Euripides in the tendency of his teaching, did not escape the notice of contemporaneous antiquity; the most eloquent expression of this felicitous insight being the tale current in Athens, that Socrates was accustomed to help Euripides in poetising. Both names were mentioned in one breath by the adherents of the "good old time," whenever they came to enumerating the popular agitators of the day: to whose influence they attributed the fact that the old Marathonian stalwart capacity of body and soul was more and more being sacrificed to a dubious enlightenment, involving progressive degeneration of the physical and mental powers. It is in this tone, half indignantly and half contemptuously, that Aristophanic comedy is wont to speak of

13: An Analysis of The Failure of Western Thought in Science

> both of them—to the consternation of modern men, who would indeed be willing enough to give up Euripides, but cannot suppress their amazement that Socrates should appear in Aristophanes as the first and head *sophist,* as the mirror and epitome of all sophistical tendencies; in connection with which it offers the single consolation of putting Aristophanes himself in the pillory, as a rakish, lying Alcibiades of poetry. Without here defending the profound instincts of Aristophanes against such attacks, I shall now indicate, by means of the sentiments of the time, the close connection between Socrates and Euripides. With this purpose in view, it is especially to be remembered that Socrates, as an opponent of tragic art, did not ordinarily patronise tragedy, but only appeared among the spectators when a new play of Euripides was performed. The most noted thing, however, is the close juxtaposition of the two names in the Delphic oracle, which designated Socrates as the wisest of men, but at the same time decided that the second prize in the contest of wisdom was due to Euripides.

This paragraph, to my reading, does nothing more than advance Nietzsche's claim that Euripides' work was strongly influenced by Socrates' aesthetics.

> Sophocles was designated as the third in this scale of rank; he who could pride himself that, in comparison with Æschylus, he did what was right, and did it, moreover, because he *knew* what was right. It is evidently just the degree of clearness of this *knowledge,* which distinguishes these three men in common as the three "knowing ones" of their age.

Socrates and the Value of Consciousness

Now he begins to elucidate Socrates' thinking, and he says that, according to Socrates, it is not enough to do what is right but that it is even better to do what is right knowing that it is right, with the emphasis on knowledge or *consciousness* of doing right.

Socrates and the Indiscriminate Lust for Knowledge

Keep in mind that common sense tells us that knowledge is a good thing. But knowledge comes to us on its own, like a mood. And there are times when we need knowledge and seek it out. However, common sense does not assign an inordinate value to knowledge and then urge us to lustfully seek it out like a miner would look for gold, regardless of need or usefulness, as if knowledge possessed a certain beauty and luster that, by itself, made it worth seeking and possessing. That inordinate value and that lust is what Socrates taught and legislated. And

13: AN ANALYSIS OF THE FAILURE OF WESTERN THOUGHT IN SCIENCE

if you agree that all knowledge is worth seeking and possessing, then, quite simply, you have bought into Socrates' evaluation, which has been taught to us for two thousand years and is called science. It is possible to look at the value of knowledge differently and to view it as a tool with which to advance the progress of life. And that is a value and a perspective that you can only learn via an undertaking of Nietzsche's dithyrambic drama.

> The most decisive word, however, for this new and unprecedented esteem of knowledge and insight was spoken by Socrates when he found that he was the only one who acknowledged to himself that he *knew nothing* while in his critical pilgrimage through Athens, and calling on the greatest statesmen, orators, poets, and artists, he discovered everywhere the conceit of knowledge. He perceived, to his astonishment, that all these celebrities were without a proper and accurate insight, even with regard to their own callings, and practised them only by instinct. "Only by instinct": with this phrase we touch upon the heart and core of the Socratic tendency. Socratism condemns therewith existing art as well as existing ethics; wherever Socratism turns its searching eyes it beholds the lack of insight and the power of illusion; and from this lack infers the inner perversity and objectionableness of existing

> conditions. From this point onwards, Socrates believed that he was called upon to, correct existence; and, with an air of disregard and superiority, as the precursor of an altogether different culture, art, and morality, he enters single-handed into a world, of which, if we reverently touched the hem, we should count it our greatest happiness.

Two very important points are worth noting here: one is the disdain for instinct, and the other is the contempt for actuality and the belief that actuality can be altered and "fixed" via knowledge.

- "… calling on the greatest statesmen, orators, poets, and artists, he discovered everywhere the conceit of knowledge. He perceived, to his astonishment, that all these celebrities were without a proper and accurate insight, even with regard to their own callings, and practised them only by instinct. "Only by instinct": with this phrase we touch upon the heart and core of the Socratic tendency."

- "From this point onwards, Socrates believed that he was called upon to, correct existence…."

> Here is the extraordinary hesitancy which always seizes upon us with regard to Socrates, and again and again invites us to ascertain the sense and purpose of this most questionable phenomenon of antiquity.

13: AN ANALYSIS OF THE FAILURE OF WESTERN THOUGHT IN SCIENCE

> Who is it that ventures single-handed to disown the Greek character, which, as Homer, Pindar, and Æschylus, as Phidias, as Pericles, as Pythia and Dionysus, as the deepest abyss and the highest height, is sure of our wondering admiration? What demoniac power is it which would presume to spill this magic draught in the dust? What demigod is it to whom the chorus of spirits of the noblest of mankind must call out: "Weh! Weh! Du hast sie zerstört, die schöne Welt, mit mächtiger Faust; sie stürzt, sie zerfällt!"[18]

It is important to recognize the fact that Socrates' teaching of science was widely legislated and exists as a supreme value even today because it drastically altered our way of thinking, both about ourselves and about the world.

Nietzsche vs. Socrates on the Value of Instinct

> A key to the character of Socrates is presented to us by the surprising phenomenon designated as the "daimonion" of Socrates. In special circumstances, when

---

[18] Woe! Woe!
Thou hast it destroyed,
The beautiful world;
With powerful fist;
In ruin 'tis hurled!
Faust, trans. of Bayard Taylor.—TR.

his gigantic intellect began to stagger, he got a secure support in the utterances of a divine voice which then spake to him. This voice, whenever it comes, always *dissuades*. In this totally abnormal nature instinctive wisdom only appears in order to hinder the progress of conscious perception here and there. While in all productive men it is instinct which is the creatively affirmative force, consciousness only comporting itself critically and dissuasively; with Socrates it is instinct which becomes critic; it is consciousness which becomes creator—a perfect monstrosity *per defectum!* And we do indeed observe here a monstrous *defectus* of all mystical aptitude, so that Socrates might be designated as the specific *non-mystic,* in whom the logical nature is developed, through a superfoetation, to the same excess as instinctive wisdom is developed in the mystic. On the other hand, however, the logical instinct which appeared in Socrates was absolutely prohibited from turning against itself; in its unchecked flow it manifests a native power such as we meet with, to our shocking surprise, only among the very greatest instinctive forces. He who has experienced even a breath of the divine naïveté and security of the Socratic course of life in the Platonic writings, will also feel

13: AN ANALYSIS OF THE FAILURE OF WESTERN THOUGHT IN SCIENCE

that the enormous driving-wheel of logical Socratism is in motion, as it were, *behind* Socrates, and that it must be viewed through Socrates as through a shadow. And that he himself had a boding of this relation is apparent from the dignified earnestness with which he everywhere, and even before his judges, insisted on his divine calling. To refute him here was really as impossible as to approve of his instinct-disintegrating influence. In view of this indissoluble conflict, when he had at last been brought before the forum of the Greek state, there was only one punishment demanded, namely exile; he might have been sped across the borders as something thoroughly enigmatical, irrubricable and inexplicable, and so posterity would have been quite unjustified in charging the Athenians with a deed of ignominy. But that the sentence of death, and not mere exile, was pronounced upon him, seems to have been brought about by Socrates himself, with perfect knowledge of the circumstances, and without the natural fear of death: he met his death with the calmness with which, according to the description of Plato, he leaves the symposium at break of day, as the last of the revellers, to begin a new day; while the sleepy companions remain behind on the

> benches and the floor, to dream of Socrates, the true eroticist. *The dying Socrates* became the new ideal of the noble Greek youths,—an ideal they had never yet beheld,—and above all, the typical Hellenic youth, Plato, prostrated himself before this scene with all the fervent devotion of his visionary soul.

- In special circumstances, when his gigantic intellect began to stagger, he got a secure support in the utterances of a divine voice which then spake to him. This voice, whenever it comes, always *dissuades.*

The axion "trust your instinct" was anathema to Socrates.

- "While in all productive men it is instinct which is the creatively affirmative force, consciousness only comporting itself critically and dissuasively; with Socrates it is instinct which becomes critic; it is consciousness which becomes creator—a perfect monstrosity *per defectum!* "

It is, indeed, the case with most people that they trust their instinct, which may tell them to make one choice over another, and that, afterward, their consciousness then may dissuade them from their instinctive choice with doubt. And the doubt comes from their consciousness. In Socrates, for whatever reason, the reverse is what happens. He believes that the best choice can only come from consciousness, in which knowledge is undisputed, and that instinct is a source of diversion from this knowledgeable choice that subsequently instills doubt.

13: AN ANALYSIS OF THE FAILURE OF WESTERN THOUGHT IN SCIENCE

- "And we do indeed observe here a monstrous *defectus* of all mystical aptitude, so that Socrates might be designated as the specific *non-mystic,* in whom the logical nature is developed, through a superfoetation, to the same excess as instinctive wisdom is developed in the mystic."

This re-evaluation of consciousness and instinct constitutes an anomaly that is peculiar to Socrates, who then legislated the re-evaluation as one of the highest values.

In contrast, Nietzsche views consciousness as a realm of human nature in which that which exists in actuality encounters a problem, and it is the problem that brings the issue into consciousness. It is important to note that there is a very efficient and quick flow of inner events that occurs instinctively and communicates itself to the mind intuitively without any interruption, any intervention, or any mediation whatsoever. And with regard to the flow of events within actuality, that is the best realm in which events play out successfully. It is only when the event is raised into consciousness — for the purpose of mediation — that the possibility exists for things to go awry. Again, this is best understood as an apprehension rather than as a concept, and you will experience that apprehension yourself as an actor within Nietzsche's dithyrambic drama. And when you do experience that apprehension, you will understand that instinctive and intuitive thought is much quicker and much more efficient than reasoned or interventional thought. And, sometimes, logical thought is abjectly inadequate, especially within the intuitive, capricious, and leapfrogging process of artistic creation by which the supra-Self appears out of nowhere, like magic. As such, this artistic process is necessarily a mystical process, in which conscious and calculating thought is completely absent. And, given the advantage that mysticism imparts to life, which is definitively the creation of supra-Self, Nietzsche argues in favor of mysticism (instinct and intuition) and against logic (calculating thought that requires prerequisite knowledge). More importantly, as we are about to see, the mode of thought that Socrates taught killed the art form called tragedy.

14: Science in Tragedy

Tragedy Requires Mysticism

> Let us now imagine the one great Cyclopean eye of Socrates fixed on tragedy, that eye in which the fine frenzy of artistic enthusiasm had never glowed—let us think how it was denied to this eye to gaze with pleasure into the Dionysian abysses—what could it not but see in the "sublime and greatly lauded" tragic art, as Plato called it? Something very absurd, with causes that seemed to be without effects, and effects apparently without causes; the whole, moreover, so motley and diversified that it could not but be repugnant to a thoughtful mind, a dangerous incentive, however, to sensitive and irritable souls. We know what was the sole kind of poetry which he comprehended: the *Æsopian fable*: and he did this no doubt with that smiling complaisance with which the good honest Gellert sings the praise of poetry in the fable of the bee and the hen:—

14: SCIENCE IN TRAGEDY

> "Du siehst an mir, wozu sie nützt,
> Dem, der nicht viel Verstand besitzt,
> Die Wahrheit durch ein Bild zu sagen."[19]

- "Something very absurd [speaking of tragedy], with causes that seemed to be without effects, and effects apparently without causes...."

This is a reference to the mystical nature of tragedy, in which events play out beyond the scope of consciousness, so that the actor reaches an achievement by which, for instance, he brings an overwhelming subliminal fear into his consciousness, overcomes it by moving his will beyond it (say, into supra-individuation), but then consciously experiences nothing more than the pleasure that results from overcoming and then, later, experiences a profoundly deeper sophrosyne than what he knew before the overcoming. This is an example of cause without effect and effects without causes.

> But then it seemed to Socrates that tragic art did not even "tell the truth": not to mention the fact that it addresses itself to him who "hath but little wit"; consequently not to the philosopher: a twofold reason why it should be avoided. Like Plato, he reckoned it among the seductive arts which only represent the agreeable, not the useful, and hence he required of his disciples abstinence and strict separation from such

---

[19] In me thou seest its benefit,—
To him who hath but little wit,
Through parables to tell the truth.

> unphilosophical allurements; with such success that the youthful tragic poet Plato first of all burned his poems to be able to become a scholar of Socrates. But where unconquerable native capacities bore up against the Socratic maxims, their power, together with the momentum of his mighty character, still sufficed to force poetry itself into new and hitherto unknown channels.

Given the obvious and plentiful benefits of tragedy, especially as a healing agent, it is difficult to understand how Socrates, if Nietzsche is correct in the above appraisal, would not have understood those obvious benefits, unless the practice of tragedy had long ago ended by Socrates' time and, with it, any comprehension of it and all hope for its resurrection.

> An instance of this is the aforesaid Plato: he, who in the condemnation of tragedy and of art in general certainly did not fall short of the naïve cynicism of his master, was nevertheless constrained by sheer artistic necessity to create a form of art which is inwardly related even to the then existing forms of art which he repudiated. Plato's main objection to the old art—that it is the imitation of a phantom,[20] and hence belongs to a sphere still lower than the empiric world—could not at all apply to the new art: and so we find Plato endeavouring to go

---

[20] Scheinbild = $ειδολον$.—TR.

beyond reality and attempting to represent the idea which underlies this pseudo-reality. But Plato, the thinker, thereby arrived by a roundabout road just at the point where he had always been at home as poet, and from which Sophocles and all the old artists had solemnly protested against that objection. If tragedy absorbed into itself all the earlier varieties of art, the same could again be said in an unusual sense of Platonic dialogue, which, engendered by a mixture of all the then existing forms and styles, hovers midway between narrative, lyric and drama, between prose and poetry, and has also thereby broken loose from the older strict law of unity of linguistic form; a movement which was carried still farther by the *cynic* writers, who in the most promiscuous style, oscillating to and fro betwixt prose and metrical forms, realised also the literary picture of the "raving Socrates" whom they were wont to represent in life. Platonic dialogue was as it were the boat in which the shipwrecked ancient poetry saved herself together with all her children: crowded into a narrow space and timidly obsequious to the one steersman, Socrates, they now launched into a new world, which never tired of looking at the fantastic spectacle of this procession. In very truth, Plato has given to all posterity the prototype of a new form of art, the

> prototype of the *novel* which must be designated as the infinitely evolved Æsopian fable, in which poetry holds the same rank with reference to dialectic philosophy as this same philosophy held for many centuries with reference to theology: namely, the rank of *ancilla*. This was the new position of poetry into which Plato forced it under the pressure of the demon-inspired Socrates.

Nietzsche focuses on the Platonic dialogue as a new art form, with its admixture of dialectic (or logic, reasoning) and poetry (not necessarily as in rhyming poetry but perhaps more so as poignant poetry), that evolved from fable, which Socrates endorsed, and which continued to evolve after Plato into the modern novel.

> Here *philosophic thought* overgrows art and compels it to cling close to the trunk of dialectics. The *Apollonian* tendency has chrysalised in the logical schematism; just as something analogous in the case of Euripides (and moreover a translation of the *Dionysian* into the naturalistic emotion) was forced upon our attention. Socrates, the dialectical hero in Platonic drama, reminds us of the kindred nature of the Euripidean hero, who has to defend his actions by arguments and counter-arguments, and thereby so often runs the risk of forfeiting our tragic pity; for who could mistake

> the *optimistic* element in the essence of dialectics, which celebrates a jubilee in every conclusion, and can breathe only in cool clearness and consciousness: the optimistic element, which, having once forced its way into tragedy, must gradually overgrow its Dionysian regions, and necessarily impel it to self-destruction—even to the death-leap into the bourgeois drama. Let us but realise the consequences of the Socratic maxims: "Virtue is knowledge; man only sins from ignorance; he who is virtuous is happy": these three fundamental forms of optimism involve the death of tragedy. For the virtuous hero must now be a dialectician; there must now be a necessary, visible connection between virtue and knowledge, between belief and morality; the transcendental justice of the plot in Æschylus is now degraded to the superficial and audacious principle of poetic justice with its usual *deus ex machina*.

The Socratic Version of Tragedy

He speaks of optimism and cheerfulness as a necessary feature of tragedy. In other words, wherever we find tragedy, we must also find a certain cheerfulness. Nietzsche developed the point quite extensively that the cheerfulness and optimism that derives from tragedy is due to it enabling the individual to escape the bounds of individuation and become one with his inner nature. But, under Socrates, that cheerfulness and optimism is replaced with the cheerfulness and optimism that derives from dialectic, "which celebrates a jubilee in every conclusion, and can breathe only in cool clearness and consciousness," a clearly Socratic value. Again, under Socrates, the tragic hero is not one who transcends the barriers beyond which justice is delivered, but rather the tragic hero is now one who is able to *explain* everything and transcendental justice is delivered via the deus ex machina.

> How does the *chorus,* and, in general, the entire Dionyso-musical substratum of tragedy, now appear in the light of this new Socrato-optimistic stage-world? As something accidental, as a readily dispensable reminiscence of the origin of tragedy; while we have in fact seen that the chorus can be understood only as the cause of tragedy, and of the tragic generally. This perplexity with respect to the chorus first manifests itself in Sophocles—an important sign that the Dionysian basis of tragedy already begins to disintegrate with him. He no longer ventures to entrust to the chorus the main share of the effect, but limits its sphere to such an extent that it now appears almost co-ordinate with the actors, just as if it were elevated from the orchestra into the scene: whereby of course its character is completely destroyed, notwithstanding that Aristotle countenances this very theory of the chorus. This alteration of the position of the chorus, which Sophocles at any rate

14: Science in Tragedy

> recommended by his practice, and, according to tradition, even by a treatise, is the first step towards the *annihilation* of the chorus, the phases of which follow one another with alarming rapidity in Euripides, Agathon, and the New Comedy. Optimistic dialectics drives *music* out of tragedy with the scourge of its syllogisms: that is, it destroys the essence of tragedy, which can be explained only as a manifestation and illustration of Dionysian states, as the visible symbolisation of music, as the dream-world of Dionysian ecstasy.

- "Optimistic dialectics drives *music* out of tragedy with the scourge of its syllogisms: that is, it destroys the essence of tragedy, which can be explained only as a manifestation and illustration of Dionysian states, as the visible symbolisation of music, as the dream-world of Dionysian ecstasy."

Dialectic Uprooted the "Musical" Foundation of Tragedy

Remember that when Nietzsche speaks of the chorus being the foundation of tragedy, he means that "music" is the foundation of tragedy. And by music, he means actuality, which lies beyond reality. Remember also that reality is an illusion, insofar as it is founded by mythical Self, a fictive being which itself is an illusion. Thus, actuality is more fundamental than reality. And actuality is the actual interplay of desire, mood, volition, passion, and the conflict of passion — absent the influence of mind, by which I mean the principium individuationis, an edifying sense and idea of one's being. That which we call "mind" is everything that is Apollonian (i.e., fictive and ideational) and it is entirely a development, a growth, that arises wholly out of "music," actuality, as an ideational reflection of that "music," which is everything that is emotional, especially the human will. Raw and stark actuality is not something that can be communicated via a language that celebrates itself in syllogisms. Thus, the introduction of dialectic into tragedy obliterated its "musical" foundation.

In its heyday, tragedy seduced its admirers into an engagement via the optimism and hope that it imparted to man. When that optimism and hope (for a reunion with one's innermost nature) was replaced with the cheerfulness imparted by dialectic, tragedy lost its "musical" foundation in human will and was destroyed — and it was Socrates and his science that destroyed it.

Culture Requires the Co-Existence of Science and Art

> If, therefore, we are to assume an anti-Dionysian tendency operating even before Socrates, which received in him only an unprecedentedly grand expression, we must not shrink from the question as to what a phenomenon like that of Socrates indicates: whom in view of the Platonic dialogues we are certainly not entitled to regard as a purely disintegrating, negative power. And though there can be no doubt whatever that the most immediate effect of the Socratic

14: SCIENCE IN TRAGEDY

> impulse tended to the dissolution of Dionysian tragedy, yet a profound experience of Socrates' own life compels us to ask whether there is *necessarily* only an antipodal relation between Socratism and art, and whether the birth of an "artistic Socrates" is in general something contradictory in itself.

Nietzsche poses the question as to whether an "artistic Socrates" is even a possibility. In other words, is it possible for a staunchly scientific mind to embrace the sensational nature of tragedy along with its necessary mysticism?

> For that despotic logician had now and then the feeling of a gap, or void, a sentiment of semi-reproach, as of a possibly neglected duty with respect to art. There often came to him, as he tells his friends in prison, one and the same dream-apparition, which kept constantly repeating to him: "Socrates, practise music." Up to his very last days he solaces himself with the opinion that his philosophising is the highest form of poetry, and finds it hard to believe that a deity will remind him of the "common, popular music." Finally, when in prison, he consents to practise also this despised music, in order thoroughly to unburden his conscience. And in this frame of mind he composes a poem on Apollo and turns a few Æsopian fables into verse. It was something similar to the

> demonian warning voice which urged him to these practices; it was because of his Apollonian insight that, like a barbaric king, he did not understand the noble image of a god and was in danger of sinning against a deity—through ignorance. The prompting voice of the Socratic dream-vision is the only sign of doubtfulness as to the limits of logical nature. "Perhaps "—thus he had to ask himself—"what is not intelligible to me is not therefore unreasonable? Perhaps there is a realm of wisdom from which the logician is banished? Perhaps art is even a necessary correlative of and supplement to science?"

- "Perhaps there is a realm of wisdom from which the logician is banished? Perhaps art is even a necessary correlative of and supplement to science?"

And to the question Nietzsche posed as to whether it was possible for a staunchly scientific mind to embrace tragedy, he answers that the scientist should ask himself it there exists, perhaps, a realm of wisdom greater than that obtained by the pursuit of scientific knowledge. And that is what you, the reader, should ask yourself. And is it possible that art, and specifically tragedy, must exist alongside science for some critical and fundamental reason that presently escapes us? Are we doomed if we allow science to proceed upon its advance *unchallenged and unchecked*? Indeed, I say, and Nietzsche says, we are.

15: Theoretical Man

Theoretical Man Cannot Understand Tragic "Music"

In the sense of these last portentous questions it must now be indicated how the influence of Socrates (extending to the present moment, indeed, to all futurity) has spread over posterity like an ever-increasing shadow in the evening sun, and how this influence again and again necessitates a regeneration of *art,*—yea, of art already with metaphysical, broadest and profoundest sense,—and its own eternity guarantees also the eternity of art.

Before this could be perceived, before the intrinsic dependence of every art on the Greeks, the Greeks from Homer to Socrates, was conclusively demonstrated, it had to happen to us with regard to these Greeks as it happened to the Athenians with regard to Socrates. Nearly every age and stage of culture has at some time or other sought with deep displeasure to free itself from the

15: THEORETICAL MAN

Greeks, because in their presence everything self-achieved, sincerely admired and apparently quite original, seemed all of a sudden to lose life and colour and shrink to an abortive copy, even to caricature. And so hearty indignation breaks forth time after time against this presumptuous little nation, which dared to designate as "barbaric" for all time everything not native: who are they, one asks one's self, who, though they possessed only an ephemeral historical splendour, ridiculously restricted institutions, a dubious excellence in their customs, and were even branded with ugly vices, yet lay claim to the dignity and singular position among the peoples to which genius is entitled among the masses. What a pity one has not been so fortunate as to find the cup of hemlock with which such an affair could be disposed of without ado: for all the poison which envy, calumny, and rankling resentment engendered within themselves have not sufficed to destroy that self-sufficient grandeur! And so one feels ashamed and afraid in the presence of the Greeks: unless one prize truth above all things, and dare also to acknowledge to one's self this truth, that the Greeks, as charioteers, hold in their hands the reins of our own and of every culture, but that almost always chariot and horses are of too poor material and incommensurate with the glory of their guides, who then will deem it sport to run such a team into an abyss: which they themselves clear with the leap of Achilles.

In order to assign also to Socrates the dignity of such a leading position, it will suffice to recognise in him the type of an unheard-of form of existence, the type of the *theoretical man,* with regard to whose meaning and purpose it will be our next task to attain an insight. Like the artist, the theorist also finds an infinite satisfaction in what *is* and, like the former, he is shielded by this satisfaction from the practical ethics of pessimism with its lynx eyes which shine only in the dark. For if the artist in every unveiling of truth always cleaves with raptured eyes only to that which still remains veiled after the unveiling, the theoretical man, on the other hand, enjoys and contents himself with the cast-off veil, and finds the consummation of his pleasure in the process of a continuously successful unveiling through his own unaided efforts. There would have been no science if it had only been concerned about that *one* naked goddess and nothing else. For then its disciples would have been obliged to feel like those who purposed to dig a hole straight through the earth: each one of whom perceives that with the utmost lifelong exertion he is able to excavate only a very little of the enormous depth, which is again filled up before his eyes by the labours of his successor, so that a third man seems to do well when on his own account he selects a new spot for his attempts at tunnelling. If now some one proves conclusively that the antipodal goal cannot be attained in this direct way, who will still care to toil on in the old depths, unless he has learned to content himself in the meantime with finding precious stones or discovering natural laws? For that reason Lessing, the most honest theoretical man, ventured to say that he cared more for the search after truth than for truth itself: in saying which he revealed the fundamental secret of science, to the astonishment, and indeed, to the vexation of scientific men. Well, to be sure, there stands alongside of this detached perception, as an excess of honesty, if not of presumption, a profound *illusion* which first came to the world in the person of Socrates, the imperturbable belief that, by means of the clue of causality, thinking reaches to the deepest abysses of being, and that thinking is able not only to perceive being but even to *correct* it. This sublime metaphysical illusion is added as an instinct to science and again and again leads the latter to its limits, where it must change into *art; which is*

> *really the end, to be attained by this mechanism.*

- "In order to assign also to Socrates the dignity of such a leading position, it will suffice to recognise in him the type of an unheard-of form of existence, the type of the *theoretical man*...."

In order to understand his use of the term "theoretical man," of which Socrates was the ultimate example, we need to consider it in contrast to the "intuitive man." And I do not think that needs much elaboration other than to say that the former deals in concept and reason and the latter deals in apprehensions and leaps of thought arising out of mystical insight that no measure of logic can achieve, of which Nietzsche is the best example, at least in our time. The point he will eventually move to make is that the "musical" foundation of tragedy, which is a representation of the human will, is walled off to theoretical man.

- "For if the artist in every unveiling of truth always cleaves with raptured eyes only to that which still remains veiled after the unveiling, the theoretical man, on the other hand, enjoys and contents himself with the cast-off veil, and finds the consummation of his pleasure in the process of a continuously successful unveiling through his own unaided efforts."

Science as Driven by the Pleasure of Discovery

The pleasure that the scientific or theoretical man derives from science, which is what drives him forward through his train of scientific thought, is the unveiling and bare disclosure

15: THEORETICAL MAN

of anything that exists within the world in which it happens but is hidden or obfuscated in some way or other. And what is especially invigorating to the scientist is the discovery of an apparently causal relationship, especially one that was previously unknown.

- "There would have been no science if it had only been concerned about that *one* naked goddess and nothing else."

- "For that reason Lessing, the most honest theoretical man, ventured to say that he cared more for the search after truth than for truth itself...."

Nietzsche claims it is the discovery itself, not the object or the substance of the discovery, that *drives* science. Science is not oriented toward an unveiling of nature's secrets; it is oriented toward the seduction in its undressing. In other words, the seducer finds more pleasure in the effort that goes into the seduction than he finds in the seduced woman herself.

- "Well, to be sure, there stands alongside of this detached perception, as an excess of honesty, if not of presumption, a profound *illusion* which first came to the world in the person of Socrates, the imperturbable belief that, by means of the clue of causality, thinking reaches to the deepest abysses of being, and that thinking is able not only to perceive being but even to *correct* it."

Myth as a Gateway

Here, Nietzsche makes a very fundamental point that illuminates the value of myth. He points to the belief that thought can plumb the deepest depths of Nature, therewith understand its actuality, *and alter that actuality*. Quite simply, were it not for that belief, there would be no science. Insofar as that singular belief acts as a gateway through which the believer may pass as an initiate into a world of discovery that was previously not within his grasp, that belief is a myth, and specifically a mythical gateway, as opposed to a mythical being, the difference of which I explained extensively in *The Birth of Dionysia*. And myth, *always, by definition*, is an illusion. But to say that myth is an illusion is not to denigrate myth *whatsoever*. On the contrary, life requires illusion. Indeed, life cannot be lived without illusion. And, insofar as the creation of illusion is an artistic endeavor, such as we see in the creation of mythical being within a world of becoming, which, in actuality, is utterly devoid of being, then life fundamentally employs art, i.e., creativity in the face of impossibility. In the case of science, the mythical gateway is the belief that thought can plumb the deepest secrets of inner nature *and alter the phenomena*.

- "This sublime metaphysical illusion is added as an instinct to science and again and again leads the latter to its limits, where it must change into *art; which is really the end, to be attained by this mechanism.*"

Specifically, we must ask, what are the limits of science? And Nietzsche states that the limits of science are revealed in the irrefutable fact that the world, in all its unfathomable depth and breadth, is ultimately incomprehensible. The scientist may

15: THEORETICAL MAN

think that he understands some of it, but he will never be able to think that he understands all of it. But the fatal pessimism arising from that one fact is overridden by the stern and unwavering belief of science that the world is, in fact, comprehensible, which is the myth. And if the scientist should ever reach the point wherein the incomprehensibility of the world becomes stark and irrefutable, so that he succumbs to the pessimism inherent in that insight, the optimism arising from the pleasure he derives from the process of discovery quickly revives him. And it is *the beauty that the scientist finds in that process of discovery*, not in the object of the discovery, that make him an artist (one who enjoys an appearance, a spectacle) as opposed to an impartial truth-seeker.

> If we now look at Socrates in the light of this thought, he appears to us as the first who could not only live, but—what is far more—also die under the guidance of this instinct of science: and hence the picture of the *dying, Socrates*, as the man delivered from the fear of death by knowledge and argument, is the escutcheon, above the entrance to science which reminds every one of its mission, namely, to make existence appear to be comprehensible, and therefore to be justified: for which purpose, if arguments do not suffice, *myth* also must be used, which I just now designated even as the necessary consequence, yea, as the end of science.

- "... its mission [that of science], namely, to make existence appear to be comprehensible, and therefore to be justified: for which purpose, if arguments do not suffice, *myth* also must be used, which I just now designated even as the necessary consequence, yea, as the end of science."

Art Makes Life Liveable

The major point that Nietzsche is moving to make is that art (as the creation of something out of nothing, especially something that benefits life), more than anything else, and even in the form of science, is what makes life possible and livable (i.e., an aesthetic phenomenon that justifies life).

> He who once makes intelligible to himself how, after the death of Socrates, the mystagogue of science, one philosophical school succeeds another, like wave upon wave,—how an entirely unfore-shadowed universal development of the thirst for knowledge in the widest compass of the cultured world (and as the specific task for every one highly gifted) led science on to the high sea from which since then it has never again been able to be completely ousted; how through the universality of this movement a common net of thought was first stretched over the entire globe, with prospects, moreover, of conformity to law in an entire solar system;—he who realises all this, together with the amazingly high pyramid of our present-day knowledge, cannot fail to see in Socrates the turning-

> point and vortex of so-called universal history. For if one were to imagine the whole incalculable sum of energy which has been used up by that universal tendency,—employed, *not* in the service of knowledge, but for the practical, *i.e.,* egoistical ends of individuals and peoples,—then probably the instinctive love of life would be so much weakened in universal wars of destruction and incessant migrations of peoples, that, owing to the practice of suicide, the individual would perhaps feel the last remnant of a sense of duty, when, like the native of the Fiji Islands, as son he strangles his parents and, as friend, his friend: a practical pessimism which might even give rise to a horrible ethics of general slaughter out of pity—which, for the rest, exists and has existed wherever art in one form or another, especially as science and religion, has not appeared as a remedy and preventive of that pestilential breath.

In saying that art is essential to life, what makes it essential is not just its ability to make life both interpretable and livable, but, more importantly, is its ability to heal. Illusion, the child of art, provides the capacity to heal most efficaciously.

The Failure of Art Fails Life

Within the inner world of man, while illusion heals most efficaciously, as we see with the creation of Self, science does not provide any healing whatsoever — again, within the inner world. In other words, science does not heal the soul, and that is self-evident. Also, in some instances, even religion, which is certainly supposed to heal the soul, fails to do so. And, in so far as Christianity fails to heal the bad conscience and only mitigates the pain arising out of it, it could be argued that Christianity is an example of religion failing to heal the soul. I do not argue that Christianity does not mitigate man's suffering, but I would certainly argue that it does nothing decisive, fundamental, and in a transformative way to cure suffering man of his bad conscience.

- "… a practical pessimism which might even give rise to a horrible ethics of general slaughter out of pity— which, for the rest, exists and has existed wherever art in one form or another, especially as science and religion, has not appeared as a remedy and preventive of that pestilential breath."

When art as science or as religion fails to heal suffering man and at the same time becomes predominant in life, that failure leads to a most profound pessimism and resignation from life, as noted in the above last sentence of the original text. And that is the twofold jeopardy that modern man faces in both science and Christianity.

When Science Realizes its Limits, Only Art Can Save It

> In view of this practical pessimism, Socrates is the archetype of the theoretical optimist, who in the above-indicated belief

15: THEORETICAL MAN

in the fathomableness of the nature of things, attributes to knowledge and perception the power of a universal medicine, and sees in error an evil. To penetrate into the depths of the nature of things, and to separate true perception from error and illusion, appeared to the Socratic man the noblest and even the only truly human calling: just as from the time of Socrates onwards the mechanism of concepts, judgments, and inferences was prized above all other capacities as the highest activity and the most admirable gift of nature. Even the sublimest moral acts, the stirrings of pity, of self-sacrifice, of heroism, and that tranquillity of soul, so difficult of attainment, which the Apollonian Greek called Sophrosyne, were derived by Socrates, and his like-minded successors up to the present day, from the dialectics of knowledge, and were accordingly designated as teachable. He who has experienced in himself the joy of a Socratic perception, and felt how it seeks to embrace, in constantly widening circles, the entire world of phenomena, will thenceforth find no stimulus which could urge him to existence more forcible than the desire to complete that conquest and to knit the net impenetrably close. To a person thus minded the Platonic Socrates then appears as the teacher of an entirely new form of

> "Greek cheerfulness" and felicity of existence, which seeks to discharge itself in actions, and will find its discharge for the most part in maieutic and pedagogic influences on noble youths, with a view to the ultimate production of genius.

What is important for the reader to note is that science has achieved a very high level of esteem among Western values. Science lays a claim to an ability to impart sophrosyne, a profound cheerfulness that helps to maintain life's vigor, and even the production of genius. Dionysia, by the way, lays the same claim.

> But now science, spurred on by its powerful illusion, hastens irresistibly to its limits, on which its optimism, hidden in the essence of logic, is wrecked. For the periphery of the circle of science has an infinite number of points, and while there is still no telling how this circle can ever be completely measured, yet the noble and gifted man, even before the middle of his career, inevitably comes into contact with those extreme points of the periphery where he stares at the inexplicable. When he here sees to his dismay how logic coils round itself at these limits and finally bites its own tail—then the new form of perception discloses itself, namely *tragic perception,* which, in order even to be endured, requires art as a safeguard and remedy.

15: Theoretical Man

- "… the new form of perception discloses itself, namely *tragic perception,* which, in order even to be endured, requires art as a safeguard and remedy."

When science reaches its limits, from which the discharge of concept and the flow of discovery ceases, the resulting tragic perception can only be remedied by art in the form of mythopoeia.

Science Is Antipodal to Life

By tragic perception, Nietzsche means the heightened and much deeper percipience that comes into existence when the veil of Maya, the prejudices of the Ego, are cast aside via their tragic collapse. Suddenly, with tragic percipience, much more of the world and its inner workings come into view, and the creation of that view and the creativity of mythopoeia that assists the creation of that view, which is singularly and directly attributable to proto-tragedy, defies logic. Thus, the phenomenon of tragic percipience *refutes* the overestimated value of science along with its method of inquiry, namely dialectic. What's more is that proto-tragedy also lays claim to sophrosyne, a profound cheerfulness, and the production of genius.

> If, with eyes strengthened and refreshed at the sight of the Greeks, we look upon the highest spheres of the world that surrounds us, we behold the avidity of the insatiate optimistic knowledge, of which Socrates is the typical representative, transformed into tragic resignation and the need of art: while,

> to be sure, this same avidity, in its lower stages, has to exhibit itself as antagonistic to art, and must especially have an inward detestation of Dionyso-tragic art, as was exemplified in the opposition of Socratism to Æschylean tragedy.

Nietzsche notes that science is antagonistic to mythopoeia. But mythopoeia, as art, is essential to life. Thus, we have a most profound clash of values in Western thought.

> Here then with agitated spirit we knock at the gates of the present and the future: will that "transforming" lead to ever new configurations of genius, and especially of the *music-practising Socrates*? Will the net of art which is spread over existence, whether under the name of religion or of science, be knit always more closely and delicately, or is it destined to be torn to shreds under the restlessly barbaric activity and whirl which is called "the present day"?—Anxious, yet not disconsolate, we stand aloof for a little while, as the spectators who are permitted to be witnesses of these tremendous struggles and transitions. Alas! It is the charm of these struggles that he who beholds them must also fight them!

15: THEORETICAL MAN
The New Dithyramb Restores Tragedy

The question remains as to how this conflict between art and science will play out. Nietzsche's *Thus Spoke Zarathustra* offers a solution by providing an *experience* of proto-tragedy, which is itself the most convincing demonstration of its value and efficacy to life.

16: Theory of Dithyrambic Tragedy

> By this elaborate historical example we have endeavoured to make it clear that tragedy perishes as surely by evanescence of the spirit of music as it can be born only out of this spirit. In order to qualify the singularity of this assertion, and, on the other hand, to disclose the source of this insight of ours, we must now confront with clear vision the analogous phenomena of the present time; we must enter into the midst of these struggles, which, as I said just now, are being carried on in the highest spheres of our present world between the insatiate optimistic perception and the tragic need of art. In so doing I shall leave out of consideration all other antagonistic tendencies which at all times oppose art, especially tragedy, and which at present again extend their sway triumphantly, to such an extent that of the theatrical arts only the farce and the ballet, for example, put forth their blossoms, which perhaps not

> every one cares to smell, in tolerably rich luxuriance. I will speak only of the *Most Illustrious Opposition* to the tragic conception of things—and by this I mean essentially optimistic science, with its ancestor Socrates at the head of it. Presently also the forces will be designated which seem to me to guarantee *a re-birth of tragedy*—and who knows what other blessed hopes for the German genius!

What is important to note in all this writing about tragedy and science is Nietzsche's hope for a re-birth of proto-tragedy, which we find in *Thus Spoke Zarathustra*.

> Before we plunge into the midst of these struggles, let us array ourselves in the armour of our hitherto acquired knowledge. In contrast to all those who are intent on deriving the arts from one exclusive principle, as the necessary vital source of every work of art, I keep my eyes fixed on the two artistic deities of the Greeks, Apollo and Dionysus, and recognise in them the living and conspicuous representatives of *two* worlds of art which differ in their intrinsic essence and in their highest aims. Apollo stands before me as the transfiguring genius of the *principium individuationis* through which alone the redemption in appearance is to be truly attained, while by the mystical cheer of

Dionysus the spell of individuation is broken, and the way lies open to the Mothers of Being, to the innermost heart of things. This extraordinary antithesis, which opens up yawningly between plastic art as the Apollonian and music as the Dionysian art, has become manifest to only one of the great thinkers, to such an extent that, even without this key to the symbolism of the Hellenic divinities, he allowed to music a different character and origin in advance of all the other arts, because, unlike them, it is not a copy of the phenomenon, but a direct copy of the will itself, and therefore represents *the metaphysical of everything physical in the world*, the thing-in-itself of every phenomenon. (Schopenhauer, *Welt als Wille und Vorstellung,* I. 310.) To this most important perception of æsthetics (with which, taken in a serious sense, æsthetics properly commences), Richard Wagner, by way of confirmation of its eternal truth, affixed his seal, when he asserted in his *Beethoven* that music must be judged according to æsthetic principles quite different from those which apply to the plastic arts, and not, in general, according to the category of beauty: although an erroneous æsthetics, inspired by a misled and degenerate art, has by virtue of the concept of beauty prevailing in the plastic domain accustomed itself to demand of

16: Theory of Dithyrambic Tragedy

> music an effect analogous to that of the works of plastic art, namely the suscitating *delight in beautiful forms.* Upon perceiving this extraordinary antithesis, I felt a strong inducement to approach the essence of Greek tragedy, and, by means of it, the profoundest revelation of Hellenic genius: for I at last thought myself to be in possession of a charm to enable me—far beyond the phraseology of our usual æsthetics—to represent vividly to my mind the primitive problem of tragedy: whereby such an astounding insight into the Hellenic character was afforded me that it necessarily seemed as if our proudly comporting classico-Hellenic science had thus far contrived to subsist almost exclusively on phantasmagoria and externalities.

- "… I keep my eyes fixed on the two artistic deities of the Greeks, Apollo and Dionysus, and recognise in them the living and conspicuous representatives of *two* worlds of art which differ in their intrinsic essence and in their highest aims. Apollo stands before me as the transfiguring genius of the *principium individuationis* through which alone the redemption in appearance is to be truly attained, while by the mystical cheer of Dionysus the spell of individuation is broken, and the way lies open to the Mothers of Being, to the innermost heart of things."

More to the point, the Self, which is a myth, is the transfiguring genius of the principium individuationis. The Self is what individuates man and creates the being in human being, and it alone provides the "trusty rowboat" upon which man relies to prevent his falling into the abyss that lies beyond the limits and boundaries of individuated being, in other words, the collapse of mind. But once individuated being is shattered, so that man inevitably does indeed fall, to some extent, into the abyss, thereby devolving into subindividuated being, then his best hope is to shatter the redrawn or reconstructed principium individuationis in order to look beyond the veil of Maya into the same abyssal depth that is so mightily feared so as to find one's true feelings, the Dionysian substratum, the "Mothers of Being," "the innermost heart of things," out of which mythopoeia will create a new Self.

- "This extraordinary antithesis, which opens up yawningly between plastic art as the Apollonian and music as the Dionysian art, has become manifest to only one of the great thinkers, to such an extent that, even without this key to the symbolism of the Hellenic divinities, he allowed to music a different character and origin in advance of all the other arts, because, unlike them, it is not a copy of the phenomenon, but a direct copy of the will itself, and therefore represents *the metaphysical of everything physical in the world*, the thing-in-itself of every phenomenon."

16: THEORY OF DITHYRAMBIC TRAGEDY

Dithyrambic Music as a Representation of Human Will

Now we finally approach a clearer understanding of Nietzsche's use of the word "music," which is most important if we are going to understand his use of the term "dithyrambic music." And we find that he adopted this unusual concept of "music" from his teacher, Schopenhauer. Specifically, we find "music" to be closely synonymous with the will. And he identifies "will" as something intrinsic in phenomena so that an artist who wishes to recreate phenomena will be far more effective and *realistic* if he finds a way to represent the will in the phenomena as opposed to merely representing the phenomena themselves. In other words, a writer of fiction may set out to tell a story by creating characters and events that follow a course of action he himself has made up. But a writer of a different kind will find a course of action arising out of a certain willfulness, not something he made up but something already existing in nature that he uncovered, and then let the willfulness tell the story. Nietzsche refers to that already existing willfulness in nature, which exists only behind all things and not in the appearance of things, as "music."

This all becomes important with regard to mythopoeia, or the creation of myth, because myth can only be created out of "music." And insofar as the dithyramb and dithyrambic drama is an art specifically dedicated to the creation of myth within its actor, the dithyramb is composed entirely in "music," which means everything that is depicted in the dithyramb is something that is already existing within the actor himself.

Nietzsche Learns the Theory of Dithyrambic Music from Schopenhauer

Perhaps we may lead up to this primitive problem with the question: what æsthetic effect results when the intrinsically separate art-powers, the Apollonian and the Dionysian, enter into concurrent actions? Or, in briefer form: how is music related to image and concept?—Schopenhauer, whom Richard Wagner, with especial reference to this point, accredits with an unsurpassable clearness and perspicuity of exposition, expresses himself most copiously on the subject in the following passage which I shall cite here at full length[21] (*Welt als Wille und Vorstellung,* I. p. 309): "According to all this, we may regard the phenomenal world, or nature, and music as two different expressions of the same thing,[22] which is therefore itself the only medium of the analogy between these two expressions, so that a knowledge of this medium is required in order to understand that analogy. Music, therefore, if regarded as an expression of the world, is in the highest degree a universal language, which is related indeed to the universality of concepts, much as these are related to the particular things. Its

---

[21] Cf. *World and Will as Idea*, I. p. 339, trans. by Haldane and Kemp.
[22] That is "the will" as understood by Schopenhauer.—TR

universality, however, is by no means the empty universality of abstraction, but of quite a different kind, and is united with thorough and distinct definiteness. In this respect it resembles geometrical figures and numbers, which are the universal forms of all possible objiects of experience and applicable to them all *a priori*, and yet are not abstract but perceptiple and thoroughly determinate. All possible efforts, excitements and manifestations of will, all that goes on in the heart of man and that reason includes in the wide, negative concept of feeling, may be expressed by the infinite number of possible melodies, but always in the universality of mere form, without the material, always according to the thing-in-itself, not the phenomenon,—of which they reproduce the very soul and essence as it were, without the body. This deep relation which music bears to the true nature of all things also explains the fact that suitable music played to any scene, action, event, or surrounding seems to disclose to us its most secret meaning, and appears as the most accurate and distinct commentary upon it; as also the fact that whoever gives himself up entirely to the impression of a symphony seems to see all the possible events of life and the world take place in himself: nevertheless upon reflection he can find no likeness between the music and the things that passed before his mind. For, as we have said, music is distinguished from all the other arts by the fact that it is not a copy of the phenomenon, or, more accurately, the adequate objectivity of the will, but the direct copy of the will itself, and therefore represents the metaphysical of everything physical in the world, and the thing-in-itself of every phenomenon. We might, therefore, just as well call the world embodied music as embodied will: and this is the reason why music makes every picture, and indeed every scene of real life and of the world, at once appear with higher significance; all the more so, to be sure, in proportion as its melody is analogous to the inner spirit of the given phenomenon. It rests upon this that we are able to set a poem to music as a song, or a perceptible representation as a pantomime, or both as an opera. Such particular pictures of human life, set to the universal language of music, are never bound to it or correspond to it with stringent necessity, but stand to it only in the relation of an example chosen at will to a general concept. In the determinateness of the real they represent that which music expresses in the universality of mere form. For melodies are to a certain extent, like general concepts, an abstraction from the actual. This actual world, then, the world of particular things, affords the object of perception, the special and the individual, the particular case, both to the universality of concepts and to the universality of the melodies. But these two universalities are in a certain respect opposed to each other; for the concepts contain only the forms, which are first of all abstracted from perception,—the separated outward shell of things, as it were,—and hence they are, in the strictest sense of the term, *abstracta*; music, on the other hand, gives the inmost kernel which precedes all forms, or the heart of things. This relation may be very well expressed in the language of the schoolmen, by saying: the concepts are the *universalia post rem,* but music gives the *universalia ante rem,* and the real world the *universalia in re.*—But that in general a relation is possible between a composition and a perceptible representation rests, as we have said, upon the fact that both are simply different expressions of the same inner being of the world. When now, in the particular case, such a relation is actually given, that is to say, when the composer has been able to express in the universal language of music the emotions of will which constitute the heart of an event, then the melody of the song, the music of the opera, is expressive. But the analogy discovered by the composer between the two must have proceeded from the direct

> knowledge of the nature of the world unknown to his reason, and must not be an imitation produced with conscious intention by means of conceptions; otherwise the music does not express the inner nature of the will itself, but merely gives an inadequate imitation of its phenomenon: all specially imitative music does this."

I would ask the reader to note three points here regarding the above passage. The first is that Schopenhauer was Nietzsche's teacher, by which I mean that, when Nietzsche discovered his passion for philosophy and then discovered the inner world of man as the object of his passion for a lifetime of study, it was Schopenhauer who walked Nietzsche through that inner world and showed him the things that he, Schopenhauer, had been studying. The second point to note is that Nietzsche only rarely quotes Schopenhauer in his own writing, and even more rarely does he quote him to any lengthy extent as he does in this instance. So, something important is being taught here. Thirdly, the important focus of study here is the concept of music as Nietzsche viewed it and as Schopenhauer viewed it. And the reason all these points are so important is because it is Nietzsche's concept of "music," as it is highlighted in this passage of Schopenhauer's original text, that defines the concept of *dithyrambic music*. And that concept is important in order to understand the most fundamental rudiment of hermeneutics that will enable the pupil to read the dithyrambs in which *Thus Spoke Zarathustra* is composed and to begin practicing dithyrambic drama. Thus, given all that importance, I have highlighted every single sentence in this lengthy quoted passage.

16: THEORY OF DITHYRAMBIC TRAGEDY
Myth as Progenitor of Image and Concept

- "Or, in briefer form: how is music related to image and concept?"

In this simple and concise question lies the most fundamental insight into Nietzsche's metaphysica: his view of the inner workings of the world that comprises human being. But it is not a good articulation of the deeper and wider question he is actually looking to answer. What he really wants to know is how mythopoeia happens. What are the conditions under which myth is created? Myth provides the being in human being. Myth is the essence out of which life begins and proceeds. And the question of its origin, its creation, is paramount. When Nietzsche asks "how is music related to image and concept," what he is really asking is how is music related to myth because image and concept arise from out of the more fundamental myth. And the answer he will find is that myth arises out of music. Except that, by "music," he does not mean the traditional and audible music with which we are all so familiar. Rather, he means dramatic music, which is will that must be embodied to the point wherein the actor who achieves the embodiment then becomes driven by the will, the "music," so that he finds himself in the midst of a drama that proceeds upon the development of that will. That drama is Nietzsche's *Thus Spoke Zarathustra*, which is composed entirely in dramatic music and whose aim is mythopoeia within the actor who undertakes it. And by acting, I do not mean pretending but rather doing.

Concept Is a Representation of Music

- "Music, therefore, if regarded as an expression of the world, is in the highest degree a universal language, which is related indeed to the universality of concepts, much as these are related to the particular things."

Schopenhauer says two things here. He says that music is a language and it can be used to communicate innermost nature. It is universal in the sense that everyone understands it but also in the sense that everything within nature is expressible via music. He also says that concept is universal, presumably in the sense that everything that is perceptible may be communicated via concept, which anybody with the ability to conceive would understand. And then he says something that goes to the heart of our desire to understand Nietzsche's concept of *dithyrambic music*, which, in fact, is what we are aiming for in this long citation that Nietzsche chose to include here. Schopenhauer says that music is related to concept in much the same way that concept is related to the thing about which it is a conception. In other words, concept is a representation of music. The fundamental point toward which we are moving, which goes to the crux of Nietzsche's concept of both "dithyrambic music" and dithyrambic drama, is that music can be used to communicate concept.

- "Its universality [of music], however, is by no means the empty universality of abstraction, but of quite a different kind, and is united with thorough and distinct definiteness."

16: THEORY OF DITHYRAMBIC TRAGEDY

Concept Is an Abstraction but Music Is an Essence

But whereas concept can be a representation of a music, it is a mere abstraction, which is all that concept achieves in its representative capacity. But music is something more essential and deeper than a mere representation. Moreover, music possesses melos (or melody), in which that which precedes any point within it has a very definite meaning as does that which follows it. Concept is an abstraction of a point within that melos, so that the melos itself has been redacted. But it is the melos, the music, that remains the essence out of which the concept arose.

- "In this respect it [music] resembles geometrical figures and numbers, which are the universal forms of all possible objects of experience and applicable to them all *a priori*, and yet are not abstract but perceptible and thoroughly determinate."

Unlike Concept, Music Is Gripping

If we represent all of human nature mathematically, which means absent any gripping pathos or ethos, we would find every possible mathematical representation within music. Except that a musical representation of human nature, though inherently conceptual and discernible by reason and logic, also exudes life, which is gripping. Thus, a concept of Self, for instance, can be entirely cerebral and abstract, as when Descartes proclaimed "I think, therefore I am," but when that concept of Self reveals itself as reality, which is gripping and sobering, then that concept becomes musical. The capacity to grip the beholder, to grab him by the throat and force him to look *and be moved*, is the capacity that lends a musical nature to concept, which is otherwise commonly abstract.

Music Is Communicative Absent Any Manifestation

- "All possible efforts, excitements and manifestations of will, all that goes on in the heart of man and that reason includes in the wide, negative concept of feeling, may be expressed by the infinite number of possible melodies, but always in the universality of mere form, without the material, always according to the thing-in-itself, not the phenomenon,—of which they reproduce the very soul and essence as it were, without the body."

Everything that man feels can find an expression in music. The same cannot be said of concept and idea because music is a representation of reality but not all concepts and ideas are rooted in reality. Moreover, every musical representation of a state of mind that is comprised by this or that circumstance of emotion is completely and wholly expressible absent any particular instance of the representation. In other words, it is possible to feel this way or that while listening to music without seeing, for instance, an actor depicting that circumstance of emotion. It is not the instance (the actor's portrayal) that defines and qualifies the representation; it is the musical form itself, which is a higher and universal essence, that defines and qualifies the representation.

- "This deep relation which music bears to the true nature of all things also explains the fact that suitable music played to any scene, action, event, or surrounding seems to disclose to us its most secret meaning, and appears as the most accurate and distinct commentary upon it; as also the fact that whoever gives himself up entirely to the impression of a symphony seems to see all the possible events of life and the world take place in himself: nevertheless upon reflection he can find no likeness between the music and the things that passed before his mind."

Insofar as music is a higher and universal representation of inner human nature, then there are many circumstances of emotion, particular instances, that will *fit* into that representation. And it is for this reason that a particular melody will appeal to many different individuals in many different ways.

Music Is a Representation of the Thing-In-Itself, of Will

- "For, as we have said, music is distinguished from all the other arts by the fact that it is not a copy of the phenomenon, or, more accurately, the adequate objectivity of the will, but the direct copy of the will itself, and therefore represents the metaphysical of everything physical in the world, and the thing-in-itself of every phenomenon."

Here, Schopenhauer defines music as will, by which we may define further as desire, hope, volition, passion, wanting, striving, and emotional discharge in general. And he says that music is not a representation of an instance of willing but rather is a representation of the willing itself. In other words, music is not a representation of a grieving widow; music is a representation of the grief itself in which many specific instances of grieving will find a mirror of itself. Schopenhauer then goes a step further and says that music, as a representation of the willing, not a particular or phenomenal instance of the willing, is a representation of the "thing-in-itself" of every act of willing. In short, "music" is will, "Music" communicates will.

- "We might, therefore, just as well call the world embodied music as embodied will: and this is the reason why music makes every picture, and indeed every scene of real life and of the world, at once appear with higher significance; all the more so, to be sure, in proportion as its melody is analogous to the inner spirit of the given phenomenon."

Finally, in this one short sentence, Schopenhauer discloses a simple fact that is applicable to all the world: the world is embodied music. And to say that it is embodied is to infer that it possesses a life of its own, outside of human existence, outside of its embodiment. It is easy enough to understand how all the world might be said to be "embodied will," except that it would be even more sensible to say that all *the inner world* is "embodied will." Most importantly, inasmuch as Schopenhauer identifies will and music as the same thing, and insofar as Nietzsche would eventually look for a way to teach will to power, the assertion that all the inner world is embodied music or embodied will *becomes very pertinent* to a reading of *Thus*

16: THEORY OF DITHYRAMBIC TRAGEDY

Spoke Zarathustra, which is the vehicle Nietzsche eventually found (or created) to teach will to power.

Myth as Imbued Will

Notice also that Schopenhauer says that music imparts a higher significance to appearance (e.g., a painting or any spectacle). Remembering that music and will are the same thing, music is able to impart a higher significance to a spectacle by imbuing the appearance with will. And any appearance of anything (from the Apollonian realm) that is imbued with will (from the Dionysian realm), such as myth, is much more gripping than a mere abstraction that is absent that imbued will, such as concept.

- "It rests upon this that we are able to set a poem to music as a song, or a perceptible representation as a pantomime, or both as an opera. Such particular pictures of human life, set to the universal language of music, are never bound to it or correspond to it with stringent necessity, but stand to it only in the relation of an example chosen at will to a general concept. In the determinateness of the real they represent that which music expresses in the universality of mere form. For melodies are to a certain extent, like general concepts, an abstraction from the actual."

Will as Music

This statement elaborates on what is meant by the universality of music by saying that music is a more general

DIONYSIA METAPHYSICA

form of something in which many specific examples can be found.

- "This actual world, then, the world of particular things, affords the object of perception, the special and the individual, the particular case, both to the universality of concepts and to the universality of the melodies. But these two universalities are in a certain respect opposed to each other; for the concepts contain only the forms, which are first of all abstracted from perception,—the separated outward shell of things, as it were,—and hence they are, in the strictest sense of the term, *abstracta*; music, on the other hand, gives the inmost kernel which precedes all forms, or the heart of things."

I direct the reader's focus above specifically to the references to the universality of concept and the universality of melodies. The use of the word "universality" in this instance is a reference to the ubiquity of concept and melody. Here, Schopenhauer is definitively classifying all of the inner world of man into two parts: concept and melody.

Keep in mind that Nietzsche, as Schopenhauer's pupil, is reading this original text and he is learning from it. He is also developing his own ideas. And it is here, as good as it might be anywhere else, that Nietzsche found his Dionysian-Apollonian duality, except that his nomenclature obfuscated his insight. He would have done better to simply call it a duality of realms between concept or visionary image and music. But even that nomenclature obfuscates the insight that Schopenhauer articulated here. While the universality of concept is something that is clearly evident within the inner world of man, the universality of melody is not. So exactly what is Schopenhauer referring to here as "music?" He is referring to will, which is exactly what he said earlier when he equated "music" with will. And what is will? Will is emotion, specifically the emotions that *move* man toward a goal, such as desire moves him. Thus, the duality that Schopenhauer has articulated here and which Nietzsche went on to develop into a full-blown philosophy is the duality of emotion and concept. Henceforth, when Nietzsche speaks of music, let us understand that he is speaking of the Dionysian realm of emotion. And, as we will soon learn, when he speaks of dramatic music, he means will.

In order to understand dithyrambic drama, which is the most major point of this entire reiteration and of Nietzsche's disquisition itself, it is critical to understand the meaning of "dramatic music." And the first thing to understand is that it is a reference to the emotions that comprise will.

Will as Progenitor of Concept

Therefore, if we return now to the above statement by Schopenhauer, he says that concept communicates "the outward shell of things," or the appearance of things, one might say, though Schopenhauer calls it the "abstracta" of things. In contrast, "music" or will communicates "the innermost kernel" of things. And then, continuing, he says something very telling. He says that "music" communicates that essence or "heart of things" *which precedes all things*. He is referencing the will and he is saying that the will precedes all things about which we later develop a concept. In short, a desire for something precedes any conception we may later develop for that same thing. And as we are about to see, in fact, it is the desire that leads to the conceptualization. It is the desire that prompts, or creates, the concept. And, by the way, it is not "cause" that brings things into the world; it is need and affect.

- "This relation may be very well expressed in the language of the schoolmen, by saying: the concepts are the *universalia post rem,* but music gives the *universalia ante rem,* and the real world the *universalia in re.*"

- "But that in general a relation is possible between a composition and a perceptible representation rests, as we have said, upon the fact that both are simply different expressions of the same inner being of the world."

If concept and will are equal expressions of the same thing, then a representation of something in the language of will would communicate that particular same thing with the same measure of articulation as would its representation in the language of concept. That is true, both will and concept are communicative, but will is far more communicative, and Nietzsche has proven that with his dithyrambic music in *Thus Spoke Zarathustra*, which successfully communicates the whole inner world via the language of will, which is dithyrambic music. But most importantly, he communicates a whole world of concepts without ever articulating or explaining a single one. In other words, will and concept may be equally expressive of the inner world of man, but the language of will can also *provoke* concept. However, the language of concept cannot provoke will because concept is mere abstraction, while will is emotive. While concept and will can both communicate the things comprising the inner world of man, the measure of their articulation is not equal because things communicated in the language of will are represented far more robustly insofar as the will that communicates them imparts itself to their conceptual counterpart and imbues that conception with that will, whereas concept alone, by itself, absent the will, presents only the mere "abstracta." There is nothing in the nature of concept that presents imbuement. But there is something in the nature of concept that allows imbuement.

Dithyrambic Music as Will

Returning to our reiteration, in the above last statement, regarding a relation between a composition, or a work of art, and the phenomenon that the artwork aims to represent, Schopenhauer says there is success only if the artwork succeeds in communicating the innermost being of the phenomenon. And, as we have already seen, by "innermost being" he means the music or the will. In other words, good art must communicate the will that exists within something.

- "When now, in the particular case, such a relation is actually given, that is to say, when the composer has been able to express in the universal language of music the emotions of will which constitute the heart of an event, then the melody of the song, the music of the opera, is expressive."

Here is confirmation of my last statement that, in Schopenhauer's mind, good art is qualified by its communication of the will. Notice also his exact wording. He speaks of representing the emotions of the will that constitute the heart of an event. And he calls this representation of the emotions of the will "music." This is precisely where Nietzsche obtained his concept of "dramatic music," which we know as dithyrambic music.

Dithyrambic music is a representation of the emotions of the will. Thus, when we read *Thus Spoke Zarathustra*, we must look for the emotions of the will in the gesticulative metaphors in which Nietzsche composed his dithyrambic drama.

- "But the analogy discovered by the composer between the two must have proceeded from the direct knowledge of the nature of the world unknown to his reason, and must not be an imitation produced with conscious intention by means of conceptions; otherwise the music does not express the inner nature of the will itself, but merely gives an inadequate imitation of its phenomenon: all specially imitative music does this."

The Reality of Dithyrambic Music in the Melos

The dithyrambist who composes dithyrambic music must do so with knowledge of the emotions of the will that enter into a confluence that results in the creation of will. He cannot choose the elements of his representation out of thin air or out of anything that is not the "music," the will that flows within the event he seeks to represent. In other words, he must compose in reality, not fiction. And it is precisely this requirement which Euripides ignored that led to the demise of tragedy because without "music" then myth is impossible to create, and mythopoeia is the aim of tragic art, as we will see shortly. The key to understanding all of the above is the concept of melos, by which I mean an underlying unity.

16: Theory of Dithyrambic Tragedy

In order to understand the concept of melos, consider, for instance, the effect of Mozart's Requiem on someone who is grieving. The music, in the end, brings the griever to a better place within himself by helping him to grieve, by helping him to discharge his sadness. And music does that by correlating with emotion. The sound of a violin playing a single note invariably provokes an emotional reaction within the listener. And a somber note does not provoke a cheerful emotion within the listener; it provokes an equally somber emotion. Moreover, a second note can bring the listener to an anticipation of a third note even before the third note has been played or heard, but only provided that one condition has been met: there must exist between each note a melos, a connection that ties each of the notes into a melody. If the melos is lacking, the anticipation of the third note fails. Thus, the melos is a key element in the process by which the listener is brought to a new state of mind.

Concept Lacks a Melos

Concept, obviously, will also bring the beholder to grief. Thus, concept also provokes emotion. But, unlike musical notes, concepts do not flow one into another. However, there is a continuity between concepts, wherein a related concept will follow an initial concept, as when a soldier comes upon a pile of skulls and wonders what happened. His initial concept will be of death. Afterwards, he might conceive of a massacre. But between the first and second concept, an instinct arises from within the realm of emotion that prompts him to ask "why?" Afterward, the idea may come to him that the skulls he sees before him are fallen comrades, which would provoke grief in him. Thus, concept or idea can potentially provoke emotion.

Thus, this continuity or cohesion that we see in this instance above of concept is woven by emotion, or instinct. And I attribute instinct to emotion insofar as it is physical, unlike idea and concept which is fictive or cerebral. Otherwise, I see no continuity or flow in concept, and certainly no melos, as we find in music. Though there is an apparent flow in concept, but it arises from within "music."

Old and New Concept

> We have therefore, according to the doctrine of Schopenhauer, an immediate understanding of music as the language of the will, and feel our imagination stimulated to give form to this invisible and yet so actively stirred spirit-world which speaks to us, and prompted to embody it in an analogous example.

In other words, the word "music" will be used to denote the language of the will, which is comprised entirely of emotions and, as such, is immediately intuitable and does not require reason. Moreover, it is within human nature that the language of the will, or "music," manifests itself in concept. More specifically, concept arises from will as an embodiment of "an analogous example." However, there are two kinds of concept: concept that is old and concept that is new. Concept that is new, having just arisen from out of the will, is imbued with will and reverberates the will as spirit, whereas concept that is old eventually loses that spirit, given that spirit fades. Thus, concept that is old does not reverberate the will and is entirely "abstracta."

16: Theory of Dithyrambic Tragedy
Mythopoeia and "Music"

On the other hand, image and concept, under the influence of a truly conformable music, acquire a higher significance. Dionysian art therefore is wont to exercise—two kinds of influences, on the Apollonian art-faculty: music firstly incites to the *symbolic intuition* of Dionysian universality, and, secondly, it causes the symbolic image to stand forth *in its fullest significance*. From these facts, intelligible in themselves and not inaccessible to profounder observation, I infer the capacity of music to give birth to *myth,* that is to say, the most significant exemplar, and precisely *tragic* myth: the myth which speaks of Dionysian knowledge in symbols. In the phenomenon of the lyrist, I have set forth that in him music strives to express itself with regard to its nature in Apollonian images. If now we reflect that music in its highest potency must seek to attain also to its highest symbolisation, we must deem it possible that it also knows how to find the symbolic expression of its inherent Dionysian wisdom; and where shall we have to seek for this expression if not in tragedy and, in general, in the conception of the *tragic*?

- "I infer the capacity of music to give birth to *myth,* that is to say, the most significant exemplar, and precisely *tragic* myth: the myth which speaks of Dionysian knowledge in symbols."

Again, when he says "music," he means will. Thus, dithyrambic music is the communication of will. And in the above statement, he states explicitly that dithyrambic music prompts mythopoeia within the actor. This is one of the most fundamental revelations about dithyrambic drama that we can hope to find: mythopoeia is the goal of the dithyramb.

- "… music firstly incites to the *symbolic intuition* of Dionysian universality, and, secondly, it causes the symbolic image to stand forth *in its fullest significance.*"

Will prompts the formation of concept as an intuitable representation of the nature of will. Secondly, concept that arises out of willful strife is imbued by that will with a spirit denoting a higher significance that other, older, faded concepts lack.

- "From these facts, I infer the capacity of music to give birth to *myth,* that is to say, the most significant exemplar, and precisely *tragic* myth: the myth which speaks of Dionysian knowledge in symbols."

Find your Self in Dithyrambic Drama

Finally, sixteen chapters into his metaphysica, Nietzsche finally comes out with his tell-all insight: music gives birth to myth. Or, to put it another way, Self arises out of a perception of emotion, which is not news to anyone in the year 2020; "to feel is to heal." However, what *is* news is that dramatic music, as an art form, also gives rise to Self. And tragic myth is a more powerful myth because proto-tragedy affords a deeper perception of what lies beyond the veil of Maya, which is also the veil of the Ego. Therefore, learn how to read dithyrambic music and how to practice dithyrambic drama, then begin reading Nietzsche's *Thus Spoke Zarathustra*, and the book will lead you to your *deepest* Self. And that is news to everyone, herein.

But now, let us return to Nietzsche's articulation. The next point to consider is how Nietzsche's Thalesian insight that "art owes its continuous evolution to the Dionysian-Apollonian duality" relates to his tell-all insight that music gives birth to myth. By "art," he means the creation of myth, mythopoeia. And by "Dionysian," we now know that he means "music," by which he means dramatic music or the emotions of the will. And by "Apollonian," though he has been less definitive here and less explicit than he has been with "Dionysian," it will become clearer that he means concept, image, and vision, and specifically the vision of Self. Thus, the creation of myth, of the vision of Self, evolves strictly in accordance with equal expressions of the emotions of the will which then find their counterpart, their symbolic representation in concept and image. And to put that even simpler, a man who succeeds in fathoming subliminal pain or subliminal fear that has resided within his subconscious for what surely seemed like an eternity will find a vision of his deepest Self, which constitutes reality, in that pain or fear and then that newly found subliminal emotion will reverberate in that newly found vision of Self in such a way that the illusoriness of Self will heal that pain or fear.

To say that myth speaks to man about his inner nature via symbols is to say that it speaks to him intuitively and instinctively, not conceptually. (And, by the way, it is via concept that science proceeds, which makes science antithetical to tragedy.)

> From the nature of art, as it is ordinarily conceived according to the single category of appearance and beauty, the tragic cannot be honestly deduced at all; it is only through the spirit of music that we understand the joy in the annihilation of the individual. For in the particular examples of such annihilation only is the eternal phenomenon of Dionysian art made clear to us, which gives expression to the will in its omnipotence, as it were, behind the *principium individuationis,* the eternal life beyond all phenomena, and in spite of all annihilation. The metaphysical delight in the tragic is a translation of the instinctively unconscious Dionysian wisdom into the language of the scene: the hero, the highest manifestation of the will, is disavowed for our pleasure, because he is only phenomenon, and because the eternal life of the will is not affected by his annihilation. "We believe in eternal life," tragedy exclaims; while music is the proximate idea of this life. Plastic art has an altogether different object: here Apollo vanquishes the suffering of the individual by the radiant

> glorification of the *eternity of the phenomenon*; here beauty triumphs over the suffering inherent in life; pain is in a manner surreptitiously obliterated from the features of nature. In Dionysian art and its tragic symbolism the same nature speaks to us with its true undissembled voice: "Be as I am! Amidst the ceaseless change of phenomena the eternally creative primordial mother, eternally impelling to existence, self-satisfying eternally with this change of phenomena!"

Now, with this paragraph and continuing with the next chapter, we begin a disquisition of proto-tragedy, which is a word I use to differentiate from modern tragedy, which is either an entirely morally-interpreted phenomenon indicating an affront or a catastrophe to the morale of a people or an individual or a theatrical spectacle evoking a catharsis of pity and terror, neither of which resemble ancient, proto-tragedy.

- "From the nature of art, as it is ordinarily conceived according to the single category of appearance and beauty, the tragic cannot be honestly deduced at all; it is only through the spirit of music that we understand the joy in the annihilation of the individual."

Tragedy Is Celebrated in the Will, Not in the Self

The value and beauty of proto-tragedy lies not in any appearance or image but rather in the reinvigoration of the will that drives it. And the delight and optimism that derives from that reinvigoration is what qualifies tragedy as an art. It is the will that gains the most benefit from tragedy, while mind is destroyed, though it is a joyful death that leads to a greater and higher reunion and not a terminal death. It is the will that is restored by the destruction of magnificent individuality and therefore rejoices deeply in that destruction. Thus, it is only through the spirit of music, by which he means the spirit of the will, that delight in tragedy becomes perceptible and meaningful.

- "For in the particular examples of such annihilation only is the eternal phenomenon of Dionysian art made clear to us, which gives expression to the will in its omnipotence, as it were, behind the *principium individuationis,* the eternal life beyond all phenomena, and in spite of all annihilation."

It is perhaps a phenomenon unique to sub-individuated man, in whom the principium individuationis (the PI, the mind, the Self), has already collapsed and has already been replaced with a weaker PI (the Ego and the egotistical mind founded as a stopgap upon the subconscious realm), that the destruction of the PI leads directly to *a better state of existence*, And it is only better because it comes from a state of existence founded upon the Ego that is much more impoverished, impercipient, and weak-willed. Were it not for that comparison, proto-tragedy would not have the value that it has, nor would proto-tragedy even be possible. And it is for this reason, I believe, and I have yet to find anything to contradict my theory, that the reason the satyr and proto-tragedy went hand in hand is because the satyr was a caricature representing sub-individuated man, half man

16: THEORY OF DITHYRAMBIC TRAGEDY

(possessing human being) and half animal (lacking human being).

As I explained extensively in *The Birth of Dionysia*, Self is a myth that arises out of the particular circumstance wherein the perception of emoting sensations triggers the mythopoeic instinct. An understanding of myth is pivotal to an understanding of proto-tragedy and this next passage of Nietzsche's essay, wherein he explains the value of will over myth. Therefore, I urge the reader to first learn about myth and the mythopoeic instinct via *The Birth of Dionysia*.

Putting aside, then, the creation of Self, which the reader can garner from supplemental reading, what is important to understand is that mythical being, whether it be Self or Ego, draws strict boundaries around itself. Indeed, inherent in the nature of being is the need for definitive boundaries. And, as a result of those boundaries, limits are also defined. For instance, the limits of perception, particularly within sub-individuated human being, restrict the extent to which the individual can look upon the sensate realm and incorporate it into myth. And the ability to be moved by titanic emotion, which indubitably requires strength, is also subject to limits, specifically the limits of the individual's ability to brave pain and horror. However, in addition to defining boundaries and setting limits, the vision of Self also provides a horizon, beyond which there is no perception, though there may be haunting and unintelligible rumblings of subliminal torment, for sure.

Keep in mind that we are redefining tragedy by looking away from the traditional concept of a theatrical event that evokes a catharsis of pity and terror, according to Aristotle, and we are also looking away from the morally interpreted concept of tragedy as an indignant injury to the morale of an individual or a people, according to my theory of the origin of moral values. Instead, we must understand tragedy as a redemptive, spiritual event playing out within a course of growth that enables that growth. Specifically, I mean the collapse of Ego, in the case of sub-individuated man, which thereby gives rise to the truer Self, or, in that case where the truer Self has already come into existence, the collapse of the existing Self, which thereby gives rise to the supra-Self, which you can read about more extensively in *The Birth of Dionysia*.

When the boundaries or limits of the Self are broken so that the individual falls out of Schopenhauer's trusty but frail craft and into the abyss of sub-individuation, the Self collapses and the Ego arises in its place, and the limits of perception are redrawn, sometimes in a highly restrictive way, giving rise to the subconscious and wiping out a wide and deep swath of the realm of sensation and emotion. This is a condition I call dismemberment. And proto-tragedy cures dismemberment by shattering the Ego and the limits of perception that it sets, thereby allowing perception of a deeper realm of emotion. And that shattering and its resultant broader perception of reality *liberates* suffering man in two ways. First, it provides access to the subliminal suffering so that the afflicted man can finally begin to do something about it, whereas previously, in a dismembered state, he had no access and, therefore, no hope of ever overcoming his affliction. But secondly, the incorporation of the subconscious into consciousness, which is precisely what happens as a result of proto-tragedy, invigorates and strengthens the will. In dismemberment, repressed emotion that remains vaulted within the subconscious is *muted*. When repressed emotion is liberated, it is no longer muted and, instead, takes on a new *tone* that is much more pronounced and audible. And it *moves* its subject with more force than previously, so that, by adding that forceful movement to the will, the will becomes stronger.

Returning, then, to our reiteration of the above statement by Nietzsche, regarding the joy in the annihilation of the individual, the joy is, more specifically, derived from the annihilation of the principium individuationis, the Self, which separates man, as if in a trusty rowboat, from the sea of emotion atop which he lives because it invigorates and strengthens the will, *the spirit of music*. This is the joy that derives from proto-tragedy, from the destruction of individuality: that destruction leads to a deeper, more meaningful, and more rewarding existence — and a deeper, more meaningful, and more rewarding sense of Self, which, again, must face destruction one day if the process of renewal is to continue, which it must. Thus speaks tragic wisdom: behind all phenomena, all appearance, lies eternal life, if only you can learn to look beyond the horizon, with life, as a process of growth, being defined by the movement imparted by will, and specifically a will to power.

17: Theory of Supra-Self and Over-Self

Tragedy as the Greater Joy in Becoming, Not Being

Dionysian art, too, seeks to convince us of the eternal joy of existence: only we are to seek this joy not in phenomena, but behind phenomena. We are to perceive how all that comes into being must be ready for a sorrowful end; we are compelled to look into the terrors of individual existence—yet we are not to become torpid: a metaphysical comfort tears us momentarily from the bustle of the transforming figures. We are really for brief moments Primordial Being itself, and feel its indomitable desire for being and joy in existence; the struggle, the pain, the destruction of phenomena, now appear to us as something necessary, considering the surplus of innumerable forms of existence which throng and push one another into life, considering the

> exuberant fertility of the universal will. We are pierced by the maddening sting of these pains at the very moment when we have become, as it were, one with the immeasurable primordial joy in existence, and when we anticipate, in Dionysian ecstasy, the indestructibility and eternity of this joy. In spite of fear and pity, we are the happy living beings, not as individuals, but as the *one* living being, with whose procreative joy we are blended.

- "Dionysian art, too, seeks to convince us of the eternal joy of existence: only we are to seek this joy not in phenomena, but behind phenomena."

Knowing all we now know about Nietzsche's use of the word "Dionysian," that it refers to music, which is will, then we may also conclude that "Dionysian art" is a reference to art that communicates to us via the will, such as lyrical poetry and, more importantly, dithyrambic music. And Nietzsche also tells us that the pleasure we may find in Dionysian art, or, more importantly, dithyrambic music, is not in phenomena, or appearance, like the vision of Self, but rather in the will, in the emotions. And, as I have said, the pleasure to be found in will, or the emotions, is in the invigoration and strengthening of the will that results from proto-tragedy, precisely from the destruction of any existing vision of Self (or Ego, but most particularly Ego). And, if you still do not follow the logic of how that invigoration *and optimism* results from a destructive event, that is because there is no logic in it. Proto-tragedy is an illogical phenomenon, and it is most illogical in its employment of mysticism. However, if you still do not follow the derivation of pleasure in the destruction of appearance, I would ask you to go back to the preceding chapter and re-read it until you do.

- "We are to perceive how all that comes into being must be ready for a sorrowful end; we are compelled to look into the terrors of individual existence—yet we are not to become torpid: a metaphysical comfort tears us momentarily from the bustle of the transforming figures."

This goes directly to the heart of Nietzsche's supra-Self, which says that the emergence of every layer of deeper Self that results from the incremental integration of the subconscious into consciousness must certainly face a day when, due to an even deeper integration, an even deeper Self will emerge, thus causing the previous Self to collapse like a false flooring, as the deeper substratum of emotion within the even deeper subconscious — and all the terror that resides within — opens up. And yet, it is not torpidity that may result from this continual destruction. Quite the contrary, invigoration will result, along with a deep and lasting optimism that itself will drive the process along.

- "We are really for brief moments Primordial Being itself, and feel its indomitable desire for being and joy in existence; the struggle, the pain, the destruction of phenomena, now appear to us as something necessary, considering the surplus of innumerable forms of existence which throng and push one another into life, considering the exuberant fertility of the universal will. We are really for brief moments Primordial Being itself, and feel its indomitable desire for being and joy in existence; the struggle, the pain, the destruction of phenomena, now appear to us as something necessary, considering the surplus of innumerable forms of existence which throng and push one another into life, considering the exuberant fertility of the universal will."

By "Primordial Being," he means actuality, which is different from reality insofar as reality, that which we "see" and understand via Self, the mind's eye, is an illusion founded upon illusory myth, the Self.

Notwithstanding the illusory nature of Self and reality, it is important to remember that the trait of illusoriness does not in any way deprecate reality. Quite the contrary, it is illusion that enables the veil of Maya to heal. Outside of Self, subliminal sensation is a haunting rumbling of unknown origin and unknown meaning. It is only when the subliminal sensation is attributed to Self that it becomes an "emotion," a dimension of Self, so that its origin becomes known. And, more importantly, via that attribution, the unknown sensation also becomes manageable, less titanic, as it assumes the veil of Maya, which soothes and poeticizes the otherwise foreign sensations. It is a simple fact that "to feel is to heal," that one always feels better about some painful moment after crying about it.

Continuing with the reiteration of the above sentence, insofar as tragedy destroys the vision of Self and therewith opens the horizon beyond which the beholder may look more deeply into his emotions, he becomes one with actuality, with music, with will, which Nietzsche regards as "Primordial Being." However, there is no "Being" whatsoever in Nietzsche's "Primordial Being." Instead, what he means is a state of existence in which man feels one with his innermost nature, with actuality that is absent the veil of Maya.

The Over-Self as a State of Existence Granting the Highest Freedom to Will

Nietzsche then notes *twice*, in the same sentence above, our knowledge of the necessary *and continual* destruction of Self and the resultant communion and joy with "Primordial Being." This is the very rare wisdom that tragedy bestows upon its practitioners: the knowledge that all growth requires some measure of death and disintegration. And it may take a very long time indeed for the pupil to reach that level of understanding about life, given the extraordinary value *and certainty* that a bright apprehension of Self imparts to its beholder. Who among us, after spending decades trying to find his Self, and, upon succeeding, then resigns himself to its eventual loss? Indeed, what merits the commitment of decades of struggle in the first place, if the prize is inevitably destined to fade away into oblivion? These are the obstacles the pupil faces. Is there something beyond all visions of Self, beyond the deepest, brightest, and most comprehensive vision of Self that makes the long struggle worthwhile? Indeed, there is. And it is the will. "In spite of fear and pity (of the subconscious), we are the happy living beings, not as individuals, but as the *one* living being, with whose procreative joy we are blended." It is the liberation of the will, not the brightest apprehension of Self, that makes the struggle that is life itself so worthwhile, which brings us to Nietzsche's discovery of the over-Self, that state of existence that lies beyond all visions of Self and also beyond all limits and boundaries set by Self, which is what we call genius.

The history of the rise of Greek tragedy now tells us with luminous precision that the tragic art of the Greeks was really born of the spirit of music: with which conception we believe we have done justice for the first time to the original and most astonishing significance of the chorus. At the same time, however, we must admit that the import of tragic myth as set forth above never became transparent with sufficient lucidity to the Greek poets, let alone the Greek philosophers; their heroes speak, as it were, more superficially than they act; the myth does not at all find its adequate objectification in the spoken word. The structure of the scenes and the conspicuous images reveal a deeper wisdom than the poet himself can put into words and concepts: the same being also observed in Shakespeare, whose Hamlet, for instance, in an analogous manner talks more superficially than he acts, so that the previously mentioned lesson of Hamlet is to be gathered not from his words, but from a more profound contemplation and survey of the whole. With respect to Greek tragedy, which of course presents itself to us only as word-drama, I have even intimated that the incongruence between myth and expression might easily tempt us to regard it as shallower and less significant than it really is, and accordingly to postulate for it a more

> superficial effect than it must have had according to the testimony of the ancients: for how easily one forgets that what the word-poet did not succeed in doing, namely realising the highest spiritualisation and ideality of myth, he might succeed in doing every moment as creative musician! We require, to be sure, almost by philological method to reconstruct for ourselves the ascendency of musical influence in order to receive something of the incomparable comfort which must be characteristic of true tragedy. Even this musical ascendency, however, would only have been felt by us as such had we been Greeks: while in the entire development of Greek music—as compared with the infinitely richer music known and familiar to us—we imagine we hear only the youthful song of the musical genius intoned with a feeling of diffidence. The Greeks are, as the Egyptian priests say, eternal children, and in tragic art also they are only children who do not know what a sublime play-thing has originated under their hands and—is being demolished.

Now he moves to the point that myth, about which he has not provided the same measure of articulation that he has provided us with regard to *everything else*, is communicated most effectively by music, meaning will, not words and perhaps even not action.

17: THEORY OF SUPRA-SELF AND OVER-SELF

- "The history of the rise of Greek tragedy now tells us with luminous precision that the tragic art of the Greeks was really born of the spirit of music...."

The Dithyramb Communicates Will, Not Concept, which Must Be "Heard," Not "Seen"

When he says "Greek tragedy" and "the spirit of music," we must remember two things. One is that, by "Greek tragedy," he means proto-tragedy which is an inner spiritual event that enables a process of growth. And two is that, by "the spirit of music," he means the spirit of the will. Thus, the egotistical Self that derives from sub-individuation collapses not out of the formation of some special concept but rather out of an emotion rising from the deep into consciousness.

- "... for how easily one forgets that what the word-poet did not succeed in doing, namely realising the highest spiritualisation and ideality of myth, he might succeed in doing every moment as creative musician!"

Here, he is moving to the point that the artist who wishes to communicate a myth, and specifically a tragic myth, can only hope to succeed if he uses the language of will as his means of expression, which is precisely what we find in Nietzsche's dithyrambic tragedy, *Thus Spoke Zarathustra*. Therefore, a work of art that communicates a myth uses words to communicate the will, not concept. And the moment that words are used to communicate concept instead of will, then the art of tragedy fails. Therefore, to practice dithyrambic music means to find the will that is represented in the words and then to embody that will so that you become driven by it because it will lead you into an inner circumstance out of which the myth will arise within you. And that is the only way you will "see" the myth, which is an Apollonian manifestation and for that reason may be "seen" at all. That out of which the myth arises, the will, the dithyrambic music, the Dionysian side of things, cannot ever be seen in any respect whatsoever; rather, it can only be "heard."

Tragedy and Mysticism Are Closely Related

> That striving of the spirit of music for symbolic and mythical manifestation, which increases from the beginnings of lyric poetry to Attic tragedy, breaks off all of a sudden immediately after attaining luxuriant development, and disappears, as it were, from the surface of Hellenic art: while the Dionysian view of things born of this striving lives on in Mysteries and, in its strangest metamorphoses and debasements, does not cease to attract earnest natures. Will it not one day rise again as art out of its mystic depth?

What this paragraph reveals to us about dithyrambic drama is that it employs mysticism. And anyone who undertakes the drama will experience mystical thoughts and emotions arising within him from a depth that he himself as yet to reach, though he strives to reach, And being from such a great depth, those thoughts and feelings — and their arousal — will be difficult to explain or articulate, yet they will define within him his Self. And then, later and quite suddenly, a vision of a new Self will arise in the mind of the actor *out of nothing*, thereby defying

17: THEORY OF SUPRA-SELF AND OVER-SELF

logic. Comprehension in this whole process is something that will come only in the end. And any attempt to demand comprehension or logic while the process of creation is playing out will serve only to complicate or perhaps abort it.

That said, in the above paragraph, Nietzsche explores the possibility that wherever today mysticism is practiced as an art form, perhaps in India, tragedy may emerge once again as its own art form, albeit closely related to mysticism.

> Here the question occupies us, whether the power by the counteracting influence of which tragedy perished, has for all time strength enough to prevent the artistic reawaking of tragedy and of the tragic view of things. If ancient tragedy was driven from its course by the dialectical desire for knowledge and the optimism of science, it might be inferred that there is an eternal conflict between *the theoretic* and *the tragic view of things,* and only after the spirit of science has been led to its boundaries, and its claim to universal validity has been destroyed by the evidence of these boundaries, can we hope for a re-birth of tragedy: for which form of culture we should have to use the symbol *of the music-practising Socrates* in the sense spoken of above. In this contrast, I understand by the spirit of science the belief which first came to light in the person of Socrates,—the belief in the fathomableness of nature and in knowledge as a panacea.

- "Here the question occupies us, whether the power by the counteracting influence of which tragedy perished, has for all time strength enough to prevent the artistic reawakening of tragedy and of the tragic view of things."

The Danger of Science

In other words, will proto-tragedy be categorically precluded by the existence of scientific thought, and specifically science's penchant for dialectical thought and dialectic's ability to impart optimism with life, for as long as scientific thought is engaged? Or is it possible that science will meet a natural demise when scientific thought reaches its limits, specifically the limits set by the realization that nature cannot be ultimately fathomed by scientific thought? Is It possible that science will fall to the wayside when the myth that sustains it, specifically its ability as thought to unriddle the mysteries of nature and correct its anomalies, fails? Is there no possibility that the myth upon which science is founded will *ever* fail?

If proto-tragedy is the one thing that is essential to the healing of suffering man, as both Nietzsche and I propose, if proto-tragedy is the one thing without which humanity *cannot* succeed, the questions above should be of critical concern to humanity and especially the philosophers.

Nietzsche's solution to this quandary is the creation of a new myth to run alongside the science myth to see which provides the most benefit and value to mankind. And a new myth means a new culture, whose symbolization may be found in the juxtaposition of the theoretical man with the tragic man,

17: THEORY OF SUPRA-SELF AND OVER-SELF

and whose success may be found in the symbol of Socrates practicing music.

> He who recalls the immediate consequences of this restlessly onward-pressing spirit of science will realise at once that *myth* was annihilated by it, and that, in consequence of this annihilation, poetry was driven as a homeless being from her natural ideal soil. If we have rightly assigned to music the capacity to reproduce myth from itself, we may in turn expect to find the spirit of science on the path where it inimically opposes this mythopoeic power of music. This takes place in the development of the *New Attic Dithyramb,* the music of which no longer expressed the inner essence, the will itself, but only rendered the phenomenon insufficiently, in an imitation by means of concepts; from which intrinsically degenerate music the truly musical natures turned away with the same repugnance that they felt for the art-destroying tendency of Socrates. The unerring instinct of Aristophanes surely did the proper thing when it comprised Socrates himself, the tragedy of Euripides, and the music of the new Dithyrambic poets in the same feeling of hatred, and perceived in all three phenomena the symptoms of a degenerate culture. By this New Dithyramb, music has in an outrageous manner been

made the imitative portrait of phenomena, for instance, of a battle or a storm at sea, and has thus, of course, been entirely deprived of its mythopoeic power. For if it endeavours to excite our delight only by compelling us to seek external analogies between a vital or natural process and certain rhythmical figures and characteristic sounds of music; if our understanding is expected to satisfy itself with the perception of these analogies, we are reduced to a frame of mind in which the reception of the mythical is impossible; for the myth as a unique exemplar of generality and truth towering into the infinite, desires to be conspicuously perceived. The truly Dionysean music presents itself to us as such a general mirror of the universal will: the conspicuous event which is refracted in this mirror expands at once for our consciousness to the copy of an eternal truth. Conversely, such a conspicious event is at once divested of every mythical character by the tone-painting of the New Dithyramb; music has here become a wretched copy of the phenomenon, and therefore infinitely poorer than the phenomenon itself: through which poverty it still further reduces even the phenomenon for our consciousness, so that now, for instance, a musically imitated battle of this sort exhausts itself in marches, signal-

17: THEORY OF SUPRA-SELF AND OVER-SELF

> sounds, etc., and our imagination is arrested precisely by these superficialities. Tone-painting is therefore in every respect the counterpart of true music with its mythopoeic power: through it the phenomenon, poor in itself, is made still poorer, while through an isolated Dionysian music the phenomenon is evolved and expanded into a picture of the world. It was an immense triumph of the non-Dionysian spirit, when, in the development of the New Dithyramb, it had estranged music from itself and reduced it to be the slave of phenomena. Euripides, who, albeit in a higher sense, must be designated as a thoroughly unmusical nature, is for this very reason a passionate adherent of the New Dithyrambic Music, and with the liberality of a freebooter employs all its effective turns and mannerisms.

- "He who recalls the immediate consequences of this restlessly onward-pressing spirit of science will realise at once that *myth* was annihilated by it...."

Insofar as science is itself founded upon a myth, Nietzsche does not really mean to say that science destroyed myth. Instead, what he means to say is that it destroyed tragic myth. And what, exactly, is tragic myth?

I have already explained myth and mythopoeia in *The Birth of Dionysia*, so I will not repeat myself here. But, for the sake of our reiteration here, I think it is necessary to say that mythopoeia that is triggered by proto-tragedy results in that which Nietzsche denotes as tragic myth. And science, or scientific thought, precludes proto-tragedy and, with it, tragic myth. And insofar as tragic mythopoeia is a critical, fundamental, and necessary event in the process of growth that manifests itself as life within human being, science is inimical to life. And that is the problem Nietzsche is addressing in *The Birth of Tragedy*.

- "... in consequence of this annihilation, poetry was driven as a homeless being from her natural ideal soil."

Euripi-dean Tragedy Is Composed in Concept, Not Will

Moreover, if we may regard poetry as not so much to be rhyming verse but more so as the poignant articulation of the nature of human being, then it is easy to see how a dialectical articulation would distort any representation of this natural condition, especially with its demand that the logos in things be found and uncovered as well.

- "If we have rightly assigned to music the capacity to reproduce myth from itself, we may in turn expect to find the spirit of science on the path where it inimically opposes this mythopoeic power of music."

It is only "music," or the poignant articulation of actuality and the human will within it, with its most significant qualifier being the capacity to *embody* the will represented in the "music," that can successfully *communicate* the instincts, particularly the mythopoeic instinct, out of which mythopoeia

17: Theory of Supra-Self and Over-Self

happens and myth is created, which itself fundamentally constitutes that which we call art, especially art as it occurs within human being. Simply put, dialectic in no way communicates instinct or anything else that might rightly qualify as "music," or emotion that comprises will. Dialectic communicates via concept. And the language of concept, not will, is what we find in the New Dithyrambs of Euripides (and all the modern tragedies that followed after him.

- "This takes place in the development of the *New Attic Dithyramb,* the music of which no longer expressed the inner essence, the will itself, but only rendered the phenomenon insufficiently, in an imitation by means of concepts...."

As above.

- "By this New Dithyramb, music has in an outrageous manner been made the imitative portrait of phenomena, for instance, of a battle or a storm at sea, and has thus, of course, been entirely deprived of its mythopoeic power."

And,

- "... music has here become a wretched copy of the phenomenon, and therefore infinitely poorer than the phenomenon itself...."

Concept as a Copy of a Copy of the Will

Understanding the notion of a composer depicting a "copy of the phenomenon" or a "copy" of the will as opposed to actually depicting and communicating the will itself and *thus* creating the phenomena arising naturally out of that will is very important for our reiteration here. The best way I can explain it is by citing from personal experience. Forgive me for getting personal.

I have been a smoker all my life, unfortunately. In my younger days, shortly after discovering that there did indeed exist something called the subconscious, which was a most significant discovery whose moment I remember well, I was sitting at my desk wondering why I smoked. I concluded it was because of the irritation it caused in my throat. When I was a young boy discovering the habit of smoking with my two friends in the woods one day, upon taking our first puffs, which we inhaled, all of us coughed. We all "manned up" and thought that this coughing must be overcome in order to learn to smoke, which we wanted to do in order to appear as adults. One boy wouldn't. To this day, he never picked up the habit. But the other boy and I bore through the initial coughing and learned to smoke. Eventually, the irritation that smoking caused in my throat somehow weirdly and perversely became a pleasurable experience, which I not only tolerated but enjoyed on a level that I once described to my physician as "sexual," meaning the indulgence of the body in pleasure, akin also to eating excessively, like gluttony. The problem in all this was that the drug nicotine that is released into the body by smoking then makes the habit physically necessary. As I contemplated this situation, I thought that my mind was tricking me into thinking that smoking was good for me, i.e., provided pleasure, when, in fact, it was hurting me. Therefore, it was deceiving me. And knowledge of the deception triggered my desire to stop smoking, which I did — that day, until one unfortunate evening seven months later when the nicotine addiction crept up on me

17: THEORY OF SUPRA-SELF AND OVER-SELF

while I was not on guard against it and caught me again. But before that, every time the desire for the pleasure of smoking crept up on me, I was able to resist it because I knew that it was deceiving me into thinking that smoking was good for me, when, in fact, it was bad for me and would hurt me.

What I had developed in that moment of contemplation that day was a will to quit smoking, which worked. And it worked so effectively, I needed nothing to assist my effort, just my will, by which I do not mean will power, though, clearly, a rude determination was a part of it. But let's look at the other parts. First, there was the desire to quit. Secondly, I was able to isolate the crux of the desire to smoke, which was the pleasure in the irritation. Thirdly, I saw deception in my desire to smoke, which greatly discredited the desire. There is, in fact, a connection between those three elements, and it is called a melos. Out of the desire to quit flows the need to isolate the origin, the cause, or the need out of which the habit arises. And out of isolation of the origin of the habit flows the realization that the pleasure is coupled with a deception. And all three together comprise a will. Separately, they are something else, something less. *They are concepts.*

Consider what happened years later when I began trying again to quit my smoking habit. I remembered the three elements of my initial quitting experience that had succeeded so effortlessly: the desire to quit, specific identification of the pleasure in the irritation to the throat, and the deception by which the nicotine tricked me into smoking again and again. By themselves, none of the three concepts initiated the same effortless cessation that I had previously experienced. And the reason for the failure was simple to understand: concepts are a *copy* of the will but are not imbued with will. Upon their creation, and it is the will that creates them, they are something other than concepts insofar as they are more akin to the will itself, by which I meant they have an emotional substratum. But when the will fades, as it inevitably does, the *memory* of the pronounced elements of the will are transformed into concepts. What, then, is an idea at the moment it arises from out of the will and before it fades into concept? It is myth, of which there are two kinds: mythical being, like Self or God and anything whose nature implies the possession of undying being, and mythical gateway, like science and anything else that provides a gateway through whose passage the will becomes mobile and achieves ascendancy over an obstacle. And the difference between myth and concept is that will is present in myth and is transferrable by the myth, so that its apprehension imparts movement in the form of growth, and will is absent in concept, so that its comprehension does not impart movement.

The most important question posed by the value of myth and its ability to transfer the power of will to its beholder is how do you create myth? Clearly, if myth arises out of will, then will creates myth. And the only way to create myth is to find a way to represent or depict the will out of which the myth arises. That is what the dithyramb does: it depicts the will out of which myth arises.

Returning to my example of an effort to quit smoking, recalling the concepts of the three elements that helped me to quit did nothing to regain the will that had initially succeeded for me. What was necessary was to rebuild the will. And the first place to start was with the desire to quit, which was the fundament of the will. But the desire must extend deeply into your realm of emotions lest it be too weak a desire. From that desire, many options might arise. Or I could look for and follow the original ideas that arose initially from my first will to quit, those being the focus on the irritation as the pleasure I found in smoking along with a focus on the deception that the nicotine was tricking me into thinking that smoking was a good thing for me. But if I chose to focus on those two elements of the will, they would only be useful if I had captured sufficiently the will from which they arose, which meant reaching a certain depth within myself where the fundamental desire was itself sufficiently strong because, without the fundamental desire, the two elements of focus, the gateway myths, would lack sufficient meaning as elements of the will. In other words, if I started with just the fundamental will, provided it actually reached down into a meaningful depth, many different and entirely new options could arise. But if I went with already known and proven gateways, then, in a sense, I would be attempting to copy the will. And if I went with mere concepts, lacking any will whatsoever, then I would be attempting a copy of a copy — of the will, and a copy of a copy is totally impotent.

What Euripides did, which was fatal in his effort to communicate proto-tragedy, was to depict elements of the will but in the absence of the fundament of the will, the desire out of which the elements of will would naturally arise, thereby essentially providing a copy of the will that lacks the *essence* of the will. And what fiction writers today depict in their writing is a copy of a copy of the will, essentially concepts. And that precisely explains what Nietzsche meant in the above last two statements of his that I placed in bullets.

Dithyrambic Music Requires a Universality of Appeal

> In another direction also we see at work the power of this un-Dionysian, myth-opposing spirit, when we turn our eyes to the

prevalence of *character representation* and psychological refinement from Sophocles onwards. The character must no longer be expanded into an eternal type, but, on the contrary, must operate individually through artistic by-traits and shadings, through the nicest precision of all lines, in such a manner that the spectator is in general no longer conscious of the myth, but of the mighty nature-myth and the imitative power of the artist. Here also we observe the victory of the phenomenon over the Universal, and the delight in the particular quasi-anatomical preparation; we actually breathe the air of a theoretical world, in which scientific knowledge is valued more highly than the artistic reflection of a universal law. The movement along the line of the representation of character proceeds rapidly: while Sophocles still delineates complete characters and employs myth for their refined development, Euripides already delineates only prominent individual traits of character, which can express themselves in violent bursts of passion; in the New Attic Comedy, however, there are only masks with *one* expression: frivolous old men, duped panders, and cunning slaves in untiring repetition. Where now is the mythopoeic spirit of music? What is still left now of music is either excitatory music or

17: THEORY OF SUPRA-SELF AND OVER-SELF

> souvenir music, that is, either a stimulant for dull and used-up nerves, or tone-painting. As regards the former, it hardly matters about the text set to it: the heroes and choruses of Euripides are already dissolute enough when once they begin to sing; to what pass must things have come with his brazen successors?

Nietzsche now moves to an analysis of modern literature and specifically modern tragedy, by which he means a theatrical spectacle in contrast with the original proto-tragedy that was an inner, spiritual phenomenon that enabled a process of growth. And his analysis reveals the effects of Socrates' scientific mode of thinking on the form that eventually developed, with some developments intentional and some consequential.

- "... we turn our eyes to the prevalence of *character representation* and psychological refinement from Sophocles onwards. The character must no longer be expanded into an eternal type...."

In *Thus Spoke Zarathustra*, the first thing we read, in the dedication, is that the book is for "everyone" but not for any individual, which means that anyone can find their Self in the drama but no one will find their Ego, the difference being a depiction of what is universally applicable and relevant to all of human nature in contrast with a particular idiosyncratic or peculiar individual nature. In this sense, the dithyramb is a depiction of a universal type. After the demise of dithyrambic drama, the focus is moved onto a sharply defined and particular type of human nature, not a universal type.

- "Where now is the mythopoeic spirit of music?"

Mythopoeia, which is the fundamental aim of dithyrambic drama, is categorically precluded by the presence of a particular type and the absence of a universal type because embodiment of the will that is present in "music," or actuality, is no longer a possibility; there is nothing to embody. And it is strictly out of will, out of "music," that mythopoeia rises. Without will, there is no mythopoeia. Without the *need* for an idea through which the will can overcome an obstacle, there simply will not arise any idea.

> The new un-Dionysian spirit, however, manifests itself most clearly in the *dénouements* of the new dramas. In the Old Tragedy one could feel at the close the metaphysical comfort, without which the delight in tragedy cannot be explained at all; the conciliating tones from another world sound purest, perhaps, in the Œdipus at Colonus. Now that the genius of music has fled from tragedy, tragedy is, strictly speaking, dead: for from whence could one now draw the metaphysical comfort? One sought, therefore, for an earthly unravelment of the tragic dissonance; the hero, after he had been sufficiently tortured by fate, reaped a well-deserved reward through a superb marriage or divine tokens of favour. The hero had turned gladiator, on whom, after being liberally battered about and covered with wounds, freedom was

occasionally bestowed. The *deus ex machina* took the place of metaphysical comfort. I will not say that the tragic view of things was everywhere completely destroyed by the intruding spirit of the un-Dionysian: we only know that it was compelled to flee from art into the underworld as it were, in the degenerate form of a secret cult. Over the widest extent of the Hellenic character, however, there raged the consuming blast of this spirit, which manifests itself in the form of "Greek cheerfulness," which we have already spoken of as a senile, unproductive love of existence; this cheerfulness is the counterpart of the splendid "naïveté" of the earlier Greeks, which, according to the characteristic indicated above, must be conceived as the blossom of the Apollonian culture growing out of a dark abyss, as the victory which the Hellenic will, through its mirroring of beauty, obtains over suffering and the wisdom of suffering. The noblest manifestation of that other form of "Greek cheerfulness," the Alexandrine, is the cheerfulness of the *theoretical man*: it exhibits the same symptomatic characteristics as I have just inferred concerning the spirit of the un-Dionysian:—it combats Dionysian wisdom and art, it seeks to dissolve myth, it substitutes for metaphysical comfort an

> earthly consonance, in fact, a *deus ex machina* of its own, namely the god of machines and crucibles, that is, the powers of the genii of nature recognised and employed in the service of higher egoism; it believes in amending the world by knowledge, in guiding life by science, and that it can really confine the individual within a narrow sphere of solvable problems, where he cheerfully says to life: "I desire thee: it is worth while to know thee."

- "The new un-Dionysian spirit, however, manifests itself most clearly in the *dénouements* of the new dramas."

- "The *deus ex machina* took the place of metaphysical comfort."

Aside from the value of mythopoeia that proto-tragedy imparts to its *participant*, proto-tragedy also provides a comfort in the form of a reunion with "Oneness," or, as Nietzsche put it, "an overwhelming feeling of oneness, which leads back to the heart of nature" and, as I put it, a reunification with one's higher Self and one's deeper feelings, But the new tragedy, under the influence of scientific thought, provides a thoroughly non-participatory spectacle, and it is a spectacle that sparkles and delights its spectator in the form of plot twists, which are referenced here as denouements and deus ex machina. Clearly, the difference is that between a rich, meaningful, and redemptive experience and, by comparison, a more impoverished and entirely cerebral non-experience. But how is this difference manifested by science? It is manifest in the focus on detail and knowledge of the detail, which has achieved an ascendency over the ethereal, the universal, the generalized, all of which are inherent in myth and "music."

18: Theoretical Man vs. Tragic Man

Art as the Enabler of Will

It is an eternal phenomenon: the avidious will can always, by means of an illusion spread over things, detain its creatures in life and compel them to live on. One is chained by the Socratic love of knowledge and the vain hope of being able thereby to heal the eternal wound of existence; another is ensnared by art's seductive veil of beauty fluttering before his eyes; still another by the metaphysical comfort that eternal life flows on indestructibly beneath the whirl of phenomena: to say nothing of the more ordinary and almost more powerful illusions which the will has always at hand. These three specimens of illusion are on the whole designed only for the more nobly endowed natures, who in general feel profoundly the weight and burden of existence, and must be deluded into forgetfulness of their displeasure by

> exquisite stimulants. All that we call culture is made up of these stimulants; and, according to the proportion of the ingredients, we have either a specially *Socratic* or *artistic* or *tragic culture*: or, if historical exemplifications are wanted, there is either an Alexandrine or a Hellenic or a Buddhistic culture.

- "… the avidious will can always, by means of an illusion spread over things, detain its creatures in life and compel them to live on."

What is important to note here is that the forward movement of the will is the fundamental phenomenon in life, both as a process of growth and as a process of maintenance. Obstacles that prevent the forward movement of the will abound and are ubiquitous. Pain is the sensation that arises in the face of those obstacles. Pleasure is the sensation that arises in the overcoming of those obstacles. And fear is the sensation that arises in the absence of will when a situation requires will. Thus, overcoming obstacles is as fundamental as is the existence of the will. The question then is what happens in those situations where the forward movement of the will is categorically impossible. And the answer is art. Art happens. Art makes life possible. And the successful forward movement of the will justifies the efforts that go into the numerous creations of art. And two of those artistic creations are idea and myth, both of which are entirely fictive, which means they do not exist in actuality. They exist only within reality and only as illusory creations of art that cast a veil of illusion over all phenomena that then constitute reality. And the most powerful illusion is that of being, which we call Self, and which is totally non-existent in actuality. Another illusion is the foundation of that mode of thought that we call science. According to Nietzsche, the illusions out of which science arises is the illusion that actuality is knowable and alterable. And the fact that man has travelled to the moon and split the atom does not refute the illusoriness on which science is founded; rather, it affirms the quality of the illusions.

- "One is chained by the Socratic love of knowledge and the vain hope of being able thereby to heal the eternal wound of existence; another is ensnared by art's seductive veil of beauty fluttering before his eyes; still another by the metaphysical comfort that eternal life flows on indestructibly beneath the whirl of phenomena...."

- "All that we call culture is made up of these stimulants...."

By "stimulants," he means illusions that make life possible and worth living, especially in the face of insuperable obstacles.

- "... according to the proportion of the ingredients, we have either a specially *Socratic* or *artistic* or *tragic culture*: or, if historical exemplifications are wanted, there is either an Alexandrine or a Hellenic or a Buddhistic culture."

18: THEORETICAL MAN VS. TRAGIC MAN
An Assessment of Western Culture in the 21ˢᵗ Century

The most fundamental myths and ideas give rise to a mode of thought, and it is that mode of thought that also constitutes that which we call culture. In our time, we are witness to a scientific culture, a culture steeped in a love of knowledge of the world's phenomena for no other reason than possession of that knowledge, which he also calls Alexandrine, a culture steeped in beautiful forms of art, which he also calls Hellenic, and a tragic culture steeped in the metaphysical comfort that is imparted by the wisdom that the best existence is not that which is already existing or about to come into existence but rather in that universal and primordial substratum that exists beyond all appearances and out of which new existences arise and come into being, which is actuality, wherein the will is unbounded by individuation, not reality, wherein limits and boundaries are strictly enforced. To put it another way, there is in our midst today, three types of culture: a way of thinking that takes delight in that which already exists, another that takes delight in creating things and bringing them into existence, and a third that delights in the creation of new and better existences precisely and directly out of the destruction of already existing things. Or, to put it even simpler still, there are men who will find unending delight with their first discovery of Self and will look no further for a deeper Self. Others will suffice to find pleasurable distractions in place of their Self, such as those who delight in losing themselves in their work. And there are others still who will find delight not in the discovery of Self but in the discovery of deeper Self, though they are rare. And rarest of all, there are those who will find delight in that which exists beyond the deepest and highest idea and sense of Self, in that realm where all that exists is unbounded will, that which we call genius. Those rarest of human beings delight not in the vision of Self but in the freedom of will.

Lastly, we must note that he labels the culture that produces "tragic man" as a Buddhistic culture, and that makes no sense because, elsewhere in his writing, he characterizes Buddhistic culture as that of tragic resignation in the likeness described and understood by Schopenhauer, from which Nietzsche himself diverted sharply. Instead, the tragic culture that Nietzsche envisioned and went on to found with his dithyrambic drama was that which produced the mode of thought that sought the freedom of the will beyond all visions of Self, the supra-Self and ultimately the over-Self, which is far from a resigned view of life. And there is controversy in this characterization, wherein, in a revised edition, Nietzsche crossed out the word "Buddhistic."

Theoretical vs. Tragic Man in Modern Western Culture

> Our whole modern world is entangled in the meshes of Alexandrine culture, and recognises as its ideal the *theorist* equipped with the most potent means of knowledge, and labouring in the service of science, of whom the archetype and progenitor is Socrates. All our educational methods have originally this ideal in view: every other form of existence must struggle onwards wearisomely beside it, as something tolerated, but not intended. In an almost alarming manner the cultured man was here

found for a long time only in the form of the scholar: even our poetical arts have been forced to evolve from learned imitations, and in the main effect of the rhyme we still recognise the origin of our poetic form from artistic experiments with a non-native and thoroughly learned language. How unintelligible must *Faust,* the modern cultured man, who is in himself intelligible, have appeared to a true Greek,—Faust, storming discontentedly through all the faculties, devoted to magic and the devil from a desire for knowledge, whom we have only to place alongside of Socrates for the purpose of comparison, in order to see that modern man begins to divine the boundaries of this Socratic love of perception and longs for a coast in the wide waste of the ocean of knowledge. When Goethe on one occasion said to Eckermann with reference to Napoleon: "Yes, my good friend, there is also a productiveness of deeds," he reminded us in a charmingly naïve manner that the non-theorist is something incredible and astounding to modern man; so that the wisdom of Goethe is needed once more in order to discover that such a surprising form of existence is comprehensible, nay even pardonable.

And science is most definitely a culture in which other manifestations of life, like art, must struggle to exist. Notice also that he labels the man who subscribes to a mode of scientific thought as "theoretical man" because he will contrast this specimen of human nature with another that he will call "tragic man." He also contrasts theoretical man with the man of great deed, like Napoleon and Caesar, who achieved much in the way of action rather than in the way of theory and the advancement of knowledge.

> Now, we must not hide from ourselves what is concealed in the heart of this Socratic culture: Optimism, deeming itself absolute! Well, we must not be alarmed if the fruits of this optimism ripen,—if society, leavened to the very lowest strata by this kind of culture, gradually begins to tremble through wanton agitations and desires, if the belief in the earthly happiness of all, if the belief in the possibility of such a general intellectual culture is gradually transformed into the threatening demand for such an Alexandrine earthly happiness, into the conjuring of a Euripidean *deus ex machina*. Let us mark this well: the Alexandrine culture requires a slave class, to be able to exist permanently: but, in its optimistic view of life, it denies the necessity of such a class, and consequently, when the effect of its beautifully seductive and tranquillising utterances about the "dignity of man" and the "dignity of labour" is spent, it gradually drifts towards a dreadful destination. There is nothing more

18: Theoretical Man vs. Tragic Man

> terrible than a barbaric slave class, who have learned to regard their existence as an injustice, and now prepare to take vengeance, not only for themselves, but for all generations. In the face of such threatening storms, who dares to appeal with confident spirit to our pale and exhausted religions, which even in their foundations have degenerated into scholastic religions?—so that myth, the necessary prerequisite of every religion, is already paralysed everywhere, and even in this domain the optimistic spirit—which we have just designated as the annihilating germ of society—has attained the mastery.

- "Now, we must not hide from ourselves what is concealed in the heart of this Socratic culture: Optimism, deeming itself absolute!"

Science and Democracy are Doomed by their Requirement for a Slave Class

What is most interesting about this statement is that it attributes democratic ideals not to democracy but to the optimism inherent in science, which aims to establish, in addition to love of knowledge and specifically appearance, also an earthly happiness for all and good fortune arising out of a veritable deus ex machina, no doubt produced by science, for perhaps life's most difficult moments.

- "Let us mark this well: the Alexandrine culture requires a slave class, to be able to exist permanently: but, in its optimistic view of life, it denies the necessity of such a class, and consequently, when the effect of its beautifully seductive and tranquillising utterances about the "dignity of man" and the "dignity of labour" is spent, it gradually drifts towards a dreadful destination."

In other words, Alexandrine culture is doomed by the necessity for maintenance of a slave class and its inherently "happiness for all" culture.

Only Religion can Spare Impending Doom, but Science Precludes Religion

- "In the face of such threatening storms, who dares to appeal with confident spirit to our pale and exhausted religions, which even in their foundations have degenerated into scholastic religions? "

And in this doom, religion is precluded from playing a healing role because, under the influence of science, religion has devolved into an enfeebled rote dogma that is steeped in historical legitimacy but has been stripped of myth, which is the only healing power afforded by religion. When the will comes upon a truly insuperable chasm, religion performs miracles by providing it with flight. And it is myth that imparts the flight. Without myth, religion limps along most effetely, almost like a mere decoration of culture.

18: THEORETICAL MAN VS. TRAGIC MAN

Nietzsche Predicts the Demise of Science and the Advent of Tragedy

While the evil slumbering in the heart of theoretical culture gradually begins to disquiet modern man, and makes him anxiously ransack the stores of his experience for means to avert the danger, though not believing very much in these means; while he, therefore, begins to divine the consequences his position involves: great, universally gifted natures have contrived, with an incredible amount of thought, to make use of the apparatus of science itself, in order to point out the limits and the relativity of knowledge generally, and thus definitely to deny the claim of science to universal validity and universal ends: with which demonstration the illusory notion was for the first time recognised as such, which pretends, with the aid of causality, to be able to fathom the innermost essence of things. The extraordinary courage and wisdom of *Kant* and *Schopenhauer* have succeeded in gaining the most, difficult, victory, the victory over the optimism hidden in the essence of logic, which optimism in turn is the basis of our culture. While this optimism, resting on apparently unobjectionable *æterna veritates,* believed in the intelligibility and solvability of all the riddles of the world, and treated space, time, and causality as totally unconditioned laws of the most universal validity, Kant, on the other hand, showed that these served in reality only to elevate the mere phenomenon, the work of Mâyâ, to the sole and highest reality, putting it in place of the innermost and true essence of things, thus making the actual knowledge of this essence impossible, that is, according to the expression of Schopenhauer, to lull the dreamer still more soundly asleep (*Welt als Wille und Vorstellung,* I. 498). With this knowledge a culture is inaugurated which I venture to designate as a tragic culture; the most important characteristic of which is that wisdom takes the place of science as the highest end,—wisdom, which, uninfluenced by the seductive distractions of the sciences, turns with unmoved eye to the comprehensive view of the world, and seeks to apprehend therein the eternal suffering as its own with sympathetic feelings of love. Let us imagine a rising generation with this undauntedness of vision, with this heroic desire for the prodigious, let us imagine the bold step of these dragon-slayers, the proud and daring spirit with which they turn their backs on all the effeminate doctrines of optimism in order "to live resolutely" in the Whole and in the Full: would it not be necessary for the tragic man of this culture,

> with his self-discipline to earnestness and terror, to desire a new art, the art of metaphysical comfort,—namely, tragedy, as the Hellena belonging to him, and that he should exclaim with Faust:
> Und sollt' ich nicht, sehnsüchtigster Gewalt,
> In's Leben ziehn die einzigste Gestalt?[23]

In this paragraph, he is predicting the demise of the Alexandrine culture that is founded on science, which is the culture we have lived through for the last two millennia. And he predicts its demise precisely via the illogic that is drawn from the conclusions of its founding myth, which is a gateway myth: that the riddles existing in actuality are ultimately solvable and the misfortunes arising out of actuality are fixable, or, as he puts it, "... the illusory notion ... which pretends, with the aid of causality, to be able to fathom the innermost essence of things."

Science Mistakenly Enshrines Actuality Under Veil of Reality

He also points to the will-saving and will-invigorating optimism that is imparted by science, which is a fundamental optimism that validates the gateway myth that is science as a viable myth insofar as it, in turn, validates a viable mode of thought. And he points to that optimism arising from the seemingly irrefutable and eternal belief that all phenomena are ultimately intelligible and solvable, which is an illusion that

---

[23] Cf. Introduction, p. 14.

succeeds by placing the veil of Maya, the illusion of reality, like a cloak over all phenomena arising out of actuality.

- "While this optimism, resting on apparently unobjectionable *æterna veritates,* believed in the intelligibility and solvability of all the riddles of the world, and treated space, time, and causality as totally unconditioned laws of the most universal validity, Kant, on the other hand, showed that these served in reality only to elevate the mere phenomenon, the work of Mâyâ, to the sole and highest reality, putting it in place of the innermost and true essence of things, thus making the actual knowledge of this essence impossible, that is, according to the expression of Schopenhauer, to lull the dreamer still more soundly asleep (*Welt als Wille und Vorstellung,* I. 498). "

In other words, science has mishandled actuality by lending it an appearance of reality, which *fixed* appearance then precludes access to the "music," the will that drives actuality, as if by drawing a horizon around it and enclosing it. And it is only an understanding of that will that lies beyond the horizon, that enclosure, which would then lead to an understanding of the phenomena arising from within it. Science enshrines itself in reality and thereby precludes itself from both actuality and an understanding of that which drives actuality, the will.

- "With this knowledge a culture is inaugurated which I venture to designate as a tragic culture; the most important characteristic of which is that wisdom takes the place of science as the highest end...."

18: THEORETICAL MAN VS. TRAGIC MAN
Science as a Detriment to Healing Culture

Knowledge of these limitations of science necessarily leads to a collapse of the scientific mode of thought, which makes the knowledge tragic. And in every true tragedy, by which I mean not a modern, theatrical tragedy but rather an inner, enlightening rite of passage, meaningful and ameliorative redemption always follows. And what is the good that might come from the end of the scientific culture? Certainly, a production of genius will follow, which science has long pretended to aim for but failed to produce, but, most importantly, a genius of deed as much as a genius of knowledge. And no ordinary genius of knowledge! But a genius of knowledge who possesses wisdom and has the ability to discern that knowledge which is good for life and will assist life, unlike the scientist who lacks any taste for knowledge and simply seeks and devours it anywhere it is to be found, thereby often producing results that are a detriment to life, which modern man has begun to notice.

And what is the difference between wisdom and scientific knowledge? Wisdom takes into consideration the contradictions inherent in actuality, specifically its pain, while science considers only the appearance, the Apollonian side, which it renders as reality, an entirely cerebral and one-sided aspect of actuality. That is the difference. By and large, science equates the world with concept. Wisdom adds emotion to the equation. And emotion that is truly considered imparts invaluable knowledge about actuality.

Nietzsche's Use of the Phrase "Metaphysical Comfort"

- "Let us imagine a rising generation with this undauntedness of vision, with this heroic desire for the prodigious, let us imagine the bold step of these dragon-slayers, the proud and daring spirit with which they turn their backs on all the effeminate doctrines of optimism in order "to live resolutely" in the Whole and in the Full: would it not be necessary for the tragic man of this culture, with his self-discipline to earnestness and terror, to desire a new art, the art of metaphysical comfort,—namely, tragedy, as the Hellena belonging to him, and that he should exclaim with Faust: "

- "Und sollt' ich nicht, sehnsüchtigster Gewalt, In's Leben ziehn die einzigste Gestalt? "
  - "And shall not I, by mightiest desire, In living shape that sole fair form acquire? SWANWICK, trans. of *Faust*. "

Lastly, what I wish to point out most assiduously here is that Nietzsche, in this very early essay in his life, is moving to declare the aim of his life's work, which is the inauguration of a new culture to replace the Socratic culture that has finally, perhaps, run its course over the last two millennia. Of this new culture, which is the tragic culture, there is no doubt that he succeeded with its inauguration in the practice of dithyrambic drama, which is an idea to which I devoted an entire book, *The Birth of Dionysia*.

18: THEORETICAL MAN VS. TRAGIC MAN

In the above citation, when he says "Let us imagine a rising generation" resolving to live "in the Whole and in the Full," he is speaking of his "tragic man," a man born of the culture he seeks to initiate, who resolves in his heart to brave the horrors and the terrors of the subconscious realm, the Dionysian realm of emotion (the Whole and not only the dismembered parts), and to bring that which he finds *fully* into the light, into "reality," the dominion of Self, and who finds comfort not in that which distracts him from his inner Self, not in that which deludes him from his inner Self, and certainly not in that which provides escape into an otherworldly realm of entirely cerebral and ameliorative reflection and contemplation. Rather, he is speaking of the tragic man who embraces his "dark side" and then redeems it, and, in that redemption, finds a more earthly comfort, a more realistic comfort, a more tragic comfort in a sense of Self whose feelings have been colorized by illusory reality, and by that colorization made bearable.

Notice also that he quotes Faust. And he uses the same quote in the preface, but, in that other instance, he means something else entirely. And the difference can be difficult to discern leading some to think that Nietzsche contradicts himself. Therefore, we need to dissect this issue carefully.

He is clearly talking here about tragic man, in contrast with theoretical man, when he says that tragic man might say about tragedy, as a new form of art toward which he might aspire, that he would aspire to the beauty that is revealed in "Oneness with the Primal Being," which is actuality beyond the limits of percipience that is set by individuation, with a mighty desire in hopes of attaining that Oneness in the same way that an ancient Greek aspired to the beauty of the goddess Helene.

In the preface, he uses the same quote to mean something else entirely, about which I wrote extensively in *The Birth of*

Dionysia, specifically in my rendition of Zarathustra's Prologue. And, most importantly, he uses it in the same context in which he uses it in the above instance, which is the what causes the confusion about his meaning.

As it turns out, the confusion actually arises out of his use of the phrase "metaphysical comfort," which he uses to mean two completely different things. In another instance within the essay, he says:

> The metaphysical comfort,—with which, as I have here intimated, every true tragedy dismisses us—that, in spite of the perpetual change of phenomena, life at bottom is indestructibly powerful and pleasurable, this comfort appears with corporeal lucidity as the satyric chorus, as the chorus of natural beings, who live ineradicable as it were behind all civilisation, and who, in spite of the ceaseless change of generations and the history of nations, remain for ever the same.

In this instance, by "metaphysical comfort," he states explicitly what he means: that, in spite of the appearance and subsequent destruction of beautiful appearance, precisely as we see in the mythopoeic creation of Self, followed by the creation of the supra-Self in the wake of its destruction, "life at bottom is indestructibly powerful and pleasurable" *in the will more so than in appearances ...* and "this comfort appears with corporeal lucidity as the satiric chorus." And I have already reiterated how Nietzsche found music in the tragic chorus, with music being actuality or will. Thus, in this later reference in the same essay, he uses the phrase "metaphysical comfort" to mean

18: THEORETICAL MAN VS. TRAGIC MAN

the rare wisdom that tragedy derives more pleasure from the destruction of Self and the resultant rise of a stronger will in that destruction than it does from the creation of beauty in the vision of Self. The "metaphysical comfort" is in that wisdom.

But when he uses the phrase "metaphysical comfort" in the preface, he means something else entirely. He means "metaphysical comfort" as the theoretical man, the man who is driven by Ego instead of Self, means it. And the man who is driven by Ego instead of Self understands "metaphysical comfort" as appearance through and through.

In section 7 of the preface, he speaks of how a person who subscribes to the scientific way of thinking might misunderstand his essay about the birth of tragedy. "But, my dear Sir, if your book is not Romanticism, what in the world is?"

> Hear, yourself, my dear Sir Pessimist [as if the reader is speaking to Nietzsche himself] and art-deifier, with ever so unlocked ears, a single select passage of your own book [*The Birth of Tragedy*], that not ineloquent dragon-slayer passage, which may sound insidiously rat-charming to young ears and hearts. What? is not that the true blue romanticist-confession of 1830 under the mask of the pessimism of 1850? After which, of course, the usual romanticist finale at once strikes up,—rupture, collapse, return and prostration before an old belief, before the old God.... What? is not your pessimist book itself a piece of anti-Hellenism and Romanticism, something "equally intoxicating and befogging," a

> narcotic at all events, ay, a piece of music, of German music?

And then, immediately after this question, follows the dragon-slayer quote.

> Let us imagine a rising generation with this undauntedness of vision, with this heroic impulse towards the prodigious, let us imagine the bold step of these dragon-slayers, the proud daring with which they turn their backs on all the effeminate doctrines of optimism, in order "to live resolutely" in the Whole and in the Full: would it not be necessary for the tragic man of this culture, with his self-discipline to earnestness and terror, to desire a new art, the art of metaphysical comfort, tragedy as the Helena belonging to him, and that he should exclaim with Faust:
> "Und sollt ich nicht, sehnsüchtigster Gewalt,
> In's Leben ziehn die einzigste Gestalt?"
> " And shall not I, by mightiest desire,
> In living shape that sole fair form acquire?
> SWANWICK, trans. of *Faust*.[24]

To which Nietzsche answers with the hypothetical question by a Romanticist, a theoretical man, with the following:

---

[24] Cf. Introduction, p. 14.

18: THEORETICAL MAN VS. TRAGIC MAN

> "Would it not be necessary?" ... No, thrice no! ye young romanticists: it would not be necessary! But it is very probable, that things may end thus, that ye may end thus, namely "comforted," as it is written, in spite of all self-discipline to earnestness and terror; metaphysically comforted, in short, as Romanticists are wont to end, as Christians.... No! ye should first of all learn the art of earthly comfort, ye should learn to laugh, my young friends, if ye are at all determined to remain pessimists: if so, you will perhaps, as laughing ones, eventually send all metaphysical comfortism to the devil—and metaphysics first of all!

Please take notice in the above quote that his use of the phrase "earthly comfort," which is a comfort to the tragic man, not the theoretical man, is precisely what he meant by his use of the phrase "metaphysical comfort" in every other instance within the essay. He meant the comfort that derives from the brilliant Apollonian vision of supra-Self that arises as mythopoeia but only after achieving a deep gaze into the abyss that resides within the subliminal suffering of the subconscious, so that the resultant vision reverberates will. In contrast to that "earthly comfort," the theoretical man subscribes to an entirely cerebral comfort, born wholly out of a dismembered egotism, which, in this case, goes to the theory of the Identity of Thought and Being, about which you can read extensively in *The Birth of Dionysia*. And it is this cerebral and dismembered "metaphysical comfort" from which Nietzsche dissuades the reader and categorically devalues in Zarathustra's Prologue.

Nietzsche Writes an Obituary for Science

But now that the Socratic culture has been shaken from two directions, and is only able to hold the sceptre of its infallibility with trembling hands,—once by the fear of its own conclusions which it at length begins to surmise, and again, because it is no longer convinced with its former naïve trust of the eternal validity of its foundation, —it is a sad spectacle to behold how the dance of its thought always rushes longingly on new forms, to embrace them, and then, shuddering, lets them go of a sudden, as Mephistopheles does the seductive Lamiæ. It is certainly the symptom of the "breach" which all are wont to speak of as the primordial suffering of modern culture that the theoretical man, alarmed and dissatisfied at his own conclusions, no longer dares to entrust himself to the terrible ice-stream of existence: he runs timidly up and down the bank. He no longer wants to have anything entire, with all the natural cruelty of things, so thoroughly has he been spoiled by his optimistic contemplation. Besides, he feels that a culture built up on the principles of science must perish when it begins to grow *illogical,* that is, to avoid its own conclusions. Our art reveals this universal trouble: in vain does one seek help by imitating all the great productive periods

18: THEORETICAL MAN VS. TRAGIC MAN

> and natures, in vain does one accumulate the entire "world-literature" around modern man for his comfort, in vain does one place one's self in the midst of the art-styles and artists of all ages, so that one may give names to them as Adam did to the beasts: one still continues the eternal hungerer, the "critic" without joy and energy, the Alexandrine man, who is in the main a librarian and corrector of proofs, and who, pitiable wretch goes blind from the dust of books and printers' errors.

I could reiterate this as a dismal obituary of Socratic culture, but I think Nietzsche says it best, so I will let it stand on its own: "Alexandrine man, who is in the main a librarian and corrector of proofs, and who, pitiable wretch goes blind from the dust of books and printers' errors."

19: The Failure of Opera in Modern Tragedy

Let me state at the outset that this particular chapter is bare of useful insights. It is essentially a critique of opera as an art form, especially as an art form that failed tragedy, that is produced by the scientific mode of thought.

> We cannot designate the intrinsic substance of Socratic culture more distinctly than by calling it *the culture of the opera*: for it is in this department that culture has expressed itself with special naïveté concerning its aims and perceptions, which is sufficiently surprising when we compare the genesis of the opera and the facts of operatic development with the eternal truths of the Apollonian and Dionysian. I call to mind first of all the origin of the *stilo rappresentativo* and the recitative. Is it credible that this thoroughly externalised operatic music, incapable of devotion, could be received and cherished with enthusiastic favour, as a re-birth, as it were, of all true music, by the very age in which the

> ineffably sublime and sacred music of Palestrina had originated? And who, on the other hand, would think of making only the diversion-craving luxuriousness of those Florentine circles and the vanity of their dramatic singers responsible for the love of the opera which spread with such rapidity? That in the same age, even among the same people, this passion for a half-musical mode of speech should awaken alongside of the vaulted structure of Palestrine harmonies which the entire Christian Middle Age had been building up, I can explain to myself only by a co-operating *extra-artistic tendency* in the essence of the recitative.

Opera Is an Invention of Science

He notes opera as an art form that reveals the intrinsic substance of Socratic or Alexandrine culture, the present-day culture that is founded on the scientific or logical mode of thought and aims to cultivate a breed of human nature that he calls "theoretical man." And he particularly notes the stilo rappresentativo, in which speech is dramatized and made passionate by giving it an intermittently musical form rather than a merely spoken form, as most revealing insofar as he finds in it a well-fitting but totally inartistic element.

Opera Focuses on Speech and Concept

> The listener, who insists on distinctly hearing the words under the music, has his wishes met by the singer in that he speaks rather than sings, and intensifies the pathetic expression of the words in this half-song: by this intensification of the pathos he facilitates the understanding of the words and surmounts the remaining half of the music.

In opera, he contends, there is an insistence on a distinct and clear pronunciation of words, which must never be drowned out by music.

> The specific danger which now threatens him is that in some unguarded moment he may give undue importance to music, which would forthwith result in the destruction of the pathos of the speech and the distinctness of the words: while, on the other hand, he always feels himself impelled to musical delivery and to virtuose exhibition of vocal talent.

The problem with this insistence and the resulting pronouncement of speech is that the speaker may himself be overrun by the music and therefore distort his speech

> Here the "poet" comes to his aid, who knows how to provide him with abundant opportunities for lyrical interjections,

> repetitions of words and sentences, etc.,—at which places the singer, now in the purely musical element, can rest himself without minding the words.

Poetry assists the speaker who must remain faithful to speech even in the midst of passionate music with the aid of alliteration, which lends a spirit of music while still maintaining speech.

In Opera, the Combination of Concept and Music Is Unnatural

> This alternation of emotionally impressive, yet only half-sung speech and wholly sung interjections, which is characteristic of the *stilo rappresentativo,* this rapidly changing endeavour to operate now on the conceptional and representative faculty of the hearer, now on his musical sense, is something so thoroughly unnatural and withal so intrinsically contradictory both to the Apollonian and Dionysian artistic impulses, that one has to infer an origin of the recitative foreign to all artistic instincts.

As a consequence of presenting the listener with clear speech on the one hand and passionate music on the other, the listener is at one time forced to work his ability for conceptual thought and at another time his intuitive reception of immediately comprehensible music that requires no thought whatsoever. And in that admixture of conception, which requires thought, and intuition, which requires feeling, Nietzsche sees something most unnatural. However, keep in mind, that in the dithyramb, there is also an admixture of intuition and idea or vision, though not concept, but there is no rapid back and forth between the two modes of representation. Instead, there are long periods of rendering gesticulative metaphors followed by periods of willful embodiments and then, separately, long periods of visionariness and ideation. Concept happens, but it is very ancillary, not primary the way idea and vision are. But in opera, Nietzsche argues, the rapid back and forth of conception and intuition is an abomination of the artistic process. One might argue that the facial gestures presented by the speaking singer and representation of emotion or will in those gestures might present a style of representation that is agreeable with the musical representation, but, in opera, the emphasis is distinctly put upon the spoken word. The listener is pressed to hear the words and conceive their meaning. The emphasis is put on conception, not necessarily on intuitive rendition of facial gestures.

> The recitative must be defined, according to this description, as the combination of epic and lyric delivery, not indeed as an intrinsically stable combination which could not be attained in the case of such totally disparate elements, but an entirely superficial mosaic conglutination, such as is totally unprecedented in the domain of nature and experience.

In other words, in epic poetry, we have the presentation of imagery and concept. And in lyrical poetry, we have the

19: THE FAILURE OF OPERA IN MODERN TRAGEDY

presentation of passion. But in opera, we have the presentation of both, at the same time, much like a forced admixture that is unnatural, which has never happened before.

> *But this was not the opinion of the inventors of the recitative:* they themselves, and their age with them, believed rather that the mystery of antique music had been solved by this *stilo rappresentativo,* in which, as they thought, the only explanation of the enormous influence of an Orpheus, an Amphion, and even of Greek tragedy was to be found. The new style was regarded by them as the re-awakening of the most effective music, the Old Greek music: indeed, with the universal and popular conception of the Homeric world *as the primitive world,* they could abandon themselves to the dream of having descended once more into the paradisiac beginnings of mankind, wherein music also must needs have had the unsurpassed purity, power, and innocence of which the poets could give such touching accounts in their pastoral plays.

With opera, people believed they had solved the mystery of ancient music and recaptured the power of ancient music with which they could then also regain the primitive and paradisiacal beginning of civilization.

Here we see into the internal process of development of this thoroughly modern variety of art, the opera: a powerful need here acquires an art, but it is a need of an unæsthetic kind: the yearning for the idyll, the belief in the prehistoric existence of the artistic, good man. The recitative was regarded as the rediscovered language of this primitive man; the opera as the recovered land of this idyllically or heroically good creature, who in every action follows at the same time a natural artistic impulse, who sings a little along with all he has to say, in order to sing immediately with full voice on the slightest emotional excitement. It is now a matter of indifference to us that the humanists of those days combated the old ecclesiastical representation of man as naturally corrupt and lost, with this new-created picture of the paradisiac artist: so that opera may be understood as the oppositional dogma of the good man, whereby however a solace was at the same time found for the pessimism to which precisely the seriously-disposed men of that time were most strongly incited, owing to the frightful uncertainty of all conditions of life. It is enough to have perceived that the intrinsic charm, and therefore the genesis, of this new form of art lies in the gratification of an altogether unæsthetic need, in the optimistic

19: THE FAILURE OF OPERA IN MODERN TRAGEDY

> glorification of man as such, in the conception of the primitive man as the man naturally good and artistic: a principle of the opera which has gradually changed into a threatening and terrible *demand,* which, in face of the socialistic movements of the present time, we can no longer ignore. The "good primitive man" wants his rights: what paradisiac prospects!

In opera, Nietzsche sees the glorification of the "good primitive man" as the originator of opera.

> I here place by way of parallel still another equally obvious confirmation of my view that opera is built up on the same principles as our Alexandrine culture. Opera is the birth of the theoretical man, of the critical layman, not of the artist: one of the most surprising facts in the whole history of art.

Nietzsche sees opera as an invention of theoretical man, the man who subscribes to the scientific mode of thought, who, when it comes to art, is only a layman, not an artist.

> It was the demand of thoroughly unmusical hearers that the words must above all be understood, so that according to them a rebirth of music is only to be expected when some mode of singing has been discovered in which the text-word lords over the counterpoint as the master over the servant. For the words, it is argued, are as much

> nobler than the accompanying harmonic system as the soul is nobler than the body.

And the theoretical layman who invented opera saw more value in the spoken word than in the music. For such a theoretical layman, the value and power of ancient music lay in the words spoken in the drama, provided those words were properly and successfully interlaced with the accompanying music while maintaining their supremacy over the music.

In Opera, Theoretical Man Claims a Pretense of Culture

> It was in accordance with the laically unmusical crudeness of these views that the combination of music, picture and expression was effected in the beginnings of the opera: in the spirit of this æsthetics the first experiments were also made in the leading laic circles of Florence by the poets and singers patronised there. The man incapable of art creates for himself a species of art precisely because he is the inartistic man as such. Because he does not divine the Dionysian depth of music, he changes his musical taste into appreciation of the understandable word-and-tone-rhetoric of the passions in the *stilo rappresentativo,* and into the voluptuousness of the arts of song; because he is unable to behold a vision, he forces the machinist and the decorative artist into his

19: THE FAILURE OF OPERA IN MODERN TRAGEDY

> service; because he cannot apprehend the true nature of the artist, he conjures up the "artistic primitive man" to suit his taste, that is, the man who sings and recites verses under the influence of passion. He dreams himself into a time when passion suffices to generate songs and poems: as if emotion had ever been able to create anything artistic. The postulate of the opera is a false belief concerning the artistic process, in fact, the idyllic belief that every sentient man is an artist. In the sense of this belief, opera is the expression of the taste of the laity in art, who dictate their laws with the cheerful optimism of the theorist.

- "The man incapable of art creates for himself a species of art precisely because he is the inartistic man as such."

He deems theoretical man to be incapable of art and, as such, theoretical man invented an art form, specifically opera. But for what reason? To pretend that he was cultured?

- "Because he does not divine the Dionysian depth of music, he changes his musical taste into appreciation of the understandable word-and-tone-rhetoric of the passions in the *stilo rappresentativo,* and into the voluptuousness of the arts of song...."

With "Dionysian depth of music," he is referring to the depth of the will. And by "depth of will," he is referring to the horizon that is drawn around the limits of percipience by the vision of Self, so that the individual who is capable of "depth of will" is able to look beyond the surface appearance of things and see more deeply into nature. Nietzsche contends that theoretical man is incapable of looking beyond the surface appearance of things and seeing what lies beyond those appearances. On the contrary, theoretical man delights in the appearance of things, and it is precisely because of this delight that he fails to see into the essence of things.

Moreover, Nietzsche sees the essence of artistic activity, both in the composition, the communication, and in the reception in the depth of the will and particularly in taking the listener into that depth. And that is not at all, according to Nietzsche, what opera aims to do. Instead, opera aims to provide a delight in the passions via the articulation of the words and tones that complement those passions.

Nietzsche's Wall in Dithyrambic Drama Keeps Out Theoretical Man

This insight into theoretical man's delight in appearance, the bare appearance of all things, and especially the mere spoken word, speaks to the wall Nietzsche erected around his dithyrambic drama with the composition of gesticulative metaphor which, if taken literally without looking for a meaning behind the mere appearance of the words, makes no sense whatsoever. Is that not precisely what has happened in the more than a century since the drama was published? And does that failure not point to a predominance of theoretical man within our present-day culture?

In fact, there is a tendency to take delight in words within theoretical man, the best example of which is his delight in

19: THE FAILURE OF OPERA IN MODERN TRAGEDY

dialectic, which, as I have said before, is synonymous with the poet's delight in his rhythming ability.

- "… because he is unable to behold a vision, he forces the machinist and the decorative artist into his service …"

What I wish to point out in this statement is Nietzsche's belief that art is essentially the production of a vision ("because he is unable to behold a vision"), by which he means myth and specifically the mythical vision of Self. I said earlier that taking the listener more deeply into the will was the essence of the artistic activity, and it is. The production of mythical vision (but also the gateway myths) is the direct result of that transport into the depths of the will because it is only out of that depth that myth arises. Thus, the primary focus of any discussion of art anywhere in this essay should be on the production of mythical vision out of "music," by which I mean the will, which is the whole art of dithyrambic drama.

Here, above, Nietzsche criticizes opera for its lack of both artistic visionariness and musical will. And he argues that the utilization of mechanical props and overly decorous stage scenery that is evident in opera is a clue hinting directly at that inadequacy.

- "… because he cannot apprehend the true nature of the artist, he conjures up the "artistic primitive man" to suit his taste, that is, the man who sings and recites verses under the influence of passion."

In Opera, the Idyllic Shepherd Is a Lame Imitation of the Satyr

Tragic man, back in the ancient days of Greece, beheld the true nature of the artist in the satyr. And theoretical man, being an innately inartistic type, alternatively comes up with the idyllic shepherd in which the audience is meant to see itself, again, as a pretense to culture.

- "The postulate of the opera is a false belief concerning the artistic process, in fact, the idyllic belief that every sentient man is an artist. In the sense of this belief, opera is the expression of the taste of the laity in art, who dictate their laws with the cheerful optimism of the theorist. "

Alexandrine culture encourages every man who subscribes to logical thought to believe that he has an artistic side, though he does not so long as he allows logic to dominate his way of thinking. And this universal democratization of human nature is due entirely to the "cheerful optimism of" of theoretical man.

> Should we desire to unite in one the two conceptions just set forth as influential in the origin of opera, it would only remain for us to speak of an *idyllic tendency of the opera*: in which connection we may avail ourselves exclusively of the phraseology and illustration of Schiller.[25] "Nature and the ideal," he says, "are either objects of grief, when the former is represented as lost,

---

[25] Essay on Elegiac Poetry.—TR.

the latter unattained; or both are objects of joy, in that they are represented as real. The first case furnishes the elegy in its narrower signification, the second the idyll in its widest sense." Here we must at once call attention to the common characteristic of these two conceptions in operatic genesis, namely, that in them the ideal is not regarded as unattained or nature as lost Agreeably to this sentiment, there was a primitive age of man when he lay close to the heart of nature, and, owing to this naturalness, had attained the ideal of mankind in a paradisiac goodness and artist-organisation: from which perfect primitive man all of us were supposed to be descended; whose faithful copy we were in fact still said to be: only we had to cast off some few things in order to recognise ourselves once more as this primitive man, on the strength of a voluntary renunciation of superfluous learnedness, of super-abundant culture. It was to such a concord of nature and the ideal, to an idyllic reality, that the cultured man of the Renaissance suffered himself to be led back by his operatic imitation of Greek tragedy; he made use of this tragedy, as Dante made use of Vergil, in order to be led up to the gates of paradise: while from this point he went on without assistance and passed over from an imitation of the highest form of Greek art

> to a "restoration of all things," to an imitation of man's original art-world. What delightfully naïve hopefulness of these daring endeavours, in the very heart of theoretical culture!—solely to be explained by the comforting belief, that "man-in-himself" is the eternally virtuous hero of the opera, the eternally fluting or singing shepherd, who must always in the end rediscover himself as such, if he has at any time really lost himself; solely the fruit of the optimism, which here rises like a sweetishly seductive column of vapour out of the depth of the Socratic conception of the world.

- "… it would only remain for us to speak of an *idyllic tendency of the opera*…."

Just as the ancient Greek saw himself in the satyr, so, too, does the modern man supposedly see himself in the idyllic shepherd.

Opera Is a Failed Attempt to Recreate Ancient Tragedy

- "… the cultured man of the Renaissance suffered himself to be led back by his operatic imitation of Greek tragedy…."

This is Nietzsche's first and only statement in the whole essay that refers to opera as an imitation of Greek tragedy, which is precisely the reason he critiques it.

19: THE FAILURE OF OPERA IN MODERN TRAGEDY

- "... he made use of this tragedy, as Dante made use of Vergil, in order to be led up to the gates of paradise: while from this point he went on without assistance and passed over from an imitation of the highest form of Greek art to a "restoration of all things," to an imitation of man's original art-world."

And in the reference to opera as an imitation of Greek tragedy, he characterizes it as a vehicle that modern man used to become transported back to nature, back to the most natural condition of human nature, and especially back to the most natural condition of art.

- "... the comforting belief, that "man-in-himself" is the eternally virtuous hero of the opera, the eternally fluting or singing shepherd, who must always in the end rediscover himself as such, if he has at any time really lost himself...."

Modern Man as the Moral Hero in Operatic Tragedy

Thus, Nietzsche critiques operatic tragedy as an attempt to celebrate modern man as the hero in opera and to provide modern man with an opportunity to be rejoined with his innermost idyllic nature.

- "... solely the fruit of the optimism, which here rises like a sweetishly seductive column of vapour out of the depth of the Socratic conception of the world."

Once again, he speaks of the effect of the optimism inherent in theoretical man on the invention of opera. It is that optimism that created the idyllic shepherd in modern operatic tragedy and celebrated modern man as the hero of operatic tragedy.

> The features of the opera therefore do not by any means exhibit the elegiac sorrow of an eternal loss, but rather the cheerfulness of eternal rediscovery, the indolent delight in an idyllic reality which one can at least represent to one's self each moment as real: and in so doing one will perhaps surmise some day that this supposed reality is nothing but a fantastically silly dawdling, concerning which every one, who could judge it by the terrible earnestness of true nature and compare it with the actual primitive scenes of the beginnings of mankind, would have to call out with loathing: Away with the phantom! Nevertheless one would err if one thought it possible to frighten away merely by a vigorous shout such a dawdling thing as the opera, as if it were a spectre. He who would destroy the opera must join issue with Alexandrine cheerfulness, which expresses itself so naïvely therein concerning its favourite representation; of which in fact it is the specific form of art. But what is to be expected for art itself from the operation of a form of art, the beginnings of which do not at all lie in the æsthetic province; which has rather stolen over from a half-moral sphere

19: THE FAILURE OF OPERA IN MODERN TRAGEDY

into the artistic domain, and has been able only now and then to delude us concerning this hybrid origin? By what sap is this parasitic opera-concern nourished, if not by that of true art? Must we not suppose that the highest and indeed the truly serious task of art—to free the eye from its glance into the horrors of night and to deliver the "subject" by the healing balm of appearance from the spasms of volitional agitations—will degenerate under the influence of its idyllic seductions and Alexandrine adulation to an empty dissipating tendency, to pastime? What will become of the eternal truths of the Dionysian and Apollonian in such an amalgamation of styles as I have exhibited in the character of the *stilo rappresentativo*? where music is regarded as the servant, the text as the master, where music is compared with the body, the text with the soul? where at best the highest aim will be the realisation of a paraphrastic tone-painting, just as formerly in the New Attic Dithyramb? where music is completely alienated from its true dignity of being, the Dionysian mirror of the world, so that the only thing left to it is, as a slave of phenomena, to imitate the formal character thereof, and to excite an external pleasure in the play of lines and proportions. On close observation, this fatal influence of the opera on music is seen to coincide absolutely with

> the universal development of modern music; the optimism lurking in the genesis of the opera and in the essence of culture represented thereby, has, with alarming rapidity, succeeded in divesting music of its Dionyso-cosmic mission and in impressing on it a playfully formal and pleasurable character: a change with which perhaps only the metamorphosis of the Æschylean man into the cheerful Alexandrine man could be compared.

- "He who would destroy the opera must join issue with Alexandrine cheerfulness, which expresses itself so naïvely therein concerning its favourite representation; of which in fact it is the specific form of art. But what is to be expected for art itself from the operation of a form of art, the beginnings of which do not at all lie in the æsthetic province; which has rather stolen over from a half-moral sphere into the artistic domain, and has been able only now and then to delude us concerning this hybrid origin? "

What I find most interesting in this statement is the reference to the beginnings of opera in a "half-moral sphere." Unfortunately, he adds nothing to elaborate, so I will do so myself.

I have theorized the origin of moral values out of the sublimation of morale within sub-individuated man, in whom dismemberment has enfeebled the will, and the subsequent spiritualization of morale after the sublimation. Thereafter, everything that increases the morale of suffering man is morally good and everything that demoralizes him is immoral. The problem that morality presents is in its arbitrary bestowal of value upon anything that adds to man's morale and devaluation of everything that demoralizes him. For instance, suffering is made immoral and banished. But suffering, and especially its willful raising from the oblivion of the subconscious, plays an integral role both in tragedy and in life, by which I specifically mean a process of spiritual growth during which the limits of Self are extended. It is expansion of the limits of Self to gaze upon and incorporate subliminal suffering that constitutes the very process of growth that defines life in human being. And it is this categorical and unequivocal devaluation of suffering by moral values that defines the problem that morality presents for life. But equally so, its arbitrary valuation of whatever adds to man's morale presents a problem as well, precisely in its arbitrariness. The question here is: are arbitrary moral valuations being added in the invention of opera. I believe Nietzsche says "yes." I believe he sees a democratizing movement in opera, which is the moral element, insofar as it celebrates the modern man universally, in all instances, in every individual, as the hero.

- "Must we not suppose that the highest and indeed the truly serious task of art—to free the eye from its glance into the horrors of night and to deliver the "subject" by the healing balm of appearance from the spasms of volitional agitations...."

The Primary Function of Art in Life Is to Heal

Once again and consistently, Nietzsche points to art as the means of healing the eye that has looked upon horror. And to put that in more practical terms, art is the process by which the man who has looked upon a paralyzing fear that resides in his subconscious is healed. And the healing comes as an illusory vision of Self, which runs much more deeply than the Self he possessed before achieving his glance. That is the production of vision that tragedy achieves by removing the limits of existing Self, which prevent such a deep percipience, in the collapse of existing Self. Moreover, in the deeper percipience of deeper emotion, the mythopoeic instinct kicks in to produce a deeper Self, a newer Self, which is the essence of Nietzsche's supra-Self or Übermensch.

What is important to take away here is the fact that Nietzsche sees art essentially in the production of mythical vision.

> If, however, in the exemplification herewith indicated we have rightly associated the evanescence of the Dionysian spirit with a most striking, but hitherto unexplained transformation and degeneration of the Hellene—what hopes must revive in us when the most trustworthy auspices guarantee *the reverse process, the gradual awakening of the Dionysian spirit* in our modern world! It is impossible for the divine strength of Herakles to languish for ever in voluptuous bondage to Omphale. Out of the Dionysian root of the German spirit a power has arisen which has nothing in common with the primitive conditions of Socratic culture, and can neither be explained nor excused thereby, but is rather

regarded by this culture as something terribly inexplicable and overwhelmingly hostile — namely, *German music* as we have to understand it, especially in its vast solar orbit from Bach to Beethoven, from Beethoven to Wagner. What even under the most favourable circumstances can the knowledge-craving Socratism of our days do with this demon rising from unfathomable depths? Neither by means of the zig-zag and arabesque work of operatic melody, nor with the aid of the arithmetical counting board of fugue and contrapuntal dialectics is the formula to be found, in the trebly powerful light[26] of which one could subdue this demon and compel it to speak. What a spectacle, when our æsthetes, with a net of "beauty" peculiar to themselves, now pursue and clutch at the genius of music romping about before them with incomprehensible life, and in so doing display activities which are not to be judged by the standard of eternal beauty any more than by the standard of the sublime. Let us but observe these patrons of music as they are, at close range, when they call out so indefatigably "beauty! beauty!" to discover whether they have the marks of nature's darling children who are fostered and fondled in the lap of the beautiful, or

---

[26] See *Faust*, Part 1.1. 965—TR.

> whether they do not rather seek a disguise for their own rudeness, an æsthetical pretext for their own unemotional insipidity: I am thinking here, for instance, of Otto Jahn. But let the liar and the hypocrite beware of our German music: for in the midst of all our culture it is really the only genuine, pure and purifying fire-spirit from which and towards which, as in the teaching of the great Heraclitus of Ephesus, all things move in a double orbit-all that we now call culture, education, civilisation, must appear some day before the unerring judge, Dionysus.

I do not find much in this paragraph that is noteworthy except that (1) Nietzsche speaks of a coming rebirth of tragedy in German culture, and (2) he views opera as "an æsthetical pretext" to culture by a thoroughly inartistic, modern, theoretical man.

Nietzsche Predicts the Rebirth of Tragedy

> Let us recollect furthermore how Kant and Schopenhauer made it possible for the spirit of *German philosophy* streaming from the same sources to annihilate the satisfied delight in existence of scientific Socratism by the delimitation of the boundaries thereof; how through this delimitation an infinitely profounder and more serious view of ethical problems and of art was

inaugurated, which we may unhesitatingly designate as *Dionysian* wisdom comprised in concepts. To what then does the mystery of this oneness of German music and philosophy point, if not to a new form of existence, concerning the substance of which we can only inform ourselves presentiently from Hellenic analogies? For to us who stand on the boundary line between two different forms of existence, the Hellenic prototype retains the immeasurable value, that therein all these transitions and struggles are imprinted in a classically instructive form: except that we, as it were, experience analogically in *reverse* order the chief epochs of the Hellenic genius, and seem now, for instance, to pass backwards from the Alexandrine age to the period of tragedy. At the same time we have the feeling that the birth of a tragic age betokens only a return to itself of the German spirit, a blessed self-rediscovering after excessive and urgent external influences have for a long time compelled it, living as it did in helpless barbaric formlessness, to servitude under their form. It may at last, after returning to the primitive source of its being, venture to stalk along boldly and freely before all nations without hugging the leading-strings of a Romanic civilisation: if only it can learn implicitly of one people—the Greeks, of

> whom to learn at all is itself a high honour and a rare distinction. And when did we require these highest of all teachers more than at present, when we experience *a rebirth of tragedy* and are in danger alike of not knowing whence it comes, and of being unable to make clear to ourselves whither it tends.

Again, more of the same as in the preceding paragraph: he sees a rebirth of tragedy and with it a return to the beginning of time, when life was most successful, as evinced by the success of ancient Greek culture and most spectacularly with the discovery of the value and practice of proto-tragedy at that time by those people. Also, he attributes a refutation of scientific thought (specifically in its limits and consequently in the optimism it imparts) in the work of the philosophers Kant and Schopenhauer, who, therefore, ushered in the rebirth of tragedy. But there should be no doubt that, with the composition of *Thus Spoke Zarathustra*, we now have in our possession the first proto-tragedy created by modern man. Or perhaps more accurately, we should say that the publication of *Thus Spoke Zarathustra* marks the rebirth of proto-tragedy and, with it, the rebirth of tragic man and the demise of modern man, certainly the demise of Socratic man or theoretical man, which is assertible only to the extent that we recognize the value of proto-tragedy.

20: The Birth of Dionysia

Moving Forward with the Demise of Theoretical Man and the Advent of Tragic Man

> It may be weighed some day before an impartial judge, in what time and in what men the German spirit has thus far striven most resolutely to learn of the Greeks: and if we confidently assume that this unique praise must be accorded to the noblest intellectual efforts of Goethe, Schiller, and Winkelmann, it will certainly have to be added that since their time, and subsequently to the more immediate influences of these efforts, the endeavour to attain to culture and to the Greeks by this path has in an incomprehensible manner grown feebler and feebler. In order not to despair altogether of the German spirit, must we not infer therefrom that possibly, in some essential matter, even these champions could not penetrate into the core of the Hellenic nature, and were unable to

establish a permanent friendly alliance between German and Greek culture? So that perhaps an unconscious perception of this shortcoming might raise also in more serious minds the disheartening doubt as to whether after such predecessors they could advance still farther on this path of culture, or could reach the goal at all. Accordingly, we see the opinions concerning the value of Greek contribution to culture degenerate since that time in the most alarming manner; the expression of compassionate superiority may be heard in the most heterogeneous intellectual and non-intellectual camps, and elsewhere a totally ineffective declamation dallies with "Greek harmony," "Greek beauty," "Greek cheerfulness." And in the very circles whose dignity it might be to draw indefatigably from the Greek channel for the good of German culture, in the circles of the teachers in the higher educational institutions, they have learned best to compromise with the Greeks in good time and on easy terms, to the extent often of a sceptical abandonment of the Hellenic ideal and a total perversion of the true purpose of antiquarian studies. If there be any one at all in these circles who has not completely exhausted himself in the endeavour to be a trustworthy corrector of old texts or a natural-history microscopist of language, he perhaps seeks also to appropriate Grecian antiquity "historically" along with other antiquities, and in any case according to the method and with the supercilious air of our present cultured historiography. When, therefore, the intrinsic efficiency of the higher educational institutions has never perhaps been lower or feebler than at present, when the "journalist," the paper slave of the day, has triumphed over the academic teacher in all matters pertaining to culture, and there only remains to the latter the often previously experienced metamorphosis of now fluttering also, as a cheerful cultured butterfly, in the idiom of the journalist, with the "light elegance" peculiar thereto—with what painful confusion must the cultured persons of a period like the present gaze at the phenomenon (which can perhaps be comprehended analogically only by means of the profoundest principle of the hitherto unintelligible Hellenic genius) of the reawakening of the Dionysian spirit and the re-birth of tragedy? Never has there been another art-period in which so-called culture and true art have been so estranged and opposed, as is so obviously the case at present. We understand why so feeble a culture hates true art; it fears destruction thereby. But must not an entire domain of culture, namely the Socratic-Alexandrine, have exhausted its powers after contriving

> to culminate in such a daintily-tapering point as our present culture? When it was not permitted to heroes like Goethe and Schiller to break open the enchanted gate which leads into the Hellenic magic mountain, when with their most dauntless striving they did not get beyond the longing gaze which the Goethean Iphigenia cast from barbaric Tauris to her home across the ocean, what could the epigones of such heroes hope for, if the gate should not open to them suddenly of its own accord, in an entirely different position, quite overlooked in all endeavours of culture hitherto—amidst the mystic tones of reawakened tragic music.

- "It may be weighed some day before an impartial judge, in what time and in what men the German spirit has thus far striven most resolutely to learn of the Greeks...."

The question that must be answered here is: what is the value of any effort to understand the glory and power of ancient Greek culture? The answer is simple. Culture cultivates. And the value of any culture may be directly measured by what it produces and specifically what it produces in the way of individuals. Ancient Greek culture produced an extraordinary progeny of geniuses. By itself, the cultivation of genius validates a culture. But what made ancient Greek culture extraordinary was the number of geniuses it produced, which was very high. The time when ancient Greek culture flourished was the only time in all of history when genius was common, not rare. Moreover, no culture since has been as prolific in the cultivation of genius as was ancient Greek culture. That, more than anything else, is a good reason to learn from them.

- "In order not to despair altogether of the German spirit, must we not infer therefrom that possibly, in some essential matter, even these champions could not penetrate into the core of the Hellenic nature, and were unable to establish a permanent friendly alliance between German and Greek culture? "

With Nietzsche's *Thus Spoke Zarathustra*, there should be no doubt that a "permanent friendly alliance between German and Greek culture" has been very firmly established and precisely in its most valuable treasure: ancient proto-tragedy. Unfortunately, the discovery has gone unnoticed but only because Nietzsche entombed his proto-tragedy in such a way as to guarantee its discovery in only the safest hands. With that accomplished, we must now move forward by teaching our young people how to read a dithyramb and how to practice dithyrambic drama. That should be our foremost goal in a liberal arts education. Nonetheless, extreme difficulties lie ahead.

- "Never has there been another art-period in which so-called culture and true art have been so estranged and opposed, as is so obviously the case at present. We understand why so feeble a culture hates true art; it fears destruction thereby. "

20: The Birth of Dionysia
A New Culture Is upon Us

What is upon us with the rebirth of tragedy is the birth of a new culture as well, which will be called "Dionysia." The transformation will proceed slowly upon a re-evaluation of values that will occur individually, not en masse, and strictly upon the practice of dithyrambic drama. But in the existing culture that values science and logic over art and mystery, the practice may never get a chance unless we promote it.

> Let no one attempt to weaken our faith in an impending re-birth of Hellenic antiquity; for in it alone we find our hope of a renovation and purification of the German spirit through the fire-magic of music. What else do we know of amidst the present desolation and languor of culture, which could awaken any comforting expectation for the future? We look in vain for one single vigorously-branching root, for a speck of fertile and healthy soil: there is dust, sand, torpidness and languishing everywhere! Under such circumstances a cheerless solitary wanderer could choose for himself no better symbol than the Knight with Death and the Devil, as Dürer has sketched him for us, the mail-clad knight, grim and stern of visage, who is able, unperturbed by his gruesome companions, and yet hopelessly, to pursue his terrible path with horse and hound alone. Our Schopenhauer was such a Dürerian

> knight: he was destitute of all hope, but he
> sought the truth. There is not his equal.

With the rebirth of tragedy, a new hope has arisen amongst us. And it is a hope that speaks especially to those individuals in whom the bad conscience has turned most dramatically and are therewith left to wallow in torturous misery for the rest of their lives, an eternity. And the hope that tragedy provides to the man who suffers the bad conscience is the wisdom that inheres in digging deeper into the abyss into which one has fallen instead of trying to climb out of it. This is the wisdom embodied in the Phoenix myth. It is only by surrendering to the fire upon which one's personal hell burns that one will ever escape it, like the Phoenix rising anew out of his ashes. But it is a very, very difficult journey. We are fortunate that Nietzsche chartered the journey and left us with a map to navigate it ourselves. But we must build our own ship to begin the journey, and we must fill our sails ourselves with the wind to move forward. And more than anything else, it requires fortitude, the ability to endure through the most adverse conditions. Indeed, even when there is no hope, the man with fortitude will persevere.

We should not underestimate the severity of the problem that lies before us. The most fundamental hope that any culture must provide its adherents is a hope to cure the conscience that has gone bad and turned against itself, leaving its afflicted individuals to wallow in torturous misery for an eternity, which is precisely the lot in which we presently exist. What does science add to this hope?

Obviously, science has done much good for humanity, especially in the area of medicine and technology, but in numerous other areas as well, most definitely. But the value of art in life, in a process of inner, spiritual growth, has been decimated by science. And to clarify that decimation, I wish to speak now to those individuals in whom the bad conscience has turned most dramatically and in whom a profound loss of being has been most felt, those in whom the loss of Self is deemed permanent and irretrievable.

The Failure of Science as Psychiatry

In the form of psychiatry, science offers the hope of one day being whole again. But I tell you this: that which you once were is dead and will never live again. And unraveling the knot in which your conscience has become mired is not a viable option because it was not for nothing that this catastrophe happened in the first place. It happened for a reason: something new must arise in place of the slain Self, something better and stronger. And it is something which you yourself must create. It is called the over-Self, which is more a description of where your creating will take you than a reference to your new Self because the over-Self is beyond all grades of the principium individuationis. And that is the art in all this: the creating. And it is art that will make all your suffering meaningful and worthwhile. It is not enough, after an eternity of suffering, that you should merely be made whole again. It is better that you emerge from the abyss with something more and better than when you fell into it. And that is what the creation of over-Self provides.

A New Way of Thinking About the World

Allow me to clarify that I am not advocating for the elimination of science or scientific thought in life. Nor do I believe that Nietzsche advocated that elimination. But within a process of growth, with regard to human suffering and the process of growth by which it is made redeemable and meaningful, science absolutely has no place and must indeed be eliminated and replaced with art, specifically tragic art. Moreover, with the new mode of thought that inheres in a man who has embraced proto-tragedy and mastered it, we now have a new way of thinking about the physical world as well. Organic life must be understood in terms relative to a pursuit for power, for dominion, within cell life and cell destruction, which I believe would drastically improve the proficiency of thought and insight about this realm of the physical world, about physics and biology.

> But how suddenly this gloomily depicted wilderness of our exhausted culture changes when the Dionysian magic touches it! A hurricane seizes everything decrepit, decaying, collapsed, and stunted; wraps it whirlingly into a red cloud of dust; and carries it like a vulture into the air. Confused thereby, our glances seek for what has vanished: for what they see is something risen to the golden light as from a depression, so full and green, so luxuriantly alive, so ardently infinite. Tragedy sits in the midst of this exuberance of life, sorrow and joy, in sublime ecstasy; she listens to a distant doleful song—it tells of the Mothers of Being, whose names are: *Wahn, Wille, Wehe*—Yes, my friends, believe with me in

20: THE BIRTH OF DIONYSIA

> Dionysian life and in the re-birth of tragedy. The time of the Socratic man is past: crown yourselves with ivy, take in your hands the thyrsus, and do not marvel if tigers and panthers lie down fawning at your feet. Dare now to be tragic men, for ye are to be redeemed! Ye are to accompany the Dionysian festive procession from India to Greece! Equip yourselves for severe conflict, but believe in the wonders of your god!

Regarding his statement that Wahn, Wille, and Wehe are the Mothers of Being, this is an important insight, but it requires some clarification and elaboration to understand it. Most translators present the German as "delusion, will, woe" in English. I have also seen it presented as "wish, will, and woe," though I cannot find the source. And I have seen it presented as "wild delusion, wish, woe." Strictly, "wahn" translates as madness (or mania, which implies excess and wildness instead of disfunction), delusion, and illusion. The underlying assumption in this insight is that it is not cause that brings things into the world (or being) but rather it is need. The question then becomes which of the possible translations would equate with a need: delusion, mania, wish, wild delusion, madness, or illusion?

Nietzsche has already made the point that tragedy invokes mythopoeia. The major insight that the essay presents is the artistic creation of Self out of an evolution that plays out between the two realms of sensation and ideation. And Self is a mythical being, which means it is an illusion; it does not exist in actuality and is, in fact, a creation that imposes being upon a world that is entirely one of becoming. In fact, Nietzsche characterized this imposition as the highest or greatest manifestation of the will to power. And mythical Self is an illusion that heals suffering man. Nietzsche also states explicitly that the need for illusion is innate within man and that it is the spark that ignites the process of becoming, certainly with respect to the mythopoeia of Self. Moreover, in tragedy, suffering man is represented by the satyr, in whom excess and wildness are inherent. And the need for Self is most pronounced in the nature of satirical man. Thus, the need for the creation of being, of Self, is rooted first in suffering and secondly in the need for illusion, where suffering prompts the need for illusion, which, in turn, heals the suffering. And it is the will that does the work of the creation of Self. In short, I would translate Wahn, Wille, and Wehe as "wish, will and woe."

Beyond that, it will be a long time after you undertake your journey into the subconscious before you finally reach the point at which meaningful changes can begin. But when that moment finally arrives, it is quite extraordinary how easily and rapidly life begins to take hold again and the suffering individual begins to rise up again from his ashes. Within the deepest point of that abyss of that suffering, new wishes, new ambitions, a reinvigorated will, and unrepressed woe take hold like a seed suddenly made fertile, and life springs forth.

Believe in this new Dionysian culture and embrace the rebirth of tragedy that it provides to its adherents. We are entering a new age in which science will be replaced with art and logical deductions with mystical creativity. Dare to face your demons and you will be redeemed. Prepare yourself for a cataclysmic confrontation with the deepest fear and humiliation that you once knew and fled from. But have faith in the possibility that miracles happen.

21: Proto-Tragedy and the New Dithyramb as the New Hope

Gliding back from these hortative tones into the mood which befits the contemplative man, I repeat that it can only be learnt from the Greeks what such a sudden and miraculous awakening of tragedy must signify for the essential basis of a people's life. It is the people of the tragic mysteries who fight the battles with the Persians: and again, the people who waged such wars required tragedy as a necessary healing potion. Who would have imagined that there was still such a uniformly powerful effusion of the simplest political sentiments, the most natural domestic instincts and the primitive manly delight in strife in this very people after it had been shaken to its foundations for several generations by the most violent convulsions of the Dionysian demon? If at every considerable spreading of the Dionysian commotion one always perceives that the Dionysian loosing from the shackles of the individual makes itself felt first of all in an increased encroachment on the political instincts, to the extent of indifference, yea even hostility, it is certain, on the other hand, that the state-forming Apollo is also the genius of the *principium individuationis,* and that the state and domestic sentiment cannot live without an assertion of individual personality. There is only one way from orgasm for a people,— the way to Indian Buddhism, which, in order to be at all endured with its longing for nothingness, requires the rare ecstatic states with their elevation above space, time, and the individual; just as these in turn demand a philosophy which teaches how to overcome the indescribable depression of the intermediate states by means of a fancy. With the same necessity, owing to the unconditional dominance of political impulses, a people drifts into a path of extremest secularisation, the most magnificent, but also the most terrible expression of which is the Roman *imperium.*

The Apollonian Realm as a State-Forming Force on Human Nature

He is comparing the culture of India in the east, in which the Dionysian realm is predominant and mysticism is embraced, and the culture of Rome in the west, in which the Apollonian realm is predominant and individuality is embraced. And between the two, he cites ancient Greece as a culture in which the Dionysian and Apollonian realms are finely balanced. And he attributes that balance to the practice of tragedy.

Notice also that he attributes the development of the mighty political state, in the form of the Roman imperium, to a predominance of the Apollonian realm. And he explicitly characterizes the Apollonian realm as "state-forming." That, by the way, is the only clue I have ever found in all of Nietzsche's writing that explains his use of the metaphor "state" in the dithyramb entitled "Of the New Idol," which teaches the need to look beyond the horizon of percipience that is defined by the existing Self in order to find the supra-Self, though the text — on its surface — clearly *appears* to speak of "the state."

A Clue for Rendering the Dithyramb "Of the New Idol"

In that dithyramb, the dithyrambist depicts one of the first quandaries encountered by the actor in his journey to find his Self. After learning to look for his Self in his feelings, suddenly he gets stuck in his contemplation of the vision that appears before him and all growth stops. That dithyramb teaches him *to look beyond the vision of Self*, beyond the horizon drawn round his percipience by that defining vision, for deeper feelings and a deeper Self. But the metaphors appear to bespeak a lecture on the relationship between man and the state, which, of course, is a deliberate diversion that is meant to distract the dawdling, theoretically-minded reader. The question is: why did he choose the word "state" as a gesticulative metaphor that he hoped would point the actor to the newly-found vision of Self, the new idol, that had become an object pf contemplative worship that stifled his will? In the cited paragraph above, we find the only clue: a predominance of the Apollonian realm, the vision of Self, sets boundaries and limits that define the individual entity, be it Self or a political entity.

Genius as a Balance of Apollonian and Dionysian Forces

In ancient Greek culture, the practice of tragedy prevented a predominance of either the Dionysian or Apollonian realms of human nature, so that, while there was an indulgence in both unlicensed emotion and sharply defined visionariness, there was not an excess of either. And that fine balance was most exquisitely manifested in genius, where extraordinary visionariness is complemented by Herculean hopes and desires.

> Placed between India and Rome, and constrained to a seductive choice, the Greeks succeeded in devising in classical purity still a third form of life, not indeed for long private use, but just on that account for immortality. For it holds true in all things that those whom the gods love die young, but, on the other hand, it holds equally true that they then live eternally with the gods. One must not demand of what is most noble that it should possess the durable toughness of leather; the staunch durability, which, for instance, was inherent in the national character of the Romans, does not probably belong to the indispensable predicates of

> perfection. But if we ask by what physic it was possible for the Greeks, in their best period, notwithstanding the extraordinary strength of their Dionysian and political impulses, neither to exhaust themselves by ecstatic brooding, nor by a consuming scramble for empire and worldly honour, but to attain the splendid mixture which we find in a noble, inflaming, and contemplatively disposing wine, we must remember the enormous power of *tragedy,* exciting, purifying, and disburdening the entire life of a people; the highest value of which we shall divine only when, as in the case of the Greeks, it appears to us as the essence of all the prophylactic healing forces, as the mediator arbitrating between the strongest and most inherently fateful characteristics of a people.

The practice of tragedy is the one ingredient, lacking in both Roman culture and Indian culture, that made the Greeks gloriously unique in all their extraordinary cultural achievements.

> Tragedy absorbs the highest musical orgasm into itself, so that it absolutely brings music to perfection among the Greeks, as among ourselves; but it then places alongside thereof tragic myth and the tragic hero, who, like a mighty Titan, takes the entire Dionysian world on his shoulders

and disburdens us thereof; while, on the other hand, it is able by means of this same tragic myth, in the person of the tragic hero, to deliver us from the intense longing for this existence, and reminds us with warning hand of another existence and a higher joy, for which the struggling hero prepares himself presentiently by his destruction, not by his victories. Tragedy sets a sublime symbol, namely the myth between the universal authority of its music and the receptive Dionysian hearer, and produces in him the illusion that music is only the most effective means for the animation of the plastic world of myth. Relying upon this noble illusion, she can now move her limbs for the dithyrambic dance, and abandon herself unhesitatingly to an orgiastic feeling of freedom, in which she could not venture to indulge as music itself, without this illusion. The myth protects us from the music, while, on the other hand, it alone gives the highest freedom thereto. By way of return for this service, music imparts to tragic myth such an impressive and convincing metaphysical significance as could never be attained by word and image, without this unique aid; and the tragic spectator in particular experiences thereby the sure presentiment of supreme joy to which the path through destruction and negation leads; so that he thinks he hears, as

> it were, the innermost abyss of things speaking audibly to him.

The best way to understand what he is saying here is to apply it in terms relative to inner metaphysics, by which I mean how things work within us, within our mind, our Self and our emotions.

Tragic Myth as Supra-Self and Tragic Hero as Liberator of the Subconscious

First, what is comparable within us to "the highest musical orgasm?" We already know that by music he means will. Thus, what would be an example of an orgasm of will? Simply put, it would be a release of titanic emotion such as we find both in pain and in pleasure when the will's going-forward is blocked by a conflict or granted by an idea but more so by a gateway myth. For instance, if a man who seeks himself in his deeper emotions one day succeeds in embracing a deeper subliminal pain or humiliation that he has avoided all his life despite its numerous and constantly haunting rumblings, that would constitute an orgasm of will. (And we must remember that this deepening of the human soul does not occur except by virtue of the tragic collapse of the existing Self, which draws very sharp lines of percipience around itself to preserve the boundaries by which it exists.) And the embrace would likely not be merely the unpleasant experience that deep and will-nullifying humiliation provides, but that would be part of it. However, insofar as he will have become liberated from his haunts by finally embracing his deeper emotions so that he now lives through them, there would also be pleasure in his liberation and his reunion with his lost Self. All of this occurs as a result of the proto-tragic phenomenon, or, as Nietzsche puts it, proto-tragedy absorbs (accounts for, instigates, comprises) this occurrence, this "highest musical orgasm" or this highest orgasm of human will.

Simultaneous with the collapse of the existing Self and the subsequent embrace of deeper emotions, a new idea and sense of Self is made manifest so that a new vision of Self appears. Thus, when Nietzsche says that proto-tragedy "then places alongside thereof tragic myth and the tragic hero, who, like a mighty Titan, takes the entire Dionysian world on his shoulders and disburdens us thereof," he is referencing that newly risen and deeper Self as both the tragic myth and the tragic hero. And, continuing, when he says that the tragic hero "takes the entire Dionysian world on his shoulders and disburdens us thereof," he means that the new Self attributes to itself the titanic emotions within that have come to the surface in the proto-tragic embrace and takes upon itself those very compelling forces as emotions instead of haunting rumblings. And in that liberation, suffering man feels disburdened. Though he may now be in pain, at least now he is no longer dismembered, and dismemberment accounts for a host of deeply troubling malfunctions of thought.

Also simultaneous with the collapse of the existing Self via proto-tragedy is the apprehension of the new and deeper Self, which imparts a profoundly healing illusion of being upon becoming, which Nietzsche cites as the highest manifestation of art within the inner world, the imposition of being upon becoming. It is a simple and easy to understand fact of human nature that "to feel is to heal."

Proto-Tragedy as Suffering Man's Greatest Hope

And what else happens with the apprehension of the new Self and the healing it provides? Suffering man becomes exalted as he rises upon a newly-defined principium individuationis to a height that is palpably intuitable and tangibly demonstrative. In such a way tragic man is delivered from the existence he knew and lived previously and which he fought so mightily to preserve and maintain, or, as Nietzsche puts it, tragedy "deliver us from the intense longing for this [previous] existence." But more importantly, tragedy reminds us that a new and better existence is possible and is achievable precisely through destruction, not just through glory.

- "Tragedy sets a sublime symbol, namely the myth between the universal authority of its music and the receptive Dionysian hearer, and produces in him the illusion that music is only the most effective means for the animation of the plastic world of myth. "

Proto-tragedy teaches us that there exists between suffering man and the sensations that rumble within him something called Self, which is an illusion, but an illusion without which we cannot live. And it teaches us that Self gives sensation its greatest freedom and its most meaningful expression when it becomes a dimension of Self.

- "The myth protects us from the music, while, on the other hand, it alone gives the highest freedom thereto. "

Self also protects us from the brute force that is inherent in the sometimes titanic discharges that erupt within the sensate realm by cloaking them with the illusion of being, which adds a character of constancy and immovability to them, while at the same time transforming those sensations into emotions and giving them their greatest measure of movability within the confines of a strictly limited entity, which is a thoroughly illogical but highly beneficial transformation.

The Dithyramb as the Great Communicator

- "By way of return for this service, music imparts to tragic myth such an impressive and convincing metaphysical significance as could never be attained by word and image...."

Likewise, the Self that becomes animated via the assimilation of sensation into itself is profoundly transformed by that assimilation insofar as it is no longer, by nature, merely an unmoved image but is now moved, so that will achieves an extraordinary measure of importance within the workings of the inner world, which it could never achieve without the assimilation of sensation into being.

What is most important to note in these observations is that the dithyrambist who succeeds in teaching myth to the dithyrambic actor — to the extent that myth is created within him via mythopoeia — also succeeds in communicating things about the inner world of man that could never be communicated via mere word and concept. Indeed, so profound is the dithyramb as a means of communicating about the inner world of man that the dithyrambic actor, upon experiencing mythopoeia, feels and thinks "the innermost abyss of things [as if] speaking audibly to him."

> If in these last propositions I have succeeded in giving perhaps only a preliminary expression, intelligible to few at first, to this difficult representation, I must not here desist from stimulating my friends to a further attempt, or cease from beseeching them to prepare themselves, by a detached example of our common experience, for the perception of the universal proposition. In this example I must not appeal to those who make use of the pictures of the scenic processes, the words and the emotions of the performers, in order to approximate thereby to musical perception; for none of these speak music as their mother-tongue, and, in spite of the aids in question, do not get farther than the precincts of musical perception, without ever being allowed to touch its innermost shrines; some of them, like Gervinus, do not even reach the precincts by this path. I have only to address myself to those who, being immediately allied to music, have it as it were for their mother's lap, and are connected with things almost exclusively by unconscious musical relations. I ask the question of these genuine musicians: whether they can imagine a man capable of hearing the third act of *Tristan und Isolde* without any aid of word or

21: PROTO-TRAGEDY AND THE NEW DITHYRAMB AS THE NEW HOPE

> scenery, purely as a vast symphonic period, without expiring by a spasmodic distention of all the wings of the soul? A man who has thus, so to speak, put his ear to the heart-chamber of the cosmic will, who feels the furious desire for existence issuing therefrom as a thundering stream or most gently dispersed brook, into all the veins of the world, would he not collapse all at once? Could he endure, in the wretched fragile tenement of the human individual, to hear the re-echo of countless cries of joy and sorrow from the "vast void of cosmic night," without flying irresistibly towards his primitive home at the sound of this pastoral dance-song of metaphysics? But if, nevertheless, such a work can be heard as a whole, without a renunciation of individual existence, if such a creation could be created without demolishing its creator—where are we to get the solution of this contradiction?

Nietzsche now presents a tragic opera as an example of the insights he has proposed in the preceding paragraphs of this chapter. And he points out that his example will not reference the scenery, the words, or the emotions of the performers in the opera he cites but purely in the music itself. He cites Wagner's third act of Tristan und Isolde and asks if a true listener can bear the orgasmic effusion of beauty and pathos in that music without losing himself in it and throwing off his sense of individuality. And if he can, he wonders how that is possible.

Another, more tangible way to put the question is to ask how a man who finally succeeded in plumbing the depths of his subconscious and found his deepest feelings could fail to see his deeper Self in those deeper feelings. This is a purely hypothetical question because in such an instance the mythopoeic instinct would most certainly kick in and produce the vision of Self.

> Here there interpose between our highest musical excitement and the music in question the tragic myth and the tragic hero—in reality only as symbols of the most universal facts, of which music alone can speak directly. If, however, we felt as purely Dionysian beings, myth as a symbol would stand by us absolutely ineffective and unnoticed, and would never for a moment prevent us from giving ear to the re-echo of the *universalia ante rem.* Here, however, the *Apollonian* power, with a view to the restoration of the well-nigh shattered individual, bursts forth with the healing balm of a blissful illusion: all of a sudden we imagine we see only Tristan, motionless, with hushed voice saying to himself: "the old tune, why does it wake me?" And what formerly interested us like a hollow sigh from the heart of being, seems now only to tell us how "waste and void is the sea." And when, breathless, we thought to expire by a convulsive distention of all our feelings, and only a slender tie bound us to our present

21: PROTO-TRAGEDY AND THE NEW DITHYRAMB AS THE NEW HOPE

> existence, we now hear and see only the hero wounded to death and still not dying, with his despairing cry: "Longing! Longing! In dying still longing! for longing not dying!" And if formerly, after such a surplus and superabundance of consuming agonies, the jubilation of the born rent our hearts almost like the very acme of agony, the rejoicing Kurwenal now stands between us and the "jubilation as such," with face turned toward the ship which carries Isolde. However powerfully fellow-suffering encroaches upon us, it nevertheless delivers us in a manner from the primordial suffering of the world, just as the symbol-image of the myth delivers us from the immediate perception of the highest cosmic idea, just as the thought and word deliver us from the unchecked effusion of the unconscious will. The glorious Apollonian illusion makes it appear as if the very realm of tones presented itself to us as a plastic cosmos, as if even the fate of Tristan and Isolde had been merely formed and moulded therein as out of some most delicate and impressible material.

- "… myth as a symbol would stand by us absolutely ineffective and unnoticed, and would never for a moment prevent us from giving ear to the re-echo of the *universalia ante rem.* "

And he answers the question I reiterated above thusly. If, upon divining the deepest part of the subconscious, which is the proto-tragic moment, and mythopoeia did not happen with the envisioning and apprehension of Self, which is the tragic myth and the tragic hero in all of this, then we would divine the essence of actuality absent the cloaking of reality, which itself is entirely illusory.

Myth Induces a Yearning for Life

- "Here, however, the *Apollonian* power, with a view to the restoration of the well-nigh shattered individual, bursts forth with the healing balm of a blissful illusion...."

But that is not what happens. In fact, mythopoeia does indeed happen, and reality overtakes actuality. And the raw, rough, and inherently contradictory and exigent sensations are incorporated into being and thereby transformed into smooth, friendly, and contemplative emotions. And while reality, by incorporating sensation into itself, does indeed bespeak (or echo, reverberate) the wisdom inherent in the sensations, it also bespeaks the nature and wisdom inherent in the Apollonian realm, which is all of ideation. And the wisdom it speaks is that the realm of sensation is all "waste and void" and it is only the illusion of being that makes life truly worth wanting. So that, as the old Self collapses and dies and the new aborning Self rises in its wake, suffering man finds himself longing for life even while dying. Or as Zarathustra puts it, in the tragic moment, suffering man exclaims "Oh, how could I endure to live now, and how could I endure to die," which bespeaks the wisdom in tragedy that the collapse of Self leads to a deeper Self, and the illusion of being adds a longing for existence to its beholder.

Reality as Mythical Self

> • "The glorious Apollonian illusion makes it appear as if the very realm of tones presented itself to us as a plastic cosmos, as if even the fate of Tristan and Isolde had been merely formed and moulded therein as out of some most delicate and impressible material."

With the joining of the two disparate realms of human nature, the Dionysian and the Apollonian, which is a marriage that is achieved only via tragedy, then tragic myth, or Self, presents itself as a work of art molded out of Dionysian elements while, at the same time, the incorporated Dionysian realm of sensations appear also to have been shaped by the Apollonian elements. Or, to put it another way, when the Self incorporates haunting demons into itself, the haunting stops, the demons present themselves as a dimension of Self (as emotions rather than unfamiliar rumblings), the demons achieve spirit (insofar as they are reverberated by Self), and Self becomes animated and willful.

What is important to take away from these observations is that the sensations of actuality, the Dionysian realm, can be brutal and unbearable. But their cloaking within the beauty and illusion of reality, which is afforded solely by the mythical Self, transforms them and makes them bearable as well as meaningful.

> Thus does the Apollonian wrest us from Dionysian universality and fill us with

rapture for individuals; to these it rivets our sympathetic emotion, through these it satisfies the sense of beauty which longs for great and sublime forms; it brings before us biographical portraits, and incites us to a thoughtful apprehension of the essence of life contained therein. With the immense potency of the image, the concept, the ethical teaching and the sympathetic emotion—the Apollonian influence uplifts man from his orgiastic self-annihilation, and beguiles him concerning the universality of the Dionysian process into the belief that he is seeing a detached picture of the world, for instance, Tristan and Isolde, and that, *through music,* he will be enabled to *see* it still more clearly and intrinsically. What can the healing magic of Apollo not accomplish when it can even excite in us the illusion that the Dionysian is actually in the service of the Apollonian, the effects of which it is capable of enhancing; yea, that music is essentially the representative art for an Apollonian substance?

Mythical Self wrests us from exigent sensation, and the beauty of illusory being that it imparts induces a deep delight within us. That is why we rejoice in the discovery of Self. And it is Self that gives rise to personality, which is shaped strictly by the integrity of the limits and boundaries that define it, leading to a measure of wholesomeness that varies according to that integrity. Moreover, Self gives rise to a thoughtful

21: PROTO-TRAGEDY AND THE NEW DITHYRAMB AS THE NEW HOPE

contemplation of the exigent sensations that are incorporated into it and transformed into emotions, which then become dimensions of being.

It is important to note that Self does not exist and that it is a mythical illusion that is created via an artistic process of creation, which is called mythopoeia. Despite being an illusion, Self exerts its influence directly upon the Dionysian realm of sensation after incorporating it into itself, just as the Dionysian realm of sensation exerts itself upon the Apollonian realm of thought. Both are transformed. Self becomes a contemplative and non-exigent snapshot of the Dionysian realm of emotion, while simultaneously restraining emotion so as to prevent the destruction of being from titanic eruptions of sensation but also giving sensation the freedom to discharge itself as an emotional dimension of Self. What is important to note in this transformation is that the static, unmovable, and purely cerebral Apollonian Self becomes moveable, animated, and alive via the incorporation of emotion. And the wisdom that inheres in sensation, which can be so great as to be unfathomable, actually becomes fathomable so that the whole inner world of man becomes more perceptible and comprehensible so long as it is a part of Self. In this transformation, emotion becomes an object and a representation of Self.

> With the pre-established harmony which obtains between perfect drama and its music, the drama attains the highest degree of conspicuousness, such as is usually unattainable in mere spoken drama. As all the animated figures of the scene in the independently evolved lines of melody simplify themselves before us to the

distinctness of the catenary curve, the coexistence of these lines is also audible in the harmonic change which sympathises in a most delicate manner with the evolved process: through which change the relations of things become immediately perceptible to us in a sensible and not at all abstract manner, as we likewise perceive thereby that it is only in these relations that the essence of a character and of a line of melody manifests itself clearly. And while music thus compels us to see more extensively and more intrinsically than usual, and makes us spread out the curtain of the scene before ourselves like some delicate texture, the world of the stage is as infinitely expanded for our spiritualised, introspective eye as it is illumined outwardly from within. How can the word-poet furnish anything analogous, who strives to attain this internal expansion and illumination of the visible stage-world by a much more imperfect mechanism and an indirect path, proceeding as he does from word and concept? Albeit musical tragedy likewise avails itself of the word, it is at the same time able to place alongside thereof its basis and source, and can make the unfolding of the word, from within outwards, obvious to us.

21: PROTO-TRAGEDY AND THE NEW DITHYRAMB AS THE NEW HOPE

In the above paragraph, he compares the dithyrambist who communicates will via dithyrambic music with the poet who communicates concept via word. And with that, we now move to a discussion of the dithyramb, its communication of will, and the creation of myth within the dithyrambic actor.

> Of the process just set forth, however, it could still be said as decidedly that it is only a glorious appearance, namely the aforementioned Apollonian *illusion,* through the influence of which we are to be delivered from the Dionysian obtrusion and excess. In point of fact, the relation of music to drama is precisely the reverse; music is the adequate idea of the world, drama is but the reflex of this idea, a detached umbrage thereof. The identity between the line of melody and the lining form, between the harmony and the character-relations of this form, is true in a sense antithetical to what one would suppose on the contemplation of musical tragedy. We may agitate and enliven the form in the most conspicuous manner, and enlighten it from within, but it still continues merely phenomenon, from which there is no bridge to lead us into the true reality, into the heart of the world. Music, however, speaks out of this heart; and though countless phenomena of the kind might be passing manifestations of this music, they could never exhaust its essence, but would always be merely its externalised

copies. Of course, as regards the intricate relation of music and drama, nothing can be explained, while all may be confused by the popular and thoroughly false antithesis of soul and body; but the unphilosophical crudeness of this antithesis seems to have become—who knows for what reasons—a readily accepted Article of Faith with our æstheticians, while they have learned nothing concerning an antithesis of phenomenon and thing-in-itself, or perhaps, for reasons equally unknown, have not cared to learn anything thereof.

Will Produces and Empowers Myth

He makes a distinction between "music" and phenomenon, which is the same distinction as what exists between "music" and drama or "music" and appearance. Again, by "music" he means will, which is comprised entirely of emotions. And by appearance, phenomena, and drama, he means myth. And will produces myth via mythopoeia. Moreover, will illuminates myth from within to the extent that mythical Self incorporates sensation into itself as emotion when the individual perceives sensation and attributes it to Self, with Self being the "cause" of the emotion. Man simply cannot observe motion without predicating a cause to that motion. And when he perceives motion within himself, in the form of sensation, he predicates Self as the "cause" of the sensation and therewith "creates" a fictive being that does not exist outside of his predicating thought process. In such a way, when sensation becomes a part of Self, it animates and enlivens Self and therewith illuminates

21: PROTO-TRAGEDY AND THE NEW DITHYRAMB AS THE NEW HOPE

it from within. And in the same way, it may be said that "music" or will may be said to give "drama" or mythical Self its substance. Self, despite being fictive appearance through and through nonetheless defines that which we call reality. But "music" or will is the foundation upon which mythical Self (or drama) arises. Thus, "music" is the actuality of things, the essence of things, while drama is the reality or phenomenal appearance of things. Actuality is more fundamental than reality.

> Should it have been established by our analysis that the Apollonian element in tragedy has by means of its illusion gained a complete victory over the Dionysian primordial element of music, and has made music itself subservient to its end, namely, the highest and clearest elucidation of the drama, it would certainly be necessary to add the very important restriction: that at the most essential point this Apollonian illusion is dissolved and annihilated. The drama, which, by the aid of music, spreads out before us with such inwardly illumined distinctness in all its movements and figures, that we imagine we see the texture unfolding on the loom as the shuttle flies to and fro,—attains as a whole an effect which *transcends all Apollonian artistic effects*. In the collective effect of tragedy, the Dionysian gets the upper hand once more; tragedy ends with a sound which could never emanate from the realm of

> Apollonian art. And the Apollonian illusion is thereby found to be what it is,—the assiduous veiling during the performance of tragedy of the intrinsically Dionysian effect: which, however, is so powerful, that it finally forces the Apollonian drama itself into a sphere where it begins to talk with Dionysian wisdom, and even denies itself and its Apollonian conspicuousness. Thus then the intricate relation of the Apollonian and the Dionysian in tragedy must really be symbolised by a fraternal union of the two deities: Dionysus speaks the language of Apollo; Apollo, however, finally speaks the language of Dionysus; and so the highest goal of tragedy and of art in general is attained.

Given the "actual" nature of will and the fictively "real" nature of mythical Self, it should come as no surprise that mythical Self is destructible and will is indestructible. Self can and does collapse into itself. And this happens despite the restrictive dominance that Self is capable of achieving over emotion. But when that happens, will rises up again. And the whole predicating process that results in mythopoeia starts over again, which gives rise to a new Self. It is for this reason that tragic wisdom teaches man that the destruction of appearances is secondary to the eternal life of will. It is also important to note that the tragic collapse of Self necessarily leads to the Self-predicating process of mythopoeia again, which gives rise to a deeper and more comprehensive Self than what existed before. In other words, the Dionysian forces reinvigorate and

21: Proto-Tragedy and the New Dithyramb as the New Hope

strengthen the Apollonian forces, and, in this sense, the two disparate realms of human nature join forces in something like a marriage and learn to speak the other's language.

22: Theory of Genius

Man Achieves a Depth and Height of Soul from the Dionysian and Apollonian Realms, Respectively

> Let the attentive friend picture to himself purely and simply, according to his experiences, the effect of a true musical tragedy. I think I have so portrayed the phenomenon of this effect in both its phases that he will now be able to interpret his own experiences. For he will recollect that with regard to the myth which passed before him he felt himself exalted to a kind of omniscience, as if his visual faculty were no longer merely a surface faculty, but capable of penetrating into the interior, and as if he now saw before him, with the aid of music, the ebullitions of the will, the conflict of motives, and the swelling stream of the passions, almost sensibly visible, like a plenitude of actively moving lines and figures, and could thereby dip into the most tender secrets of unconscious emotions.

22: THEORY OF GENIUS

While he thus becomes conscious of the highest exaltation of his instincts for conspicuousness and transfiguration, he nevertheless feels with equal definitiveness that this long series of Apollonian artistic effects still does *not* generate the blissful continuance in will-less contemplation which the plasticist and the epic poet, that is to say, the strictly Apollonian artists, produce in him by their artistic productions: to wit, the justification of the world of the *individuatio* attained in this contemplation,—which is the object and essence of Apollonian art. He beholds the transfigured world of the stage and nevertheless denies it. He sees before him the tragic hero in epic clearness and beauty, and nevertheless delights in his annihilation. He comprehends the incidents of the scene in all their details, and yet loves to flee into the incomprehensible. He feels the actions of the hero to be justified, and is nevertheless still more elated when these actions annihilate their originator. He shudders at the sufferings which will befall the hero, and yet anticipates therein a higher and much more overpowering joy. He sees more extensively and profoundly than ever, and yet wishes to be blind. Whence must we derive this curious internal dissension, this collapse of the Apollonian apex, if not from the *Dionysian* spell, which, though

> apparently stimulating the Apollonian emotions to their highest pitch, can nevertheless force this superabundance of Apollonian power into its service? *Tragic myth* is to be understood only as a symbolisation of Dionysian wisdom by means of the expedients of Apollonian art: the mythus conducts the world of phenomena to its boundaries, where it denies itself, and seeks to flee back again into the bosom of the true and only reality; where it then, like Isolde, seems to strike up its metaphysical swan-song:—

Given the disparate nature of forces arising from within the Dionysian and Apollonian realms, their symbiosis via tragedy is reflected in a multitude of contradictions all of which defy logic. And Nietzsche cites many of those contradictions in the above paragraph. In the first, he cites how the individual who beholds *and mounts* his higher Self arising like the Phoenix out of the collapse of the old Self "felt himself exalted to a kind of omniscience." That omniscience and its accompanying exaltation are the direct result of the individuation from inner chaos arising out of mythopoeia and its simultaneous communion with inner nature, which itself arises from the incorporation of the Dionysian sensations, the emotions. In *Thus Spoke Zarathustra*, there are numerous references to Zarathustra ascending to or walking through the mountains, and it is this exaltation that is represented by the metaphor "mountains."

Notice also, in the third sentence, how he characterizes "vision" as an Apollonian trait. In other words, it is only with reference to an idea and a sense of being, which is the mythical

Self, that man has an understanding of what we call reality. Reality is comprised entirely of the illusory domain of Self, which *appears* to man as a vision and therewith imparts visibility to that which exists outside the domain, namely the forces arising from out of the Dionysian realm. But then he says that the "vision" imparted by Self, which previously seemed limited to the surface of things, confined within a strictly limited horizon, now seems to extend into the depths, by which he means the depths of the Dionysian realm, *precisely* because the aborning Self arising out of that depth derives from a deeper look into that realm and now, having extended the limits of individuation, possesses the ability to look more deeply into things.

This deeper look transforms the Apollonian realm, which takes its deepest delight in mere appearance, the beauty of that illusory appearance, and especially the contemplative delight it arouses and sustains, so that, with the incorporation of the Dionysian realm, the deeper emotions of the subconscious, *will-less* contemplation is no longer the highest aim of the Apollonian realm. Now there is added to that delight a willful animation as well, which is a major transformation of human nature — resulting in a uniquely tragic nature, so that neither ideation nor sensation are predominate but instead equally share power.

A Characterization of Tragic Man and Vision of Supra-Self

Of that new species of tragic man, Nietzsche has written the most accurate articulation I have ever come across, which I now highlight for you in its entirety, below.

DIONYSIA METAPHYSICA

- "He beholds the transfigured world of the stage and nevertheless denies it. He sees before him the tragic hero in epic clearness and beauty, and nevertheless delights in his annihilation. He comprehends the incidents of the scene in all their details, and yet loves to flee into the incomprehensible. He feels the actions of the hero to be justified, and is nevertheless still more elated when these actions annihilate their originator. He shudders at the sufferings which will befall the hero, and yet anticipates therein a higher and much more overpowering joy. He sees more extensively and profoundly than ever, and yet wishes to be blind. "

And to make the articulation just a little more palpable, I would reiterate it as follows, sentence by sentence. Tragic man beholds with wonder the newly emergent Self and yet he denies it because he knows it is a beguiling illusion and, in fact, anticipates its destruction because he knows a more brilliant vision will replace it in that destruction. He understands everything he "sees" with the vision imparted by his Self and yet yearns to become immersed once again into the incomprehensible because he knows therein lies actuality, which is beyond reality and much deeper in wisdom. Tragic man delights in his ability to fathom more deeply his most subliminal emotions and yet delights in the destruction of his existing Self as a result of that fathoming. He dreads the pain, the fear, and the humiliation that he knows awaits him in the subconscious but knows that a higher and much more overpowering joy awaits him in overcoming those titanic emotions if only he can find a way beyond them. And as his higher visions of Self emerge into apprehension, so that he sees more and more of the inner world, still, in a mysterious way, he wishes to find a depth wherein he has no vison at all because, although there may be no vision in that depth, he knows there is mighty and inexorable will in the absence of vision. Thus, in perhaps life's most primordial contradiction, tragic man years to live on due to the beauty and eternity imparted by a vision of Self and yet he also yearns to "die," to be reunited with the Oneness or Belly of Being, apart from individuation, due to the vitality and fertility that is promised by an empowerment of the will.

- *"Tragic myth* is to be understood only as a symbolisation of Dionysian wisdom by means of the expedients of Apollonian art: the mythus conducts the world of phenomena to its boundaries, where it denies itself, and seeks to flee back again into the bosom of the true and only reality...."

Tragedy gives rise to both a gateway myth that liberates the will from beguiling image and a mythical being that provides the most profound source of delightful contemplation. As such, when mythical being, or Self, emerges to create illusory reality, tragedy takes man to the boundaries of the limits defined by that reality, that Self and its horizon, and urges man to look beyond the horizon for a deeper reality, which he finds, so that he flees away from that reality and into his deeper emotions. Thus, we have a juxtaposition of reality and actuality, with actuality winning out over and over again. Out of this tragic wisdom arises a new myth, the myth of the supra-Self.

A Definition of Genius as the Incarnation of the Over-Self

> In des Wonnemeeres
> wogendem Schwall,
> in der Duft-Wellen
> tönendem Schall,
> in des Weltathems
> wehendem All—
> ertrinken—versinken
> unbewusst—höchste Lust![27]
>
> We thus realise to ourselves in the experiences of the truly æsthetic hearer the tragic artist himself when he proceeds like a luxuriously fertile divinity of individuation to create his figures (in which sense his work can hardly be understood as an "imitation of nature")—and when, on the other hand, his vast Dionysian impulse then absorbs the entire world of phenomena, in order to anticipate beyond it, and through its annihilation, the highest artistic primal joy, in the bosom of the Primordial Unity. Of

---

[27] In the sea of pleasure's
Billowing roll,
In the ether-waves
Knelling and toll,
In the world-breath's
Wavering whole—
To drown in, go down in—
Lost in swoon—greatest boon!

course, our æsthetes have nothing to say about this return in fraternal union of the two art-deities to the original home, nor of either the Apollonian or Dionysian excitement of the hearer, while they are indefatigable in characterising the struggle of the hero with fate, the triumph of the moral order of the world, or the disburdenment of the emotions through tragedy, as the properly Tragic: an indefatigableness which makes me think that they are perhaps not æsthetically excitable men at all, but only to be regarded as moral beings when hearing tragedy. Never since Aristotle has an explanation of the tragic effect been proposed, by which an æsthetic activity of the hearer could be inferred from artistic circumstances. At one time fear and pity are supposed to be forced to an alleviating discharge through the serious procedure, at another time we are expected to feel elevated and inspired at the triumph of good and noble principles, at the sacrifice of the hero in the interest of a moral conception of things; and however certainly I believe that for countless men precisely this, and only this, is the effect of tragedy, it as obviously follows therefrom that all these, together with their interpreting æsthetes, have had no experience of tragedy as the highest *art*. The pathological discharge, the catharsis of Aristotle, which philologists are at a loss whether to include under medicinal or moral phenomena, recalls a remarkable anticipation of Goethe. "Without a lively pathological interest," he says, "I too have never yet succeeded in elaborating a tragic situation of any kind, and hence I have rather avoided than sought it. Can it perhaps have been still another of the merits of the ancients that the deepest pathos was with them merely æsthetic play, whereas with us the truth of nature must co-operate in order to produce such a work?" We can now answer in the affirmative this latter profound question after our glorious experiences, in which we have found to our astonishment in the case of musical tragedy itself, that the deepest pathos can in reality be merely æsthetic play: and therefore we are justified in believing that now for the first time the proto-phenomenon of the tragic can be portrayed with some degree of success. He who now will still persist in talking only of those vicarious effects proceeding from ultra-æsthetic spheres, and does not feel himself raised above the pathologically-moral process, may be left to despair of his æsthetic nature: for which we recommend to him, by way of innocent equivalent, the interpretation of Shakespeare after the fashion of Gervinus, and the diligent search for poetic justice.

In the above, Nietzsche proposes that Aristotle's proposition that tragedy provides a catharsis of pity and terror and the moralist's proposition that tragedy exemplifies the triumph of good over evil subsequent to a heroic sacrifice for the moral good — are herewith debunked. He also mentions a "proto-phenomenon" as definitive tragedy, implying that the tragedy we have interpreted for millennia since has been something else entirely, not the original proto-phenomenon. And I would go a step further and say that the proto-phenomenon was never a theatrical spectacle or any kind of spectacle whatsoever. Proto-tragedy, in the beginning and as it has been resurrected in our time, was and is an inner, spiritual rite of passage within a process of growth that heals suffering, subindividuated man and, through that growth, *is singularly responsible* for breeding a type of human being that we call genius, by which I mean a type of man in whom the limits of individuation have been surpassed so that the Dionysian forces of ambition and hope and the Apollonian forces of idea and vision have grown to an extraordinary extent.

Dithyrambic Music and the Art of "Hearing"

> Thus with the re-birth of tragedy the *æsthetic hearer* is also born anew, in whose place in the theatre a curious *quid pro quo* was wont to sit with half-moral and half-learned pretensions,—the "critic." In his sphere hitherto everything has been artificial and merely glossed over with a semblance of life. The performing artist was in fact at a loss what to do with such a critically comporting hearer, and hence he,

as well as the dramatist or operatic composer who inspired him, searched anxiously for the last remains of life in a being so pretentiously barren and incapable of enjoyment. Such "critics," however, have hitherto constituted the public; the student, the school-boy, yea, even the most harmless womanly creature, were already unwittingly prepared by education and by journals for a similar perception of works of art. The nobler natures among the artists counted upon exciting the moral-religious forces in such a public, and the appeal to a moral order of the world operated vicariously, when in reality some powerful artistic spell should have enraptured the true hearer. Or again, some imposing or at all events exciting tendency of the contemporary political and social world was presented by the dramatist with such vividness that the hearer could forget his critical exhaustion and abandon himself to similar emotions, as, in patriotic or warlike moments, before the tribune of parliament, or at the condemnation of crime and vice:— an estrangement of the true aims of art which could not but lead directly now and then to a cult of tendency. But here there took place what has always taken place in the case of factitious arts, an extraordinary rapid depravation of these tendencies, so that for instance the tendency to employ the

> theatre as a means for the moral education of the people, which in Schiller's time was taken seriously, is already reckoned among the incredible antiquities of a surmounted culture. While the critic got the upper hand in the theatre and concert-hall, the journalist in the school, and the press in society, art degenerated into a topic of conversation of the most trivial kind, and æsthetic criticism was used as the cement of a vain, distracted, selfish and moreover piteously unoriginal sociality, the significance of which is suggested by the Schopenhauerian parable of the porcupines, so that there has never been so much gossip about art and so little esteem for it. But is it still possible to have intercourse with a man capable of conversing on Beethoven or Shakespeare? Let each answer this question according to his sentiments: he will at any rate show by his answer his conception of "culture," provided he tries at least to answer the question, and has not already grown mute with astonishment.

First, I wish to point out that my earlier statement about original proto-tragedy being an inner, spiritual event and nothing like a theatrical spectacle is borne out by Nietzsche's statement above that "... with the re-birth of tragedy the *æsthetic hearer* is also born anew, in whose place in the theatre a curious *quid pro quo* was wont to sit with half-moral and half-learned pretensions,—the "critic." The characterization of "aesthetic hearer" here needs some clarification. Exactly what is it that needs to be heard? What needs to be heard is the "music." But music is will, so it is the will that must be heard. But how does one "hear" will? It is not so much that one must hear the will but more that one must listen for it. Or, more precisely, one must learn to sense the will, which requires "listening" with one's intuition, because you will not "see" it but you can certainly sense it. You can "see" your Self because Self is something that pertains to the Apollonian realm and vision is a trait of the Apollonian realm, given that the Apollonian realm gives rise to form. But will is comprised entirely of emotion, which pertains to the Dionysian realm, and visibility is not a trait of the Dionysian realm.

Thus, the practice of proto-tragedy requires the art of "listening" for will (or music) because will is what gives rise to tragedy and it is the will that is celebrated in tragedy.

> On the other hand, many a one more nobly and delicately endowed by nature, though he may have gradually become a critical barbarian in the manner described, could tell of the unexpected as well as totally unintelligible effect which a successful performance of *Lohengrin,* for example, exerted on him: except that perhaps every warning and interpreting hand was lacking to guide him; so that the incomprehensibly heterogeneous and altogether incomparable sensation which then affected him also remained isolated and became extinct, like a mysterious star after a brief brilliancy. He then divined what the æsthetic hearer is.

23: Theoretical Man Is Banned from the New Dithyramb

Dithyrambic Music Cannot Be "Heard" by Theoretical Man

> He who wishes to test himself rigorously as to how he is related to the true æsthetic hearer, or whether he belongs rather to the community of the Socrato-critical man, has only to enquire sincerely concerning the sentiment with which he accepts the *wonder* represented on the stage: whether he feels his historical sense, which insists on strict psychological causality, insulted by it, whether with benevolent concession he as it were admits the wonder as a phenomenon intelligible to childhood, but relinquished by him, or whether he experiences anything else thereby. For he will thus be enabled to determine how far he is on the whole capable of understanding *myth,* that is to say, the

> concentrated picture of the world, which, as abbreviature of phenomena, cannot dispense with wonder. It is probable, however, that nearly every one, upon close examination, feels so disintegrated by the critico-historical spirit of our culture, that he can only perhaps make the former existence of myth credible to himself by learned means through intermediary abstractions. Without myth, however, every culture loses its healthy, creative natural power: it is only a horizon encompassed with myths which rounds off to unity a social movement. It is only by myth that all the powers of the imagination and of the Apollonian dream are freed from their random rovings. The mythical figures have to be the invisibly omnipresent genii, under the care of which the young soul grows to maturity, by the signs of which the man gives a meaning to his life and struggles: and the state itself knows no more powerful unwritten law than the mythical foundation which vouches for its connection with religion and its growth from mythical ideas.

Nietzsche sees a significant distinction between the type of person who is likely to "hear" the "music" comprising the will through which the proto-tragic phenomenon is communicated and another type of person who is more likely to come upon it and completely miss it. He calls the latter "theoretical man," by which he means someone who subscribes to the Socratic or logical or abstract way of looking at things. This would be a type of person who remains at the surface of things and does not look or listen deeply enough to hear anything that may be rumbling below the surface, which would be the "music" in this instance.

The effect of this failure to look or listen deeply beyond the mere appearance of things is most evident in the dithyrambic tragedy that Nietzsche wrote, which is his *Thus Spoke Zarathustra*. For more than a century, *no one* understood a word of it. And that is because no one *heard* the "music." No one was able to see it as a representation of will and then find a way to render that will.

Myth as Imbued Will

Lastly, he says in the above paragraph that the most important thing to take away from tragedy is myth, which he calls an abbreviature of phenomena. In other words, myth, which I have explained extensively in *The Birth of Dionysia* is a very abstract idea of the world that enables the will to exist and thrive within it. But if it is an abstract idea, why, then, is abstract (or theoretical) man unable to see it or understand it? Because it derives exclusively from will. It arises from out of the will. Myth is an abstraction, but it is an imbued abstraction. It cannot be understood except as a creation of will. In order to understand a myth, one must be moved by the will out of which it is created. In other words, myth must be apprehended; it cannot simply be comprehended, which goes back to the very first sentence of *The Birth of Tragedy* when Nietzsche calls upon the pupil to a direct apprehension rather than a mere ascertaining of the essence of tragedy, with the essence being the myth that is created.

23: Theoretical Man Is Banned from the New Dithyramb

Let us now place alongside thereof the abstract man proceeding independently of myth, the abstract education, the abstract usage, the abstract right, the abstract state: let us picture to ourselves the lawless roving of the artistic imagination, not bridled by any native myth: let us imagine a culture which has no fixed and sacred primitive seat, but is doomed to exhaust all its possibilities, and has to nourish itself wretchedly from the other cultures—such is the Present, as the result of Socratism, which is bent on the destruction of myth. And now the myth-less man remains eternally hungering among all the bygones, and digs and grubs for roots, though he have to dig for them even among the remotest antiquities. The stupendous historical exigency of the unsatisfied modern culture, the gathering around one of countless other cultures, the consuming desire for knowledge—what does all this point to, if not to the loss of myth, the loss of the mythical home, the mythical source? Let us ask ourselves whether the feverish and so uncanny stirring of this culture is aught but the eager seizing and snatching at food of the hungerer—and who would care to contribute anything more to a culture which cannot be appeased by all it devours, and in contact with which the most vigorous and wholesome nourishment is wont to change into "history and criticism"?

Nihilism Derives from the Demise of Myth

Nietzsche characterizes myth as something without which man cannot live. And, since myth derives singularly from tragedy, the death of tragedy as a result of the advent of scientific thought, also means the death of myth. But since man cannot live without it, he then seeks out old myths to satisfy the need, such as we see today with religious fundamentalists trying to establish norms that derived originally from a living myth that existed at an earlier time in history.

He also suggests that the loss of myth created a hunger for something that went missing and that the insatiable craving for knowledge that characterizes science satisfies that hunger, which would mean that tragedy originally died out for a reason other than the advent of science, such as something as simple as man losing his way, and that the advent of science ensured the death of tragedy and myth and precluded their resurrection.

> We should also have to regard our German character with despair and sorrow, if it had already become inextricably entangled in, or even identical with this culture, in a similar manner as we can observe it to our horror to be the case in civilised France; and that which for a long time was the great advantage of France and the cause of her vast preponderance, to wit, this very identity of people and culture, might compel us at the sight thereof to congratulate ourselves

23: Theoretical Man Is Banned from the New Dithyramb

> that this culture of ours, which is so questionable, has hitherto had nothing in common with the noble kernel of the character of our people. All our hopes, on the contrary, stretch out longingly towards the perception that beneath this restlessly palpitating civilised life and educational convulsion there is concealed a glorious, intrinsically healthy, primeval power, which, to be sure, stirs vigorously only at intervals in stupendous moments, and then dreams on again in view of a future awakening. It is from this abyss that the German Reformation came forth: in the choral-hymn of which the future melody of German music first resounded. So deep, courageous, and soul-breathing, so exuberantly good and tender did this chorale of Luther sound,—as the first Dionysian-luring call which breaks forth from dense thickets at the approach of spring. To it responded with emulative echo the solemnly wanton procession of Dionysian revellers, to whom we are indebted for German music—and to whom we shall be indebted for *the re-birth of German myth.*

Nietzsche theorizes the existence within his present-day German culture of something stirring within out of which tragedy might soon arise again. Obviously, he was right.

The Dithyramb is for Him Who Seeks His Self

I know that I must now lead the sympathising and attentive friend to an elevated position of lonesome contemplation, where he will have but few companions, and I call out encouragingly to him that we must hold fast to our shining guides, the Greeks. For the rectification of our æsthetic knowledge we previously borrowed from them the two divine figures, each of which sways a separate realm of art, and concerning whose mutual contact and exaltation we have acquired a notion through Greek tragedy. Through a remarkable disruption of both these primitive artistic impulses, the ruin of Greek tragedy seemed to be necessarily brought about: with which process a degeneration and a transmutation of the Greek national character was strictly in keeping, summoning us to earnest reflection as to how closely and necessarily art and the people, myth and custom, tragedy and the state, have coalesced in their bases. The ruin of tragedy was at the same time the ruin of myth. Until then the Greeks had been involuntarily compelled immediately to associate all experiences with their myths, indeed they had to comprehend them only through this association: whereby even the most immediate present necessarily appeared to them *sub specie æterni* and in a certain sense as timeless. Into this current of the timeless, however, the state as well as art plunged in order to find repose from the burden and eagerness of the moment. And a people—for the rest, also a man—is worth just as much only as its ability to impress on its experiences the seal of eternity: for it is thus, as it were, desecularised, and reveals its unconscious inner conviction of the relativity of time and of the true, that is, the metaphysical significance of life. The contrary happens when a people begins to comprehend itself historically and to demolish the mythical bulwarks around it: with which there is usually connected a marked secularisation, a breach with the unconscious metaphysics of its earlier existence, in all ethical consequences. Greek art and especially Greek tragedy delayed above all the annihilation of myth: it was necessary to annihilate these also to be able to live detached from the native soil, unbridled in the wilderness of thought, custom, and action. Even in such circumstances this metaphysical impulse still endeavours to create for itself a form of apotheosis (weakened, no doubt) in the Socratism of science urging to life: but on its lower stage this same impulse led only to a feverish search, which gradually merged into a pandemonium of myths and superstitions accumulated from all quarters: in the midst of which, nevertheless, the Hellene sat with a yearning heart till he contrived, as Græculus, to mask his fever with Greek cheerfulness and Greek levity, or to narcotise himself completely with some gloomy Oriental superstition.

We have approached this condition in the most striking manner since the reawakening of the Alexandro—Roman antiquity in the fifteenth century, after a long, not easily describable, interlude. On the heights there is the same exuberant love of knowledge, the same insatiate happiness of the discoverer, the same stupendous secularisation, and, together with these, a homeless roving about, an eager intrusion at foreign tables, a frivolous deification of the present or a dull senseless estrangement, all *sub speci sæculi,* of the present time: which same symptoms lead one to infer the same defect at the heart of this culture, the annihilation of myth. It seems hardly possible to transplant a foreign myth with permanent success, without dreadfully injuring the tree through this transplantation: which is perhaps occasionally strong enough and sound enough to eliminate the foreign element after a terrible struggle; but must ordinarily consume itself in a languishing and stunted condition or in sickly

23: THEORETICAL MAN IS BANNED FROM THE NEW DITHYRAMB

> luxuriance. Our opinion of the pure and vigorous kernel of the German being is such that we venture to expect of it, and only of it, this elimination of forcibly ingrafted foreign elements, and we deem it possible that the German spirit will reflect anew on itself. Perhaps many a one will be of opinion that this spirit must begin its struggle with the elimination of the Romanic element: for which it might recognise an external preparation and encouragement in the victorious bravery and bloody glory of the late war, but must seek the inner constraint in the emulative zeal to be for ever worthy of the sublime protagonists on this path, of Luther as well as our great artists and poets. But let him never think he can fight such battles without his household gods, without his mythical home, without a "restoration" of all German things! And if the German should look timidly around for a guide to lead him back to his long-lost home, the ways and paths of which he knows no longer—let him but listen to the delightfully luring call of the Dionysian bird, which hovers above him, and would fain point out to him the way thither.

In the last sentence, he exhorts the German who seeks his long-lost home to listen to the call of the Dionysian bird to find his way. But the exhortation goes out to anyone who seeks out his Self. And the "Dionysian bird" he should heed is an innate desire for Self. But in order to heed and be guided by an innate desire for Self, one must first be a good listener and not a theorist who seeks the best of all things in abstracta. But to put on the fast track the man who seeks out his Self, I would exhort you to Nietzsche's dithyrambic tragedy, *Thus Spoke Zarathustra*. Anyone who learns to read it will most certainly find himself in it. But in order to learn how to read dithyrambic music, one must first learn to listen to oneself. And one of the first things *Thus Spoke Zarathustra* teaches is the good skill of seeking out "one's animals," two of which are the eagle with a serpent coiled around his neck, where the "eagle" represents the desire to rise above the chaos of thought and passion within oneself and unto the omniscience that results from finding one's Self, which is represented by the wise serpent of knowledge.

24: The Birth of Tragedy from Dissonance

Salvation as a Fraternal Union of the Apollonian and Dionysian Realms

Among the peculiar artistic effects of musical tragedy we had to emphasise an Apollonian *illusion,* through which we are to be saved from immediate oneness with the Dionysian music, while our musical excitement is able to discharge itself on an Apollonian domain and in an interposed visible middle world. It thereby seemed to us that precisely through this discharge the middle world of theatrical procedure, the drama generally, became visible and intelligible from within in a degree unattainable in the other forms of Apollonian art: so that here, where this art was as it were winged and borne aloft by the spirit of music, we had to recognise the highest exaltation of its powers, and consequently in the fraternal union of

> Apollo and Dionysus the climax of the Apollonian as well as of the Dionysian artistic aims.

Regarding the first sentence above, which states that the Apollonian illusion saves us from "immediate oneness with the Dionysian music," this statement equates with Schopenhauer's analogy of Self or mind (as the principium individuationis and the highest manifestation of the Apollonian realm in the form of mythical being) preventing the individual's plunge into abyssal torment by keeping him "afloat" above that abyss or individuated from it. In another example, it equates with the individual who seeks to reclaim his dismembered subconscious emotions but finding the goal insuperable *until* he adds the perspective of Self to those emotions, whereby the illusion of Self makes them not only bearable but interpretable and manageable as well. It is the separation of subliminal emotion from the abyss in which they exist and the addition of those emotions to the perspective of Self that thereby transform those emotions into something that is much more livable, which we call reality. Thereafter, those emotions, which seemed so insuperable otherwise, before adding the perspective of Self, not only become bearable and manageable but achieve the freedom to discharge themselves as well so that they also attain to visibility and intelligence as a dimension of Self. And that proper discharge also enlivens and animates the Self through which the discharge is achieved. In both cases, insofar as the Dionysian realm of human nature is comprised of emotion and the Apollonian realm is comprised of ideation, and specifically Self, both realms become empowered by a fraternal union.

Salvation is Found in Self but Originates in Emotion

Of course, the Apollonian light-picture did not, precisely with this inner illumination through music, attain the peculiar effect of the weaker grades of Apollonian art. What the epos and the animated stone can do—constrain the contemplating eye to calm delight in the world of the *individuatio*—could not be realised here, notwithstanding the greater animation and distinctness. We contemplated the drama and penetrated with piercing glance into its inner agitated world of motives—and yet it seemed as if only a symbolic picture passed before us, the profoundest significance of which we almost believed we had divined, and which we desired to put aside like a curtain in order to behold the original behind it. The greatest distinctness of the picture did not suffice us: for it seemed to reveal as well as veil something; and while it seemed, with its symbolic revelation, to invite the rending of the veil for the disclosure of the mysterious background, this illumined all-conspicuousness itself enthralled the eye and prevented it from penetrating more deeply He who has not experienced this,—to have to view, and at the same time to have a longing beyond the viewing,—will hardly be able to conceive how clearly and definitely these two processes coexist in the contemplation of tragic myth and are felt to be conjoined; while the truly æsthetic spectators will confirm my assertion that among the peculiar effects of tragedy this conjunction is the most noteworthy. Now let this phenomenon of the æsthetic spectator be transferred to an analogous process in the tragic artist, and the genesis of *tragic myth* will have been understood. It shares with the Apollonian sphere of art the full delight in appearance and contemplation, and at the same time it denies this delight and finds a still higher satisfaction in the annihilation of the visible world of appearance. The substance of tragic myth is first of all an epic event involving the glorification of the fighting hero: but whence originates the essentially enigmatical trait, that the suffering in the fate of the hero, the most painful victories, the most agonising contrasts of motives, in short, the exemplification of the wisdom of Silenus, or, æsthetically expressed, the Ugly and Discordant, is always represented anew in such countless forms with such predilection, and precisely in the most youthful and exuberant age of a people, unless there is really a higher delight experienced in all this?

Returning to the two examples I provided above, regarding the individuating effect of the Apollonian realm on the emotions, one being a presence of mind that must never be breached and the other being an apprehension of Self that makes unbearable suffering bearable, there is a vast difference in the effect of the individuating Self on the abyssal subconscious that is defined by the perspective of the *approach* to that fundamental delineation, whether from above or from below. And that perspective is defined by whether or not the principium individuationis has ever been breached. In those individuals in whom it has not, the maintenance of the principium individuationis must be achieved at all costs. But in those individuals in whom it has been breached, which is subindividuated man, the priorities are vastly different.

Subindividuated man who seeks out his Self amidst the swirling maelstrom of subliminal emotions has actually experienced the creation of Self or mythopoeia in that search, and he knows that it is an illusion, albeit a quite necessary illusion, and that it defines that which we call reality. He knows that the perception of sensation triggers mythopoeia and that the perception of deeper, stronger subliminal emotions triggers the mythopoeia of a deeper, stronger Self, provided he can look beyond the horizon of percipience that is defined by the existing Self, which, again, is reality. In such a way, he engages life in a meaningful and artistic way, as a hero advancing the process of growing myth, which is the whole process of life.

The beguiling image of Self, to him, is not merely an object of delightful contemplation but rather an illusory construction that exists as a waystation, beyond which lies a deeper, richer reality. He knows that creation and destruction are integrally entwined, as are compelling emotion and restrained Self-presence. That is the wisdom that distinguishes the subindividuated man who has become tragic man. Insofar as a deeper perception of actuality results in a deeper sense of reality, emotion or will, over Self-presence, offers the greater reward.

A Metaphysical Supplement as an Aesthetic Phenomenon that Justifies Life

> For the fact that things actually take such a tragic course would least of all explain the origin of a form of art; provided that art is not merely an imitation of the reality of nature, but in truth a metaphysical supplement to the reality of nature, placed alongside thereof for its conquest. Tragic myth, in so far as it really belongs to art, also fully participates in this transfiguring metaphysical purpose of art in general: What does it transfigure, however, when it presents the phenomenal world in the guise of the suffering hero? Least of all the "reality" of this phenomenal world, for it says to us: "Look at this! Look carefully! It is your life! It is the hour-hand of your clock of existence!"

If it is the natural course of things which undergo life that they throw off that which they became earlier in order to become something more later, that alone would not explain the origin of tragedy as an art form because art is not merely the imitation of life. Instead, it is a process of creation that adds something new to life as a transfiguring redemption, as healing. But exactly what is the transformation, the redemptive element that is created, which makes art as mythopoeia *meaningful* in life and which enables us to overcome actuality?

Nietzsche finds the transfiguring redemption in an aesthetic pleasure, a delight, which arises partly from illusion and partly from the triumph of the will over whatever obstructs its advance.

Dissonance of Will as the Spirit of Tragedy out of which Tragedy Is Born

> And myth has displayed this life, in order thereby to transfigure it to us? If not, how shall we account for the æsthetic pleasure with which we make even these representations pass before us? I am inquiring concerning the æsthetic pleasure, and am well aware that many of these representations may moreover occasionally create even a moral delectation, say under the form of pity or of a moral triumph. But he who would derive the effect of the tragic exclusively from these moral sources, as was usually the case far too long in æsthetics, let him not think that he has done anything for Art thereby; for Art must above all insist on purity in her domain. For the explanation of tragic myth the very first requirement is that the pleasure which characterises it must be sought in the purely æsthetic sphere, without encroaching on the domain of pity, fear, or the morally-

24: THE BIRTH OF TRAGEDY FROM DISSONANCE

> sublime. How can the ugly and the discordant, the substance of tragic myth, excite an æsthetic pleasure?

Self, as the Apollonian vision-giving realm of human nature, makes the inner world of sensation visible and knowable as a dimension of being, as emotion. But to what aim are we meant to see the horror that exists within the sublimated subconscious? How does that which is most ugly and most discordant lead to aesthetic pleasure?

Here we now approach the idea of musical dissonance and, more importantly, dissonance of the will. And I propose it is precisely this phenomenon, dissonance, that prompted Nietzsche to attribute the birth of tragedy to the spirit of music. Thus, the idea is very important to grasp.

> Here it is necessary to raise ourselves with a daring bound into a metaphysics of Art. I repeat, therefore, my former proposition, that it is only as an æsthetic phenomenon that existence and the world, appear justified: and in this sense it is precisely the function of tragic myth to convince us that even the Ugly and Discordant is an artistic game which the will, in the eternal fulness of its joy, plays with itself. But this not easily comprehensible proto-phenomenon of Dionysian Art becomes, in a direct way, singularly intelligible, and is immediately apprehended in the wonderful significance of *musical dissonance:* just as in general it is music alone, placed in contrast to the

> world, which can give us an idea as to what is meant by the justification of the world as an æsthetic phenomenon. The joy that the tragic myth excites has the same origin as the joyful sensation of dissonance in music. The Dionysian, with its primitive joy experienced in pain itself, is the common source of music and tragic myth.

If we go back to the second forward of this essay wherein Nietzsche elaborates on musical dissonance as an overabundance of optimism that *necessarily* leads to a yearning for pessimism, then we begin to see the origin of proto-tragedy, wherein a man who has achieved an extraordinary measure of self-empowerment as a direct result of having also achieved an extraordinary delineation of Self begins to yearn for the opposite. This is not a common experience in most people's lives, though it is a common experience in Nietzsche's dithyrambic tragedy. But it does have a certain ring to it that should appeal easily to people's common sense. However, a more tangible analogy by which to grasp the phenomenon as a naturally occurring phenomenon would be to consider what happens while listening to any musical movement that is building to a crescendo and one can instinctively anticipate the moment when the crescendo falls into dissonance. Musical dissonance is an instinctively occurring phenomenon, and so is proto-tragedy, if it is not first precluded by scientific thought.

Tragedy as the Originator of the Supra-Self

Horror and pain that has been sublimated into the subconscious provides the dissonant moment that is needed when empowerment by an apprehension of Self has reached a maximum capacity, provided that one condition has been met: the individual who achieves maximum self-empowerment must have achieved the condition through willful struggle. He is the tragic hero who has struggled through the chaos of thought and passion to delineate his Self, found it in its scattered parts within that chaos, and knows that the willful integration of those parts results in the creation of the Self he has built, like an artistic process of creation. And that is why maximum self-empowerment leads to the tragic moment when the Self collapses into a deeper perception of the subconscious — because deeper and more powerful emotions reside within the subconscious and they comprise the scattered parts of a deeper and more powerful vision of Self that he has yet to achieve. And this bit of tragic wisdom comes to him instinctively and mystically. That is the role that "the Ugly and the Discordant" play in life and tragedy. And insofar as those two elements lead directly to a greater apprehension of Self, wherein an aesthetic pleasure in delightful illusion is achieved while at the same time granting those previously sublimated emotions their freedom to discharge, thus they contribute to a meaningful and aesthetic justification of life.

> Is it not possible that by calling to our aid the musical relation of dissonance, the difficult problem of tragic effect may have meanwhile been materially facilitated? For we now understand what it means to wish to view tragedy and at the same time to have a longing beyond the viewing: a frame of mind, which, as regards the artistically employed dissonance, we should simply

> have to characterise by saying that we desire to hear and at the same time have a longing beyond the hearing. That striving for the infinite, the pinion-flapping of longing, accompanying the highest delight in the clearly-perceived reality, remind one that in both states we have to recognise a Dionysian phenomenon, which again and again reveals to us anew the playful up-building and demolishing of the world of individuals as the efflux of a primitive delight, in like manner as when Heraclitus the Obscure compares the world-building power to a playing child which places stones here and there and builds sandhills only to overthrow them again.

As I explained earlier, in contrast with an individual who has experienced the threat of the principium individuationis being broached, which is what we might call wholesome man or individuated man, the individual who has undergone the breach already and then risen up from subindividuated chaos unto an apprehension of Self from its scattered parts is no longer merely subindividuated man but has truly become a tragic man, And the difference that makes him a tragic man is his possession of the tragic wisdom I elucidated above, which I will repeat again to avoid any loss of clarity. "The beguiling image of Self, to him [to tragic man], is not merely an object of delightful contemplation but rather an illusory construction that exists as a waystation, beyond which lies a deeper, richer reality. He knows that creation and destruction are integrally entwined, as are compelling emotion and restrained Self-presence." And it is out

24: THE BIRTH OF TRAGEDY FROM DISSONANCE

of that tragic wisdom that there arises a vision of genius, the supra-Self, which is Nietzsche's Übermensch. For the tragic man, life's process of growing myth aims not for the creation of the first Self but rather for the creation of a multitude of Selves, each deeper in emotion and higher in omniscience than the previous, with each previous Self, each previous tragic hero, dying in the long process. And that is what his dithyrambic tragedy, *Thus Spoke Zarathustra*, teaches.

> Hence, in order to form a true estimate of the Dionysian capacity of a people, it would seem that we must think not only of their music, but just as much of their tragic myth, the second witness of this capacity. Considering this most intimate relationship between music and myth, we may now in like manner suppose that a degeneration and depravation of the one involves a deterioration of the other: if it be true at all that the weakening of the myth is generally expressive of a debilitation of the Dionysian capacity. Concerning both, however, a glance at the development of the German genius should not leave us in any doubt; in the opera just as in the abstract character of our myth-less existence, in an art sunk to pastime just as in a life guided by concepts, the inartistic as well as life-consuming nature of Socratic optimism had revealed itself to us. Yet there have been indications to console us that nevertheless in some inaccessible abyss the German spirit still

> rests and dreams, undestroyed, in glorious health, profundity, and Dionysian strength, like a knight sunk in slumber: from which abyss the Dionysian song rises to us to let us know that this German knight even still dreams his primitive Dionysian myth in blissfully earnest visions. Let no one believe that the German spirit has for ever lost its mythical home when it still understands so obviously the voices of the birds which tell of that home. Some day it will find itself awake in all the morning freshness of a deep sleep: then it will slay the dragons, destroy the malignant dwarfs, and waken Brünnhilde—and Wotan's spear itself will be unable to obstruct its course!

Mankind's Greatest Gift

There exists a veritable danger to the creation of myth as an art form, by which one may hope to find and finally behold one's long lost Self, in the existence of theoretical man and his delight in concept and his insatiable thirst for knowledge indiscriminately and regardless of taste, which has run amok for two thousand years. But out of nineteenth century German culture, most astoundingly, there has arisen a new hope for a rebirth of tragedy and with it the emergence among human kind of a progeny of genius *like never before*.

> My friends, ye who believe in Dionysian music, ye know also what tragedy means to us. There we have tragic myth, born anew

> from music,—and in this latest birth ye can hope for everything and forget what is most afflicting. What is most afflicting to all of us, however, is—the prolonged degradation in which the German genius has lived estranged from house and home in the service of malignant dwarfs. Ye understand my allusion—as ye will also, in conclusion, understand my hopes.

We must learn to *hear* dithyrambic music so as to learn as well how to practice dithyrambic drama, as we find them both in *Thus Spoke Zarathustra*, the world's only existing proto-tragedy. And we are blessed to have this new hope for ourselves. I would venture to vouch for Nietzsche's statement that he has given us our greatest gift in that book. And let us not be led astray in the service of society when what we truly seek is culture.

25: Dionysia and Redemption

Prepare for a Cataclysmic Confrontation via Dithyrambic Drama Followed by Redemption

> Music and tragic myth are equally the expression of the Dionysian capacity of a people, and are inseparable from each other. Both originate in an ultra Apollonian sphere of art; both transfigure a region in the delightful accords of which all dissonance, just like the terrible picture of the world, dies charmingly away; both play with the sting of displeasure, trusting to their most potent magic; both justify thereby the existence even of the "worst world." Here the Dionysian, as compared with the Apollonian, exhibits itself as the eternal and original artistic force, which in general calls into existence the entire world of phenomena: in the midst of which a new transfiguring appearance becomes necessary, in order to keep alive the animated world of individuation. If we could conceive an incarnation of

25: DIONYSIA AND REDEMPTION

> dissonance—and what is man but that?—then, to be able to live this dissonance would require a glorious illusion which would spread a veil of beauty over its peculiar nature. This is the true function of Apollo as deity of art: in whose name we comprise all the countless manifestations of the fair realm of illusion, which each moment render life in general worth living and make one impatient for the experience of the next moment.

A person who undertakes Nietzsche's dithyrambic tragedy will learn to raise up the most frightening, the most painful, and the most humiliating subliminal emotions that reside deep within his subconscious, all of which represent the most "terrible picture of the world," and he will learn how to redeem those monsters, thereby justifying the existence of the "'worst world,'" so that the worst he has suffered, regardless of its depth and duration, will be made *worthwhile*. And that is justice unlike any justice he will ever have experienced, even if he had lived for two thousand years.

With each incremental step forward into the deep, into evil, a new vision of Self will appear to him as a way to redeem that suffering revealed in that small step. And as he steps forward even more deeply, an even deeper and richer redemptory vision will reveal itself to him so that a time will come when he grows impatient via a lust for power to attain to the next Self.

> At the same time, just as much of this basis of all existence—the Dionysian substratum of the world—is allowed to enter into the

DIONYSIA METAPHYSICA

> consciousness of human beings, as can be surmounted again by the Apollonian transfiguring power, so that these two art-impulses are constrained to develop their powers in strictly mutual proportion, according to the law of eternal justice. When the Dionysian powers rise with such vehemence as we experience at present, there can be no doubt that, veiled in a cloud, Apollo has already descended to us; whose grandest beautifying influences a coming generation will perhaps behold.

And let me assure anyone who undertakes this drama that every step forward on this journey to redemption will be marked by an emergence of grueling suffering from the subconscious and into consciousness *in strict proportion* with the actor's ability to redeem it with the discovery of Self that resides therein so that true danger will always be kept at bay. Indeed, always remember in that moment of difficult endurance amongst titanic suffering that, just as surely, the redeeming vision of Self is not far off, by virtue of the union that exists between ideation and sensation, as elucidated in this disquisition.

> That this effect is necessary, however, each one would most surely perceive by intuition, if once he found himself carried back—even in a dream—into an Old-Hellenic existence. In walking under high Ionic colonnades, looking upwards to a horizon defined by clear and noble lines, with reflections of his transfigured form by

> his side in shining marble, and around him solemnly marching or quietly moving men, with harmoniously sounding voices and rhythmical pantomime, would he not in the presence of this perpetual influx of beauty have to raise his hand to Apollo and exclaim: "Blessed race of Hellenes! How great Dionysus must be among you, when the Delian god deems such charms necessary to cure you of your dithyrambic madness!"—To one in this frame of mind, however, an aged Athenian, looking up to him with the sublime eye of Æschylus, might answer: "Say also this, thou curious stranger: what sufferings this people must have undergone, in order to be able to become thus beautiful! But now follow me to a tragic play, and sacrifice with me in the temple of both the deities!"

- "… what sufferings this people must have undergone, in order to be able to become thus beautiful!"

In the raising of the ugliest aspect of your existence, which is that which resides in the deepest depth of the subconscious, and its redemption, you will achieve a beauty of the soul that you never would have thought possible. Indeed, via an undertaking of Nietzsche's dithyrambic tragedy, the actor himself becomes a work of art. And that goes back to the very first sentence of this reiteration regarding how beauty manifests itself within human being, which completes our work here.

www.ingramcontent.com/pod-product-compliance
Lightning Source LLC
Chambersburg PA
CBHW070534230426
43665CB00014B/1684